Let the Bible Speak

God is Calling Us to Himself

R. W. Alderson

Table of Contents

Preface 3
Introduction 7
Chapter 1   A Finished Work 17
Chapter 2   A Reconciled Mind 25
Chapter 3   Grace or Works 29
Chapter 4   Incorruptible 37
Chapter 5   A New Covenant 45
Chapter 6   Introducing Christianity to the Jews 60
Chapter 7   Free at Last 69
Chapter 8   Work Out Your Salvation 77
Chapter 9   Perspective 85
Chapter 10   A Hebrew Inheritance 90
Chapter 11   From Egypt to Canaan 98
Chapter 12   Partakers of Christ 102
Chapter 13   Possessing Your Inheritance 114
Chapter 14   Approaching God: Duty or Identity 121
Chapter 15   Living in Absolutes 130
Chapter 16   Priesthood of the Believer 139
Chapter 17   The Eighth Day 145
Chapter 18   Quality of Life and the Land of the Living 150
Chapter 19   Mountains 160
Chapter 20   The Storehouses 165
Chapter 21   Determination 170
Chapter 22   The Harvest is Plentiful 178
Chapter 23   Forevermore 187
Chapter 24   Death and Resurrection 193

Chapter 25	Judge Not	202
Chapter 26	Session of Christ	209
Chapter 27	Spiritual Leadership & Divine Authority	218
Chapter 28	No Private Interpretation	230
Chapter 29	Filling Man's Poverty with God's Riches	241
Chapter 30	Three that Remain: Faith, Hope & Love	246
Chapter 31	When Willingness Meets Divine Purpose	254
Chapter 32	Where Deep Calls to Deep	260
Chapter 33	In Your Presence	269

Preface

"Cease striving and know that I am God; I will be exalted among the nations, I will be exalted in the earth." The Lord of hosts is with us; the God of Jacob is our stronghold.
Psalm 46:10-11

Many great Christian believers do not find the fullness of a relationship with Christ as one who abides in Christ early in their walk with God, but it usually comes after years of trying to be the man or woman God wants him or her to be without being fully enveloped in the life of Christ – the exchanged life. Most often, the revelation comes after a period of the believer falling short of his expectation of how he should be living. One such example is Hudson Taylor.

One of the greatest missionaries of the modern Christian age is (James) Hudson Taylor, who spent 51 years in China and was responsible for bringing over 800 missionaries to the country and began 125 schools, which directly resulted in 18,000 Christian conversions, as well as the establishment of more than 300 stations of work with more than 500 local helpers in all eighteen provinces.

According to Billy Graham, "Few men have been used to touch China for God as Hudson Taylor was. He willingly broke with tradition and adopted Chinese dress. Eagerly, he built teams across denominational lines. His vision was always to penetrate new frontiers with the gospel. His motivation was neither reckless adventure nor self-fulfillment, but a deep concern for those without Christ. His life was impelled by a growing confidence in the faithfulness of God." Kenneth Scott LaTourette said, "Hudson Taylor was...one of the greatest missionaries of all time, and... one of the four or five most influential foreigners who came to China in the nineteenth century for any purpose."

After 15 years of serving in China, Taylor went through a spiritual crisis that created in him a deep depression regarding his relationship with God and victory over sin. In 1869, he stated, "I felt the ingratitude, the danger, the sin of not living nearer to God." According to Roger Steer in his biography, *J. Hudson Taylor, A Man in Christ*, "He prayed, he agonized, he fasted, he tried to do better, he made resolutions. He read the Bible more carefully; he ordered his life to give more time for rest and meditation. But all this had little effect. He saw that both he himself and the CIM [China Inland Mission] needed more holiness, life, and power."

Taylor stated, "Every day, almost every hour, the consciousness of sin oppressed me. I knew that if only I could abide in Christ, all would be well, but I could not." These thoughts created a spiral that brought him to a place of more weakness and failure. He remained passionate about his ministry, and Christ remained precious, but with constant feelings of personal failure. "I felt assured that there was in Christ all I needed, but the practical question was how to get it out."

In 1869, Hudson read a book called "Christ is All" by Henry Law and was influenced by a passage on personal holiness sent to him by a fellow missionary, John McCarthy. "*The Lord Jesus received is holiness begun; the Lord Jesus cherished is holiness advancing; the Lord Jesus counted upon as never absent would be holiness complete.*" Taylor recalled, "As I read, I saw it all! 'If we believe not, He abideth faithful.' I looked to Jesus and saw (and when I saw, oh, how joy flowed!) that He had said, 'I will never leave you.' Ah, there is rest!" I thought *I have striven in vain to rest in Him. I'll strive no more. For has He not promised to abide with me – never to leave me, never to fail me?*

This new understanding of continually abiding in Christ endured for the rest of his life. He had found true holiness not in human perfection but in a continual trusting in the power and plan of his abiding Christ. He found the reality that "It is finished!" At the time, he was quoted by fellow missionary Charles Henry Judd as saying: "Oh, Mr. Judd, God has made me a new man!"

John Lennon of the Beatles wrote a song entitled "Rain" in which he clarifies the difference between rain and shine: "I can show you that when it starts to rain, everything's the same." "Can you hear me, that when it rains and shines, it's just a state of mind." God is calling us to Himself, a state of mind in which He is always with us so that we can rest in Him.

Isaac Watts, a prolific hymnwriter of the 17th and 18th centuries, was responsible for more than 750 hymns, some still sung in churches today. He wrote the words below to exemplify the essence of the abiding relationship in Christ. It takes all the weight off of man's works and places them squarely on his faith in who Jesus is and what He did:

> No more, my God, I boast no more
> Of all the duties I have done;
> I quit the hopes I held before,
> To trust the merits of Thy Son.
>
> Now, for the love I bear His name,
> What was my gain I count my loss;
> My former pride I call my shame,
> And nail my glory to His cross.

Yes, and I must and will esteem
All things but loss for Jesus' sake:
O may my soul be found in Him,
And of His righteousness partake!

The best obedience of my hands
Dares not appear before Thy throne;
But faith can answer Thy demands
By pleading what my Lord has done.

Introduction

Orthodoxy can be defined as adherence to a purported "correct" or otherwise mainstream or generally accepted creed. Within Christianity, orthodoxy refers to the acceptance of doctrines defined by various creeds and ecumenical councils in antiquity. However, different Churches accept different creeds and councils. The point is that there is no singular mainstream or generally accepted belief. Instead, Christianity is a conglomeration of factions that have a hard time agreeing on many things, even the requirements of being a Christian. A significant portion of Christian doctrine is subject to private interpretation. Since Jesus and the New Testament writers are basically silent on any hierarchy of New Testament doctrine, this work is left to the Holy Spirit. As a result, each believer needs to develop a capacity to hear the voice of the Holy Spirit.

My journey to experience God's presence and hear His voice has included a series of major life challenges that seemed to accompany the teachings I received in my Bible college classrooms. God was bringing to life the Biblical truths I was now learning, and it was up to me to accept them as true, not just theologically but personally. It has taken the extended classroom of my life's details to make them real in a personal sense. Through this process, the Word of God comes alive, and I am now able to hear Him personally speak to me through the thoughts that He gently whispers to my spirit (the still small voice of 1 Kings 19:12). No longer are they idle thoughts, but His voice is directing me in the details of life by the Holy Spirit. In Romans 10:17, the Bible says, *So, faith comes from hearing and hearing by the word* [rhema – that which is spoken by the Holy Spirit] *of Christ.* Faith is built on hearing the Spirit of Christ illuminate the Word of God. This process is uniquely personal.

Your Sins are Forgiven

> When He had come back to Capernaum several days afterward, it was heard that He was at home. And many were gathered together so that there was no longer room, not even near the door, and He was speaking the word to them. And they came, bringing to Him a paralytic, carried by four men. Being unable to get to Him because of the crowd, they removed the roof above Him, and when they had dug an opening, they let down the pallet on which the paralytic was lying. And Jesus, seeing their faith, said to the paralytic, "Son, your sins are forgiven." But some of the scribes were sitting there and reasoning in their hearts, "Why does this man speak that way? He is blaspheming; who can forgive sins but God alone?" Immediately, Jesus, aware in His spirit that they were reasoning that way within themselves, said to them, "Why are you reasoning about these things in your hearts? "Which is easier, to say to the paralytic, 'Your sins are forgiven'; or to say, 'Get up, and pick up your pallet and walk'?
>
> "But so that you may know that the Son of Man has authority on earth to forgive sins,"—He said to the paralytic, "I say to you, get up, pick up your pallet, and go home." And he got up and immediately picked up the pallet and went out in the sight of everyone so that they were all amazed and were glorifying God, saying, "We have never seen anything like this." **Mark 2:1-12**

The public ministry of Jesus centered on His teaching the twelve and the masses. As the mediator of a new covenant, He was bringing new understanding to the Scriptures as He revealed Himself as the Messiah, the Son of God. The Jewish leadership of His day completely rejected His claim to deity and, therefore, all of His words. There is a vivid picture of this process in the passage above. A paralytic is lowered into a crowded room where Jesus was teaching, looking for healing. Jesus observed the effort of the four men to get that paralytic before Him and told the man his sins were forgiven. The reaction of the scribes in the room was predictable, accusing Jesus of blasphemy. To confirm the authority of His words, Jesus said to the paralytic, *"I say to you, get up, pick up your pallet, and go home,"* after he had healed him. When the hearer recognizes the authority of the Word, written or spoken, it has supernatural power. Paul observed this attitude among believers in 1 Thessalonians 2:13, where they received the Word spoken from the pulpit as if God had spoken it directly.

God promised the Jews that they would walk in His ways, and it would be well with them **if** they would *"obey My voice, and I will be your God, and you will be My people."* Both the Hebrew and Greek words translated *obey* have the basic meaning of "listening closely with the intention to obey." When the Jews did not incline their ear to God's words, they went backward (Jeremiah 7:23-24). This principle holds just as true for the New Testament believer as well.

Inspired by God

In the church age, believers have the distinct advantage of living in a new covenant, secured by the completed work of Christ on Calvary's cross. We also enjoy access to the full canon of Scripture, which affords us a deeper understanding of the character and nature of God through the doctrines addressed and further defined in both the Old and New Testaments. In 2 Timothy 3:16, Paul addresses all Scripture as *"inspired by God and profitable for doctrine, for reproof, for correction, for training in righteousness*."The study of Scripture doctrinally (teaching by category) brings the believer into a more in-depth comprehension of His thoughts on a particular subject. This approach to the Word of God provides the framework that enables believers to hear and understand His voice.

In Deuteronomy 5:24, Moses says, *"Behold, the Lord our God has shown us His glory and His greatness, and we have heard His voice from the midst of the fire; we have seen today that God speaks with man, yet he lives"*. The reference is to Moses hearing the voice of God from Mount Sinai and receiving the Law in Exodus 20, but it also speaks to His voice in the midst of the fires of man's living experiences – and he still lives. **To hear the voice of God is to recognize His greatness and glory**.

Diligence

Be diligent [*spoudazo* – to make every effort to do one's best] *to present yourself approved to God as a workman who does not need to be ashamed, accurately handling* [*orthotomeo* – handle correctly] *the word of truth.*
2 Timothy 2:15

The fulfillment of God's life in each believer is related to diligence and a willingness to pursue, to seek after truth with an attention to accuracy as a critical part of the process. It includes a proper exegesis, the critical explanation or interpretation of a text, especially in relation to biblical works. It involves careful study to uncover the intended meaning of the text by analyzing its historical and cultural context. Through this process, the Bible becomes *the word of truth*.

A Finished Work Foundation

As I urged you upon my departure for Macedonia, remain on at Ephesus so that you may instruct [paraggello – advance an order to] *certain men not to teach strange doctrines, nor to pay attention to myths and endless genealogies, which give rise to mere speculation* [zetesis – exchange of words, philosophies instead of pursuit of truth] *rather than furthering the administration of God which is by faith. But the goal* [telos – termination or objective, goal] *of our instruction* [paraggelia – order, command] *is love* [agape – brotherly affection which Jesus commands and inspires] *from a pure* [katharos – clean, pure, unsoiled] *[heart and a good conscience* [conscience of integrity] *and a sincere* [anupokritos – genuine, without hypocrisy] *faith.* **1 Timothy 1:3-5**

The new covenant relationship with God is predicated on the premise that the work of Christ was complete, as evidenced by Jesus's declaration on the cross, "It is Finished." He meant that His work of redemption for all believers was perfect, leaving nothing to be accomplished by the believer in this life. Sanctification is not merely living under the rules and regulations of God's laws but instead receiving His grace as a free gift and allowing it to cause the believer to honor God in their life. In Titus 2:12, it is the grace of God that instructs the believer to surrender to God's will and live sensibly, righteously, and godly since he is able to deny ungodliness and worldly desires. The finished work of Christ produces the proper foundation for anyone wanting to be connected to His love. Paul defines it most completely in 1 Corinthians 3:10-11, *According to the grace of God which was given to me, like a wise master builder I laid a foundation, and another is building on it. But each man must be careful how he builds on it. For no man can lay a foundation other than the one which is laid, which is Jesus Christ.* Consider the following:

Albert Einstein once said, "Everybody is a genius. But if you judge a fish by its ability to climb a tree, it will live its whole life believing that it is stupid." This comes from a genius – a genius who didn't talk until he was four or read until he was seven. Einstein's teachers labeled him "slow" and "mentally handicapped." He may have been last in his class to do what the rest could, but certainly, Einstein wasn't any less than his peers. He just had his own way of thinking — a way of thinking that would earn him the Nobel Prize and change the way we understand our world.

When the teaching a believer receives is not founded on the finished work of Christ, he will be asked to fulfill God's desire for a spiritual life without the spiritual ability to accomplish it. Romans 8:3-4 tells us, *For what the Law could not do, weak as it was through the flesh, God did: sending His own Son in the likeness of sinful flesh and as an offering for sin, He condemned sin in the flesh, so that the requirement of the Law might be fulfilled in us, who do not walk according to the flesh but according to the Spirit.* Walking according to the Spirit is possible only when the believer is convinced that his position before God is perfect and is the basis of his life in Christ. Einstein had a mindset that allowed him to be the great thinker he became; the finished work of Christ provides the same spiritual mindset leading to *a pure heart, and a good conscience, and a sincere faith.*

Love Fulfills the Law

Owe nothing to anyone except to love [agapao – to esteem, place high value on] one another, for he who loves his neighbor has fulfilled the law. For this, "YOU SHALL NOT COMMIT ADULTERY, YOU SHALL NOT MURDER, YOU SHALL NOT STEAL, YOU SHALL NOT COVET," and if there is any other commandment, it is summed up in this saying, "YOU SHALL LOVE YOUR NEIGHBOR AS YOURSELF." Love does no wrong to a neighbor; therefore, love is the fulfillment of the law. **Romans 13:8-10**

We love, because He first loved us (1 John 4:19). Paul recognized that the Law of Moses is fulfilled in the love of others. The ability to esteem or place high value on others, even those who don't deserve love, stems from our acceptance that God loves us unconditionally. The Apostle John understood this kind of love like no other New Testament writer and illuminates some of these thoughts below:

But whoever keeps [tereo – guards, observes] His word [logos – the revelation of God's will], in him the love of God has truly been perfected [teleioo – matured, completed]. By this, we know that we are in Him: the one who says he abides [meno – remains, continues] in Him ought himself to walk in the same manner [kathos – according as, equivalent to the way] as He walked. Beloved, I am not writing a new commandment to you, but an old commandment which you have had from the beginning; the old commandment is the word which you have heard. On the other hand, I am writing a new commandment to you, which is true in Him and in you, because the darkness is passing away and the true Light is already shining. The one who says he is in the Light and yet hates his brother is in the darkness until now. The one who loves his brother abides in Light and there is no cause for stumbling in him. But the one who hates his brother is in the darkness and walks in the darkness, and does not know where he is going because the darkness has blinded his eyes. **1 John 2:5-11**

John wants the new covenant believer to be convinced that loving others is central to his relationship with God. The one who observes with great intention to obey the revelation of God's will in his life is completed in the love God has demonstrated to him. It brings his perfect position into his experience. He can *walk in the Light as He Himself is in the Light* (1 John 1:7), an openness and responsiveness to the Light. This creates intimacy and fellowship between Jesus and the believer, *and the blood of Jesus, His Son, cleanses us from all sin.*

John also speaks of an old commandment *which you have had from the beginning,* found in Leviticus 19:18: *'You shall not take vengeance, nor bear any grudge against the sons of your people, but you shall love your neighbor as yourself; I am the Lord."* He is bringing this commandment to the forefront of the new covenant relationship with God, in agreement with Jesus's words to a Pharisee in Matthew 22:37-40. In response to his question, *"Teacher, which is the great commandment in the Law?"* Jesus said, *"YOU SHALL LOVE THE LORD YOUR GOD WITH ALL YOUR HEART, AND WITH ALL YOUR SOUL, AND WITH ALL YOUR MIND,"* and *"YOU SHALL LOVE YOUR NEIGHBOR AS YOURSELF."* Later, Jesus gave His disciples the new commandment in John 13:34-35: *A new commandment I give to you, that you love one another, even as I have loved you, that you also love one another. By this, all men will know that you are My disciples if you have love for one another."* Loving God and others is the most significant evidence of a finished work relationship with God. As Paul concludes his first letter to the Corinthians, *let all that you do be done in love* (1 Corinthians 16:14).

Knowledge Makes Arrogant

Now, concerning things sacrificed to idols, we know that we all have knowledge. Knowledge makes arrogant, but love edifies. If anyone supposes that he knows anything, he has not yet known as he ought to know; but if anyone loves God, he is known by Him. **1 Corinthians 8:1-3**

Too much of preaching in evangelical churches today is preoccupied with Biblical knowledge without purpose. There are 31,102 verses in the Protestant Bible and billions of messages to be extracted by the preacher to enlighten the congregation. However, biblical knowledge without a divine purpose does not promote the believer's walk with God; the central theme should always be motivated by love. Love edifies. In James 1:27, *Pure and undefiled religion in the sight of our God and Father is this: to visit orphans and widows in their distress and to keep oneself unstained by the world*. It all comes down to loving God (*keep oneself unstained*) and loving others.

The Spiritual Man

This book is 33 chapters long representing the 33 years Jesus lived on the earth. It is intended to define the highest quality of life that God has ordained for everyone this side of heaven. It is through the recognition that the person and work of Christ and the personal reality of a living faith are the foundation of the spiritual man. Jesus spoke these words to Nicodemus in John 3:6: *That which is born of the flesh is flesh, and that which is born of the* [Holy] *Spirit is spirit* [spiritual]. The spiritual man receives his guidance from the Holy Spirit and acts accordingly. Any other motivation is just flesh producing more flesh.

> Oh God, You are my God
> And I will ever praise You
> Oh God, You are my God
> And I will ever praise You
> I will seek You in the morning
> And I will learn to walk in Your ways
> And step by step You'll lead me
> And I will follow You all of my days

These words were written by Rich Mullins, a contemporary Christian songwriter in his song "Sometimes by Step." The essence of a daily walk can be refined to a simple approach of seeking Him daily, in the simplicity of the details of life, and. thereby learn that each step is an opportunity to be led by His Spirit, in every situation Except where noted, all scriptural references are from the New American Standard Bible (NASB95).

Chapter 1
A Finished Work

The night before His crucifixion, Jesus prayed to His Father, *"I glorified You on the earth, having accomplished the work which You have given Me to do"* (John 17:4). Throughout His public ministry, Jesus was preoccupied with this work as He said that His food was to do the will of His Father and *"to accomplish His work"* (John 4:34). This divine work, planned before the foundation of the world by *"the predetermined plan and foreknowledge of God"* (Acts 2:23), is the central part of God's plan of redemption for all mankind. It requires a victorious Messiah to be the Pascal Lamb (1 Corinthians 5:7). When Jesus said on the cross, *"It is finished!"* in John 19:30, He spoke about more than His work on earth.

The Passover Fulfilled

So much of Jesus's last week of human life was the fulfillment of many Scriptures. The Last Supper was a Passover Seder, and at the center of the service was an unblemished lamb that needed to be slain so that blood would be shed. When Paul identified Christ as our Passover, he was linking last week's events to the requirements of the first Passover from Exodus 12. Jay Mack's "Life of Christ Commentary" below captures the fulfillment of the Passover lamb:

"At the feast of the Passover, the man of the house was commanded to examine a lamb for the Passover meal (Exodus 12:3-6). For five days, from the tenth of Nissan to the fourteenth he was to examine the lamb to make sure it was without defect or blemish and worthy to be the Pesach sacrifice. Jesus entered Jerusalem on Sunday, the tenth of Nissan and was examined by the Jews for five days. As far as the Jewish religious leaders were

concerned, they had two goals. They would question Yeshua in front of the multitude to turn the people against Him, and they looked for a specific way to charge Him with a crime so they could put Him to death by Roman law. But it was not successful. After those five days of examination by the Pharisees, by the Sadducees, by the Torah-teachers and by the Herodians, Jesus answered all their objections and questions; therefore, He was found to be without defect or blemish. Christ ate the Seder meal on the night of the Passover, the same night that all the Jewish people ate it. But because the Son of God qualified as the Pesach Lamb, He was slaughtered on the day of the Passover, the fifteenth of Nissan."

When John the Baptist saw Jesus approaching him to be baptized in John 1:29, he said, "*Behold the Lamb of God who takes away the sins of the world*". Long before Jesus fulfilled the promise of being the Passover lamb, John the Baptist already recognized Jesus that way. But what is the significance of being the Lamb of God? The importance of the lamb is identified by Isaiah in 53:7. When referring to the coming Messiah,. He said, "*Like a lamb that is led to slaughter, and like a sheep that is silent before its shearers, so He did not open His mouth.*" The significance of a lamb is that it was intended to be slaughtered.

Ransom

The concept of being redeemed in Greek is *exagorazo,* and means *to release on receipt of a ransom*. Jesus acknowledged to His disciples that He came "*not to be served, but to serve and give His life a ransom for many*" (Mark 10:45). Jesus was the ransom that releases the believer from the curse of sin as Paul defines it in Galatians 3:13-14. The result of that redemption is to open up the blessings of Abraham to all believers, Jews and Gentiles, who put their trust in the completed work of Christ and may now receive the Holy Spirit by faith. It also means that believers have been *"bought at a price"* (1 Corinthians 6:20) so that they may recognize that they no longer belong to themselves but to the Redeemer.

A remarkable passage in the Talmud says: "*It was a famous and old opinion among the ancient Jews that the day of the new year, which was the beginning of the Israelites' deliverance out of Egypt, should in future time be the beginning of the redemption by the Messiah.*" The foundation of the new covenant is that redemption of men is fully accomplished and therefore, *"FOR I WILL BE MERCIFUL TO THEIR INIQUITIES, AND I WILL REMEMBER THEIR SINS NO MORE"* (Hebrews 8:12). Forgiveness of sins for all new covenant believers is dependent on the completion of the work of redemption.

Worthy is the Lamb

From the time of Calvary forward, Jesus would be recognized as the slain Lamb in honor of His fulfilled sacrifice, the lamb's innocence speaking to the fact that He remained silent despite the false accusations. In Revelation 5:5-12, taking place in heaven during the Tribulation period, the elders with the four living creatures recognize Messiah first as the Lion of Judah (verse 5), representing His second coming, and then as the Lamb slain, representing His first coming. It is important to note that the book in verse 7 symbolizes the future, which could only be opened by the Lamb. In verse 9, they sang a new song: *Worthy is the Lamb!* Why? Because the slain Lamb had *"purchased for God with Your blood from every tribe and tongue and people and nation."* And in verse 10, the Lamb has "*made them be a kingdom and priests to our God.*" This is a powerful passage illustrating the completed work of the Pascal Lamb, resulting in worship, not just from men but from angels as well. When Jesus said, "*It is finished,*" He was opening the door for all men, Jews, and Gentiles, based on faith, to be able to *"reign in life through the One, Jesus Christ"* (Romans 5:17), as is referenced in verse 10 above.

> *"And behold, the veil of the temple was torn in two from top to bottom; and the earth shook, and the rocks were split. The tombs were opened, and many bodies of the saints who had fallen asleep were raised; and coming out of the tombs after His resurrection, they entered the holy city and appeared to many. Now, the centurion and those who were with him keeping guard over Jesus when they saw the earthquake and the things that were happening, became very frightened and said, "Truly this was the Son of God!"*
> **Matthew 27:51-54**

The moment of Jesus's death on the cross caused several profound things to take place, as the Matthew account above reveals. In verse 51, "*the veil of the temple was torn in two from top to bottom.*" This is a profound statement since that veil was the curtain that separated the Holy of Holies from the Holy Place in the temple. It also was torn from the top, not the bottom, signifying that it was God's work and not men's. The Holy of Holies was the place restricted to God Himself and only available to the High Priest one day of each year, the Day of Atonement (Yom Kippur). The moment of Jesus's death opened the Holy of Holies, the location of the presence of God to all believers. This principle is further illuminated in Hebrews 10:20 when the writer tells us that the veil symbolizes Jesus's flesh, providing "*a new and living way*"! The completed work of Christ at Calvary through the sacrifice of His flesh immediately gave each believer full access to God (Ephesians 2:18).

More Evidence

At the same time, an earthquake occurred, resulting in rocks being split. Jesus's sacrificial death resulted in a statement to all living beings, not just the religious crowd. The Matthew account is the only one that includes the raising of many bodies of dead believers to enter Jerusalem after His resurrection, "*appearing to many.*" It appears that the earthquake opened the graves and resurrected the bodies from their graves after the resurrection of Christ. Since they were recognizable to many, these saints demonstrate Jesus's victory over death. All of these events caused those Roman soldiers (probably pagans) who were keeping guard to testify, "*Truly this was the Son of God.*" The power of this event was on display for all interested to observe!

> *"And his father Zacharias was filled with the Holy Spirit, and prophesied, saying: "Blessed be the Lord God of Israel, for He has visited us and* **accomplished redemption for His people**, *and has raised up a horn of salvation for us in the house of David His servant."* **Luke 1:67-69**

The prophecy of Zacharias was that the Redeemer was to visit, and He would "*accomplish redemption for His people.*" Although He was to be rejected by His own (John 1:11), He still came for His people, which defines the greatest work of redemption! No one is left behind when it comes to the accomplished work of the Redeemer at Calvary, not even those who have completely rejected Him. The believer can have full assurance that God requires nothing on his/her behalf to complete redemption. **By faith in His work**, "*It is finished*".

Atonement

> *But the Lord was pleased to crush Him, putting Him to grief; if He would render Himself as a guilt offering, He will see His offspring, He will prolong His days, and the good pleasure of the Lord will prosper in His hand. As a result of the anguish of His soul, He will see it and be satisfied; by His knowledge, the Righteous One, My Servant, will justify* [sadaq – declare righteous] *the many, as He will bear their iniquities.*

Therefore, I will allot Him a portion with the great, and He will divide the booty with the strong; because He poured out Himself to death, and was numbered with the transgressors; yet He Himself bore the sin of many, and interceded for the transgressors. **Isaiah 53:10-12**

That *the Lord was pleased to crush Him* confirms that it was His perfect will despite the pain and suffering the Son of God would endure. The Law of Moses commanded that acts of sin require an offering for sin, evidenced by blood. *For it is the blood by reason of the life that makes atonement* (Leviticus 17:11). A guilt offering was required for sins committed; *so, the priest shall make atonement [kapar – cover over sin] on his behalf for his sin* (Leviticus 5:6). In Romans 3:25, *whom God displayed publicly as a propitiation in His blood through faith. This was to demonstrate His righteousness, because* **in the forbearance of God He passed over the sins previously committed**. It means that prior to the offering of Jesus on the cross, all offerings were temporary, covering over the sin, anticipating the perfect offering.

Redemption & Righteousness

He made Him who knew no sin to be sin on our behalf, so that we might become the righteousness of God in Him.
2 Corinthians 5:21

But by His doing, you are in Christ Jesus, who became to us wisdom from God, and righteousness and sanctification, and redemption. **1 Corinthians 1:30**

Faith in God is what man offers to God; God's righteousness is something bestowed upon man. Redemption is the ground of God's righteousness, and God's righteousness is the result of redemption. Redemption satisfies God's justice, God's righteousness makes man blessed; the first was finished upon the cross, the second happens at salvation and is experienced *from faith to faith* (Romans 1:17). Christ's offering provides every believer the environment whereby he can overcome everything that separates him from a loving God.

> *Surely, His salvation is near **to those who fear** [reverence] **Him**, that glory may dwell in our land. Lovingkindness and truth have met together; righteousness and peace have kissed each other. Truth springs from the earth, and righteousness looks down from heaven. Indeed, the Lord will give what is good, and our land will yield its produce. Righteousness will go before Him and will make His footsteps into a way.* **Psalm 85:9-13**

Romans 9:8 tells us that faith in the promises of God, a willingness to trust God for something one could not accomplish on his own, is always the basis of a relationship with God. Psalm 85:9 refers to it as a reverence for God, recognizing Him as savior and deliverer. Just as Paul wrote of all the fantastic supernatural blessings associated with salvation in Ephesians 1, this psalm gives us an inside view of what salvation looks like. Regarding this passage, Keil and Delitzsch Commentary on the Old Testament says:

> *The glory that has been far removed again takes up its abode in the land. Mercy or loving-kindness walks along the streets of Jerusalem, and there meets fidelity, like one guardian angel meeting the other. Righteousness and peace or prosperity, these two inseparable brothers kiss each other there and fall lovingly into each other's arms. The poet pursues this charming picture of the future further. After God's emet, i.e., faithfulness to the promises, has descended like dew, His faithfulness to the covenant springs up*

out of the land, the fruit of that fertilizing influence. And sedeq, gracious justice, looks down from heaven, smiling favor and dispensing blessing.

It appears that the above passage from Psalm 85 is a spiritual view of what Jesus accomplished on Calvary.

Chapter 2
A Reconciled Mind

When Jesus made his famous statement on the cross, *"It is finished"* in John 19:30, He was saying more than His work on earth was completed. The finished work of Christ addresses the full scope of God's justice in directly dealing with the matter separating man from his God – sin! The Greek word *katallasso* is translated "reconciled" and basically means that God has taken upon Himself the work and has become an atonement. It possesses the idea of a total change not dependent on the receiver. The sense is that God has laid aside or withdrawn His wrath so that man no longer has to worry that the wrath may be restored at some later date based on his failure. *"It is finished"*!

To experience reconciliation is to believe on and trust in the atoning work of Christ, that Jesus is God and that His work was enough. In Romans 5:10-11, Paul writes, *"For if while we were enemies we were reconciled to God through the death of His Son,* **much more**, *having been reconciled, we shall be saved by His life. And not only this, but we also exult in God through our Lord Jesus Christ, through whom we have now received the reconciliation"*. If I am to live in the full (much more) effect of reconciliation, my mind must accept the reality that my previous, current, or future failures cannot revive the wrath of God toward me. My position is secure.

The constant reminders of my shortcomings in daily life can cause me to doubt God's promises, so I need a regular renewal of mind (the organ of mental perception and apprehension). Paul refers to this process in Romans 12:1-2 when he urges us to *"present your bodies a living and holy sacrifice"* as an integral part of our worship.

He continues by recommending separation from this world's influences by keeping on being *"transformed by the renewing of your mind"* (present passive imperative), representing a total change in thinking. The world is outwardly conforming us to its agenda while transformation (metamorphosis) is the inward assimilation of the image and character of Christ. In the process, the believer proves the good, acceptable, and perfect will of God.

So long as one remains square in the middle of the influences of this world, his mind will be being conformed to its value system. Again, Paul teaches that sanctification, a willingness to be separated from the world for God's purposes is the will of God (1 Thessalonians 4:3). If one is to come to *"know how to possess his own vessel in sanctification and honor* [respect]" (verse 4), he prioritizes purity as a path of life. The world says that a life of purity is either strange or impossible. In Colossians 1:21-22, *"And you, who once were alienated and enemies **in your mind** by wicked works, yet now He has reconciled in the body of His flesh through death, to present you holy, and blameless, and **above reproach in His sight"*** Reconciliation is the avenue through which we are seen by God as above reproach. Purity does not happen by accident, but is realized when the believer agrees with God in how he conducts himself in this life.

> *Beloved, now we are children of God, and it has not appeared as yet what we will be. We know that when He appears, we will be like Him, because we will see Him just as He is. And everyone who has this hope fixed on Him purifies himself, just as He is pure.* **1 John 3:2-3**

For the believer in Christ, the transformation process will be completed, *because we will see Him just as He is.* In the meantime, the one who looks with an expectation that His return is eminent and his desire is to honor Christ with his life, he walks in His purity, His devotion to follow His Father. This believer looks forward to his future life in eternity with Christ as a forgone conclusion.

Take a look at the Hebrew nation in Exodus 14. God had initiated ten plagues to finally get Pharaoh to let the people go. Now He is leading them to a place that requires a supernatural result to complete the process. Moses brings them to the edge of the Red Sea, and the Egyptian army is in view, coming after them. The people started complaining that this would be the end of them and that being back in bondage in Egypt would have been better. But God was showing them that He wanted to separate them from their past bondages to a new place. In verses 13-14, Moses said, *"Do not fear! Stand by and see the salvation of the Lord, which He will accomplish for you today; for the Egyptians whom you have seen today, you will never see them again forever. "The Lord will fight for you while you keep silent."* The sea parted, the people crossed over, and Pharaoh's army was destroyed. A reconciled mind sees the promised land and the divine future in front and the bondages of the past in the rearview mirror. He now can see clearly the purity of an ordained life since God did it supernaturally.

> *To the pure, all things are pure, but to those who are defiled and unbelieving, nothing is pure, but both their mind and their conscience are defiled. They profess to know God, but by their deeds, they deny Him, being detestable and disobedient and worthless for any good deed.* **Titus 1:15-16**

The reconciled mind is secure because of what Christ did and recognizes that purity is not only an option for living but, more importantly, the best option. By the power of God's presence in one's life, he can devote himself to God's will and find that pure pathway that is able to face his current failures (sin) without discouragement. The serpent who deceived Eve is also at work to remove believers from the *"simplicity and purity of devotion to Christ"* (2 Corinthians 11:3). The world system is designed to corrupt the mind of each believer so as to destroy the simplicity of a walk with God defined by devotion. There is a simplicity in purity. The end result of a reconciled mind is the ministry that God has for us to affect others' lives. In 2 Corinthians 5:18-19, *"Now all these things are from God, who reconciled us to Himself through Christ and gave us the ministry of reconciliation, namely, that God was in Christ reconciling the world to Himself, not counting their trespasses against them, and He has committed to us the word of reconciliation."* Verse 18 speaks of a ministry to the world and is defined by God's work to reconcile the world to Himself. The ministry that God has had to us becomes our ministry to others. And it is all possible through a reconciled mind, walking in a devotion to Christ that manifests the life of God to others. This is not religious, but spiritual.

Chapter 3
Grace or Works

> *But if it is by grace* [charis - a favor done without expectation of return; the absolutely free expression of the lovingkindness of God to men finding its only motive in the bounty and benevolence of the Giver; unearned and unmerited favor], *it is no longer on the basis of works* [ergon - work, performance, the result or object of employment]; *otherwise, grace is no longer grace.* **Romans 11:6**

Grace stands in direct antithesis to works; the two are mutually exclusive. God's grace affects man's sinfulness, forgiving the repentant sinner and bringing joy and thankfulness to Him. It changes the individual into a new creature without destroying his individuality. Grace, God's free gift, is the environment where man can experience eternal life simply based on faith in who Jesus is and what He did. Works are not part of the equation, as Ephesians 2:8-9 reports: *For by grace, you have been saved through faith; and that not of yourselves, it is the gift of God; not as a result of works, so that no one may boast.*

Faith and Works

What use is it, my brethren, if someone says he has faith but he has no works? Can that faith save him? If a brother or sister is without clothing and in need of daily food, and one of you says to them, "Go in peace, be warmed and be filled," and yet you do not give them what is necessary for their body, what use is that? Even so, faith, if it has no works, is dead, being by itself. **James 2:14-17**

The Apostle James, the half-brother of Jesus and leader of the church in Jerusalem in the early first century, identifies the importance of practical attention to the duties of religion and the assurance that men cannot be saved by a mere speculative opinion or merely by following a prescribed program or set of rules. ... *in humility, receive the word implanted, which is able to save [sozo – rescue from death] your souls. But prove yourselves doers of the word, and not merely hearers who delude themselves* (James 1:21-22). Salvation from physical death or human calamity versus salvation from hell and unto eternal life are two aspects of salvation and the Christian experience. They represent the distinction between faithfulness as a lifestyle and faith as a state of mind. In the above passage, James refers to the faithful one as the one who acts out his faith on the stage of life and is saved from many of life's consequences.

A Law of Righteousness

What shall we say then? Gentiles who did not pursue righteousness attained righteousness, even the righteousness which is by faith, but Israel, **pursuing a law of righteousness**, *did not arrive at that law. Why? Because* **they did not pursue it by faith but as though it were by works**. *They stumbled over the stumbling stone, just as it is written, "BEHOLD, I LAY IN ZION A STONE OF STUMBLING AND A ROCK OF OFFENSE, AND HE WHO BELIEVES IN HIM WILL NOT BE DISAPPOINTED."* **Romans 9:30-33**

By the time of Paul's third missionary journey, the church included Jewish as well as Gentile believers, and the increasing rejection of the gospel by the Jews and the predominance of Gentiles in the church led the apostle to speak of Gentiles as antithetical to Israel. The Jews continued to pursue a Law of righteousness but had not yet attained it. *A Law of righteousness* refers to the Mosaic Law (see Romans 7:7,12 & 14). To seek to attain righteousness by observing the Law requires that it be kept perfectly, or as James says, he will become guilty of all (James 2:10). Why did Israel not attain it? Because they pursued it not by (*ek* – out of) faith but as if it were by (*ek* – out of) works. The Israelites did not admit their inability to keep the Law perfectly and willingly turned their faith to God for forgiveness. Instead, a few kept trying to keep the Law through their own efforts. Consequently, they stumbled over a *STONE OF STUMBLING*. Paul quoted from Isaiah 8:14 and 28:16, which referenced the coming Messiah. They were unwilling to acknowledge that Jesus was the Messiah and put their trust in Him.

Pursuing Righteousness

Brethren, my heart's desire and my prayer to God for them is for their salvation. For I testify about them that they have a zeal for God, but not in accordance with knowledge [epignosis – knowledge which enables one to avoid error]. For not knowing about God's righteousness and seeking to establish their own, **they did not subject themselves to the righteousness of God***. For Christ is the end of the law for righteousness to everyone who believes. For Moses writes that the man who practices [obeys] the righteousness which is based on law* **shall live by that righteousness***. But the righteousness based on faith speaks as follows: "DO NOT SAY IN YOUR HEART, 'WHO WILL ASCEND INTO HEAVEN?' (that is, to bring Christ down), or 'WHO WILL DESCEND INTO THE ABYSS?' (that is, to bring Christ up from the dead)." But what does it say? "THE WORD IS NEAR YOU [easily obtained], IN YOUR MOUTH AND IN YOUR HEART"—that is, the word of faith which we are preaching, that if you confess with your mouth Jesus as Lord, and believe in your heart that God raised Him from the dead, you will be saved; for* *with the heart a person believes, resulting in righteousness, and with the mouth he confesses, resulting in salvation. For the Scripture says, "WHOEVER BELIEVES IN HIM WILL NOT BE DISAPPOINTED." For there is no distinction between Jew and Greek; for the same Lord is Lord of all, abounding in riches for all who call on Him, for "WHOEVER WILL CALL ON THE NAME OF THE LORD WILL BE SAVED."* **Romans 10:1-13**

The Apostle Paul never disavowed his Jewish heritage, always recognizing himself as a redeemed Jew, one who had found Jesus as the Messiah, and his priority was to see his fellow countrymen do the same. In the above passage, he identifies the spiritual problem that holds them back from accepting Jesus: *they have a zeal for God, but not in accordance with knowledge.* That knowledge is defined by the Law of Moses versus God's righteousness as a means of knowing God. They knew about God, but they didn't *subject themselves to the righteousness of God*. All of their efforts to uphold the law of righteousness would only produce self-righteousness since it was man's work.

By quoting from Deuteronomy 30:11-14, Paul was explaining that the people had their answer right from Moses himself:

> *"For this commandment which I command you today is not too difficult for you, nor is it out of reach. "It is not in heaven that you should say, 'Who will go up to heaven for us to get it for us and make us hear it, that we may observe it?' "Nor is it beyond the sea that you should say, 'Who will cross the sea for us to get it for us and make us hear it, that we may observe it?' "But the word is very near you, in your mouth and in your heart, that you may observe it.*

In preparing the people for their entry into the promised land, Moses instructed them that *the word of faith* was all they would need to succeed in the promised land without Moses. Paul defines this as confessing with the mouth that Jesus is Lord and trusting from the heart, as Abraham had demonstrated, which results in righteousness—a right standing before God. One's Jewish heritage was not a requirement for salvation but rather a calling on the name (His character and nature) of the Lord (Joel 2:32). Access to Yahweh is no longer through the Torah but through Jesus Christ, the Messiah (John 14:6).

Hunger and Thirst

O God, You are my God; I shall seek You earnestly; my soul thirsts for You, my flesh yearns for You, in a dry and weary land where there is no water. Thus, I have seen You in the sanctuary to see Your power and Your glory. Because Your lovingkindness is better than life, my lips will praise You. So, I will bless You as long as I live; I will lift up my hands in Your name. My soul is satisfied as with marrow and fatness, and my mouth offers praises with joyful lips. **Psalm 63:1-5**

When speaking the Sermon on the Mount, Jesus instructed believers that the one who hungers and thirsts for righteousness will be blessed by being satisfied (Matthew 5:6). He was telling them that success in the kingdom of heaven was a continuous, daily pursuit of the right standing of God (present active participle). The emphasis is on the relationship with Jesus rather than religious activity. Proverbs 15:9, *The way of the wicked is an abomination to the Lord, but He loves one who pursues righteousness.* Proverbs 21:21, *He who pursues righteousness and loyalty finds life, righteousness, and honor.*

Instructed by Grace

> *For **the grace of God** has appeared, bringing salvation to all men, **instructing us** to deny ungodliness and worldly desires and to live sensibly, righteously, and godly in the present age, looking for the blessed hope and the appearing of the glory of our great God and Savior, Christ Jesus, who gave Himself for us to redeem us from every lawless deed, and to purify for Himself a people for His own possession, zealous for good deeds.* **Titus 2:11-14**

The first coming of Christ can be characterized by grace, a free gift of God to humanity that does not deserve it. This grace is also their instructor, not the Law of Moses, to lead each one into a sensible, righteous, and godly life. This instruction produces an expectation of His Second Coming, *looking for the blessed hope,* who will *purify for Himself a people for His own possession, zealous for good deeds.* Good deeds will result from a consistent walk in His righteousness. Paul saw this in the church at Thessaloniki: *constantly bearing in mind your work of faith and labor of love and steadfastness of hope in our Lord Jesus Christ in the presence of our God and Father* (1 Thessalonians 1:3).

The Horn and the Ear

We find the following statement in the Talmud: "The camel went in search of horns and got its ears nipped off instead." In the Bible, horns usually symbolize spiritual achievement or material success. Overall, they are symbolic of all the good things that people desire. The camel represents a person who desires what someone else has and attempts to acquire it for himself.

However, it doesn't end well for the camel. Not only is the camel unable to attain horns, but it also injures its ears. Ears, in this case, represent our ability to hear God's Word. The lesson is that when we occupy ourselves with chasing after what someone else has, we lose our ability to hear God's plan for our lives. Chasing after life's advantages apart from God will distort our perception of the real blessings God intends for each one. In Matthew 18:23-35, Jesus tells the story of a man who is forgiven much, but is not willing to forgive others; he has not found God's righteousness:

> *"For this reason, the kingdom of heaven may be compared to a king who wished to settle accounts with his slaves. When he had begun to settle them, one who owed him ten thousand talents was brought to him. But since he did not have the means to repay, his lord commanded him to be sold, along with his wife and children and all that he had, and repayment to be made. So, the slave fell to the ground and prostrated himself before him, saying, 'Have patience with me, and I will repay you everything.' And the lord of that slave felt compassion and released him and forgave him the debt. But that slave went out and found one of his fellow slaves who owed him a hundred denarii, and he seized him and began to choke him, saying, 'Pay back what you owe.' So, his fellow slave fell to the ground and began to plead with him, saying, 'Have patience with me, and I will repay you.' But he was unwilling and went and threw him in prison until he should pay back what was owed. So, when his fellow slaves saw what had happened, they were deeply grieved and came and reported to their lord all that had happened. Then, summoning him, his lord said to him, 'You wicked slave, I forgave you all that debt because you pleaded with me. Should you not also have had mercy on your fellow slave in the same way that I had mercy on you?' And his lord, moved with anger, handed him over to the torturers until he should repay all that was owed him. My heavenly Father will also do the same to you if each of you does not forgive his brother from your heart."*

Trials

In this you greatly rejoice, even though now for a little while, if necessary, you have been distressed by various trials, so that the proof of your faith [faithfulness], *being more precious than gold which is perishable, even though tested by fire, may be found to result in praise and glory and honor at the revelation of Jesus Christ; and though you have not seen Him, you love Him, and though you do not see Him now, but believe in Him, you greatly rejoice with joy inexpressible and full of glory,* **1 Peter 1:6-8**

Faithfulness is demonstrated and proven through trials and produces *praise, glory, and honor at the revelation of Jesus Christ*. Faithful perseverance in suffering will be fulfilled in honor of Christ, and joy will be *inexpressible and full of glory*. The believer obtains true deliverance of the soul as he is *tested by fire*. By his own free will, the believer determines the level of intimacy in his relationship with the Lord, and although *you have not seen Him, you love Him*.

Chapter 4
Incorruptible

Now I say this, brethren, that flesh and blood cannot inherit the kingdom of God, nor does the perishable inherit the **imperishable** *[aphtharsía - incorruptible]. Behold, I tell you a mystery; we will not all sleep, but we will all be changed, in a moment, in the twinkling of an eye, at the last trumpet; for the trumpet will sound, and the dead will be raised* **imperishable** *[incorruptible], and we will be changed. For this perishable must put on the* **imperishable** *[incorruptible], and this mortal must put on immortality [athanasía - without death].*

> *But when this perishable will have put on the* **imperishable** *[incorruptible], and this mortal will have put on immortality, then will come about the saying that is written, "DEATH IS SWALLOWED UP in victory. "O DEATH, WHERE IS YOUR VICTORY? O DEATH, WHERE IS YOUR STING?" The sting of death is sin, and the power of sin is the law, but thanks be to God, who gives us the victory through our Lord Jesus Christ.* **1 Corinthians 15:50-57**

Romans 8:20-21 says that *creation was subjected to futility, not willingly, but because of Him who subjected it, in hope that the creation itself also will be set free from its slavery to corruption into the freedom of the glory of the children of God*. When Adam and Eve fell in the Garden of Eden, God cursed the ground (Genesis 3:17), so man became subject to that curse until there would be freedom through the seed of the woman (Genesis 3:15). Romans 5:12 *Therefore, just as through one man, sin entered into the world, and death through sin, and so death spread to all men because all sinned*. Since the fall, mankind has been subject to death because of his corruption (sin).

The Change

Paul was given amazing insight into details surrounding the rapture of the church and the changes that would take place in man in the above passage (see also 1 Thessalonians 4:13-17). Everything associated with the corruption of man would be left behind so that he would live in immortality in a perfect state and incorruptible, with no sin, no death, and no corruption. *"DEATH IS SWALLOWED UP in victory."* In 1 Corinthians 15:42-44, *So also is the resurrection of the dead. It is sown a perishable body; it is raised an imperishable* [incorruptible] *body; it is sown in dishonor, it is raised in glory; it is sown in weakness, it is raised in power; it is sown a natural body, it is raised a spiritual body. If there is a natural body, there is also a spiritual body.* The transition from natural body to spiritual body must travel through resurrection.

For we know that if the earthly tent, which is our house is torn down, we have a building from God, a house not made with hands, eternal in the heavens. For indeed, in this house, we groan, longing to be clothed with our dwelling from heaven, inasmuch as we, having put it on, will not be found naked. For indeed, while we are in this tent, we groan, being burdened, because we do not want to be unclothed but to be clothed so that what is mortal will be swallowed up by life. Now He who prepared us for this very purpose is God, who gave to us the Spirit as a pledge. **2 Corinthians 5:1-5**

Man's earthly tent represents not only his physical body but also everything associated with his natural existence, including human reason and wisdom (James 3:15). The spiritual man longs for his freedom from the burden of his earthly existence to experience eternal life in all its fullness. As Job laments in Job

14:14-17, *"If a man dies, will he live again? All the days of my struggle, I will wait until my change comes. "You will call, and I will answer You; You will long for the work of Your hands. "For now, You number my steps; You do not observe my sin. "My transgression is sealed up in a bag, and You wrap up my iniquity*. Death would be like an honorary discharge or a changing of the guard. A person continues to exist after death, for he is transferred from one condition to another. In the meantime, *You number my steps*, meaning God counts his steps as a sign of His care. In Job 31:5-6, *"If I have walked with falsehood, and my foot has hastened after deceit, let Him weigh me with accurate scales, and let God know my integrity."* The pledge of the Holy Spirit anticipates an inheritance and a higher quality of life prepared for each believer on the other side of the natural life and resurrection.

Receiving Mercy

Blessed be the God and Father of our Lord Jesus Christ, who, according to His great mercy, has caused us to be born again to a living hope through the resurrection of Jesus Christ from the dead, to obtain an inheritance which is imperishable [incorruptible] *and undefiled and will not fade away, reserved in heaven for you, who are protected by the power of God through faith for a salvation ready to be revealed in the last time.* **1 Peter 1:3-5**

Peter understood that the believer's access to the Father was through the mercy exemplified by His Son. 1 John 2:2 tells us that Jesus is our mercy seat (*hilasmos*), the propitiation for our sins. In 1 Peter 2:10, *for you once were NOT A PEOPLE, but now you are THE PEOPLE OF GOD; you had NOT RECEIVED MERCY, but now you have RECEIVED MERCY.* Paul spoke clearly on the importance of mercy concerning Jews and Gentiles when he wrote in Romans 11:30-32, *For just as you once were disobedient to God, but now have been shown mercy because of their disobedience, so these also now have been disobedient, that because of the mercy shown to you they also may now be shown mercy. For God has shut up all in disobedience so that He may show mercy to all.* Both Peter and Paul acknowledge that salvation is a free gift, motivated by God's mercy and love, and must be received through Christ's sacrifice. Any effort on man's part to earn salvation in any way is connected to the natural man and not the spiritual man and corrupts the perfect work of Christ.

Citizenship

Jesus answered and said to him, "Truly, truly, I say to you, unless one is born again [anothen - from above], he cannot see the kingdom of God." Nicodemus said to Him, "How can a man be born when he is old? He cannot enter a second time into his mother's womb and be born, can he?" Jesus answered, "Truly, truly, I say to you, unless one is born of water and the Spirit, he cannot enter into the kingdom of God. That which is born of the flesh is flesh, and that which is born of the Spirit is spirit. **John 3:3-6**

The new birth, as described by Jesus to Nicodemus in the above passage, is characterized by a spiritual birth, that is, by the Holy Spirit, and comes to the believer from above or from heaven. This relationship originates from heavenly places and defines the believer's life both in the present life and the life to come as Paul recognizes that the believer's citizenship is in heaven while those of the world (enemies of the cross) set their mind on earthly things (Philippians 3:19-20). Barnes Notes explains it this way:

The idea is that there are two great communities in the universe-that of the world and that of heaven: that governed by worldly laws and institutions, and that by the laws of heaven; that associated for worldly purposes, and that associated for heavenly or religious purposes; and that the Christian belonged to the latter—the enemy of the cross, though in the church, belonged to the former. Between true Christians, therefore, and others, there is all the difference which arises from belonging to different communities, being bound together for different purposes, subject to different laws; and altogether under a different administration. There is more difference between them than there is between the subjects of two earthly governments.

The believer's connection to his citizenship is directly related to his mindset. F*or those who are according to the flesh set their minds on the things of the flesh, but those who are according to the Spirit,* [set their minds on] *the things of the Spirit* (Romans 8:5). The incorruptible relationship gives the believer the strength and ability to walk with a holy God. Watermark, a contemporary Christian artist, wrote the following words to the song "Incorruptible:"

Not Redeemed by Corruptible Things

Incorruptible, indescribable
Salvation's calling when I was longing...
Now, You're the strength that holds my life
With a love that will never die and never fade like the flowers...
It is a love that stands forever!

Oh, I am not redeemed by corruptible things
Not by silver, not by gold, and not by aimless tradition
But by the blood of God's sacred Son Jesus ...
Oh, You alone are my living hope, and my inheritance is...
Incorruptible

Incomparable, inconceivable
Your plans for me shall always be...
And for the day that You're revealed
My heart is forever sealed with the promise of mercy...
And the hope of all Your glory!

Oh, sacred Son, Who paid the price
Oh, may I live a grateful life
That magnifies Your name forever!

Glory of God

Knowing that He who raised the Lord Jesus will raise us also with Jesus and will present us with you. For all things are for your sakes, so that the grace which is spreading to more and more people may cause the giving of thanks to abound to the glory [doxa] *of God.*   **2 Corinthians 4:14-15**

There is a vital link between the quality of a believer's relationship with God and God's glory. *It was for this He called you through our gospel that you may gain the glory of our Lord Jesus Christ* (2 Thessalonians 2:14). Paul saw clearly that one's relationship to Christ was a wonderful connection to His glory in Colossians 1:27, *to whom God willed to make known what is the riches of the glory of this mystery among the Gentiles, which is Christ in you, the hope of glory.* Spiros Zodhiates explains the meaning of doxa as follows:

Christ in You, the Hope of Glory

Basically, in the Bible, [doxa] *refers to the recognition, honor, or renown belonging to a person. When we read in Rom 3:23 that they "come short of [or lack] the glory of God," it means they are not what God intended them to be. They lack His image and character. The predominant meaning of the noun dóxa in Scripture is recognition. It may denote form, aspect, or that appearance of a person or thing which catches the eye, attracts attention, or commands recognition. It is thus equivalent to splendor, brilliance, glory attracting the gaze, which makes it a strong synonym of eikœn, image (Rom 1:23). Dóxa embraces all which is excellent in the divine nature, coinciding with God's self-revelation. It comprises all that God will manifest Himself to be in His final revelation to us (Luke 2:9; Rom 5:2; 6:4; Rev 21:23). God's glory revealed itself in and through Jesus Christ (John 1:14; 2 Cor 4:6; Heb 1:3).*

Spiros Zodhiates

God has chosen to make known this mystery to New Testament saints. He willed in His sovereign mercy to reveal His eternal purpose with all its glorious riches. It is an amazing thing that this was being revealed among the Gentiles, whereas previously, God's special revelation was to the Jews. In Ephesians 2:13, *But now in Christ Jesus, you who formerly were far off have been brought near by the blood of Christ.* Those *having no hope and without God* (Ephesians 2:12) have been given a glorious hope, which is Christ in you [Gentiles]. Because of the riches of the glory, believers are indwelt by Christ, *the hope of glory*. They are thus "in Christ," and Christ is in them. Because of Christ, believers look forward to sharing His glory.

Not Disqualified

Everyone who competes [agonízomai - to contend for victory, straining every nerve to the uttermost] in the games exercises self-control in all things. They then do it to receive a perishable wreath, but we an imperishable [incorruptible]. *Therefore, I run in such a way as not without aim [adelos -* without attending to the prescribed marks or lines]; *I box in such a way as not beating the air; but I discipline* [bring into subjection to hardship] *my body and make it my slave so that after I have preached to others, I myself will not be disqualified* [adokimos - unworthy, unapproved]. **1 Corinthians 9:25-27**

The Apostle Paul was passionate about the call he received from his mother's womb to serve the living God and bring the gospel's good news to the Gentile world. He was more than willing to suffer much for that highest of purposes. An athlete and a boxer characterize the terminology he uses in describing his commitment. His priority is the heralding of the gospel to anyone who will listen. He recognizes that his running is with a particular goal: winning souls to Christ. The goal is the ultimate, incorruptible prize.

But remember the former days when, after being enlightened, you endured a great conflict of sufferings, partly by being made a public spectacle through reproaches and tribulations and partly by becoming sharers with those who were so treated. For you showed sympathy to the prisoners and accepted joyfully the seizure of your property, knowing that you have for yourselves a better possession and a lasting one. Therefore, do not throw away your confidence, which has a great reward. For you have need of endurance so that when you have done the will of God, you may receive what was promise. **Hebrews 10:32-36**

Chapter 5
A New Covenant

There seems to be no real consensus about the year each of the gospels was written, but it is fairly clear that the synoptic gospels of Matthew, Mark, and Luke were written before A.D. 65, while John's Gospel was not written until somewhere between A.D. 90 – 100. At the end of the first century, the Christian world was made up mainly of Gentiles, while the early gospels appeared during a time dominated by Jewish Christians. In addition, the 30+ year time difference represented a maturing of the Christian community regarding its understanding of doctrine since the lion's share of New Testament works had been circulating among the churches for many years. It also meant that doctrinal deviations and heresies were appearing. John's Gospel and his letters addressed some of these heresies, including Gnosticism and Docetism, which challenged the humanity of Christ and the value of the material realm. Ultimately, John accepted and acknowledged to others his agreement with the facts presented in the first three gospels; the Holy Spirit inspired him to address certain events and miracles that would speak to believers on a deeper level.

> *Therefore, many other signs [semeion – miracles with a spiritual end and purpose] Jesus also performed in the presence of the disciples, which are not written in this book, but these have been written so that you may believe that Jesus is the Christ, the Son of God; and that believing you may have life in His name.* **John 20:30-31**

The four Gospels record 35 different miracles. John selected seven for special consideration so that people might come to believe that Jesus is the Christ, the promised Messiah, and the Son of God. These seven symbolize the introduction of the new covenant to the Jew and the Gentile and essential elements that define the unique features that make it far superior to the old covenant as defined by the Law of Moses. *For what the Law could not do, weak as it was through the flesh, God did: sending His own Son in the likeness of sinful flesh, and as an offering for sin, He condemned sin in the flesh so that the requirement of the Law might be fulfilled in us, who do not walk according to the flesh but **according to the Spirit*** (Romans 8:3-4). The Holy Spirit takes this new covenant into the supernatural realm, where the power of God is unleashed in the believer based on his faith that Jesus is *the Christ, the Son of God*.

1. Changing Water into Wine

> *Jesus said to them, "Fill the waterpots with water." So, they filled them up to the brim. And He said to them, "Draw some out now and take it to the headwaiter." So, they took it to him. When the headwaiter tasted the water, which had become wine and did not know where it came from (but the servants who had drawn the water knew), the headwaiter called the bridegroom and said to him, "Every man serves the good wine first, and when the people have drunk freely, then he serves the poorer wine; but you have kept the good wine until now." This beginning of His signs Jesus did in Cana of Galilee, and manifested His glory, and His disciples believed in Him.*
> **John 2:7-11**

The first and second of Jesus's miracles occur in Cana of Galilee, the birthplace of Nathanael. This location corresponds to present-day Kerr Kenna, about 15 miles northwest of Tiberias and 6 miles northeast of Nazareth. When Jesus changed the water into wine at the wedding, He revealed one of His priorities in His first coming: introducing the new covenant as spoken to Jeremiah (31:31-34). It is no coincidence that it would take place at a wedding since the fulfillment of the new covenant for the Church will be the Marriage Supper of the Lamb (Revelation 19:7-9). The new covenant believer will be married to Jesus, the Messiah, at that event.

The Gospel of Mark tells us that the water pots were a requirement of the old covenant for the cleansing of people as well as the washing of kitchen utensils. (*And when they come from the marketplace, they do not eat unless they cleanse themselves; and there are many other things which they have received in order to observe, such as the washing of cups and pitchers and copper pots*) (Mark 7:4). The wine symbolizes the new covenant: *The Lord of hosts will prepare a lavish banquet for all peoples on this mountain, a banquet of aged wine, choice pieces with marrow, and refined, aged wine* (Isaiah 25:6). Jesus was introducing a change of covenants. He would fulfill that covenant (Matthew 5:17) to reveal a new relationship with God through Jesus as Messiah. The event also illustrates that the new covenant is not a modification of the old covenant but rather totally new.

2. Healing a Royal Official's Son

Therefore, He came again to Cana of Galilee, where He had made the water wine. And there was a royal official whose son was sick at Capernaum. When he heard that Jesus had come out of Judea into Galilee, he went to Him and was imploring Him to come down and heal his son, for he was at the point of death. So, Jesus said to him, "Unless you people see signs and wonders, you simply will not believe." The royal official said to Him, "Sir, come down before my child dies." Jesus said to him, "Go, your son lives." The man believed the word that Jesus spoke to him and started off. As he was now going down, his slaves met him, saying that his son was living. So, he inquired of them the hour when he began to get better. Then they said to him, "Yesterday at the seventh hour, the fever left him." So, the father knew that it was at that hour in which Jesus said to him, "Your son lives," and he himself believed and his whole household. This is again a second sign that Jesus performed when He had come out of Judea into Galilee. **John 4:46-54**

The second miracle describes an important aspect of the new covenant: faith in God is dependent upon believing God's promises. Jesus told this royal official that his son was healed without Jesus visiting the child: *"Go, your son lives."* The Apostle Paul explained in Romans 4 and Galatians 3 that the covenant made with Abraham in Genesis 17:1-5, a covenant dependent on believing the promises of God, would be integral within the new covenant:

> *For the promise to Abraham or to his descendants that he would be heir of the world was not through the Law but through the righteousness of faith. For if those who are of the Law are heirs, faith is made void, and the promise is nullified; for the Law brings about wrath, but where there is no law, there also is no violation. For this reason, it is by faith, in order that it may be in accordance with grace, so that the promise will be guaranteed to all the descendants, not only to those who are of the Law but also to those who are of the faith of Abraham, who is the father of us all.*
> **Romans 4:13-16**

God made promises to Abraham in Genesis 12:1-3 and Genesis 17:4-5 that the covenant made to him was for *all the families of the earth.* Although the covenant known as the Law of Moses came more than 400 years after the Abrahamic Covenant, it was not nullified by the Law since it depended on faith. In Genesis 17:4, the Lord told Abraham, *"As for Me, behold, My covenant is with you, and you will be the father of a multitude of nations."* The *righteousness of faith* is His righteousness that comes to each believer as a gift and on the basis of the believer's faith in who Jesus is and what He accomplished. The new covenant is extended beyond the Jew to all *those who are of the faith of Abraham.*

3. Healing a Paralytic

A man was there who had been ill for thirty-eight years. When Jesus saw him lying there, and knew that he had already been a long time in that condition, He said to him, "Do you wish to get well?" The sick man answered Him, "Sir, I have no man to put me into the pool when the water is stirred up, but while I am coming, another steps down before me." Jesus said to him, "Get up, pick up your pallet, and walk." Immediately, the man became well and picked up his pallet, and began to walk. Now, it was the Sabbath on that day. **John 5:5-9**

"**Grace** keeps giving me things I don't deserve; **mercy** keeps withholding things I do" – Wayne Watson

These words come from Wayne Watson's song, "Grace," and says that because of grace, I get things I do not deserve, and because of mercy, I do not get what I deserve. That covers much ground and reminds us that He is always trying to find ways to bless each one despite personal shortcomings. The paralytic wrestled with his condition for 38 years, waiting for someone to help him into the pool at Bethesda (Hebrew meaning "house of mercy"), where he might be healed. When Jesus observed his struggle, He asked the man, *"Do you wish to get well?"* His answer was yes, and Jesus healed him on the spot. In the process, Jesus illustrated to those watching that salvation is a free gift given to each believer by grace and based on his faith. Ephesians 2:8-9 tells the story: *For by grace, you have been saved through faith; and that not of yourselves, it is the gift of God; not as a result of works, so that no one may boast*. Human effort is not a part of the equation.

Later in this John 5 account, Jesus spoke to this man and said, *"Behold, you have become well, do not sin anymore, so that nothing worse happens to you"* in verse 14. What a picture of the saved man! Salvation provides forgiveness for sins, but committing sin has a negative effect on a man's walk. This is why we need confession. Our position before God is perfect, but our experience still needs to be cleansed. In 1 John 1:9, when we confess our sins, He is faithful to forgive and to cleanse us from all unrighteousness. Because sins have an inherent energy to be repeated, the cleansing process deals with the proclivity to repeat the effects of sin.

4. Feeding the 5,000

Therefore, Jesus, lifting up His eyes and seeing that a large crowd was coming to Him, said to Philip, "Where are we to buy bread so that these may eat?" This He was saying to test him, for He Himself knew what He was intending to do. Philip answered Him, "Two hundred denarii worth of bread is not sufficient for them, for everyone to receive a little." One of His disciples, Andrew, Simon Peter's brother, said to Him, "There is a lad here who has five barley loaves and two fish, but what are these for so many people?" Jesus said, "Have the people sit down." Now, there was much grass in the place. So, the men sat down, in number about five thousand. Jesus then took the loaves, and having given thanks, He distributed to those who were seated; likewise, also of the fish as much as they wanted. When they were filled, He said to His disciples, "Gather up the leftover fragments so that nothing will be lost." So, they gathered them up and filled twelve baskets with fragments from the five barley loaves which were left over by those who had eaten. Therefore, when the people saw the sign which He had performed, they said, "This is truly the Prophet who is to come into the world." **John 6:5-14**

The account of Jesus feeding the 5,000 is one of the few that all four gospels cover. Upon crossing the Sea of Galilee with his disciples, Jesus sits down and recognizes a large crowd joining them. Then Jesus asks Philip where the food to feed them will come from since the crowd will need to be fed. Philip suggests that two hundred denarii could not buy enough bread to feed the crowd. Instead, the young lad provided five barley loaves (bread) and two fish, and Jesus miraculously made that enough to feed everyone, with leftovers.

To give more insight into these events, Mark 6:40-41 says that the people were divided into fifties and hundreds, and the disciples received the food from Jesus and delivered it to the people. When the meal was over, the disciples collected twelve baskets full of leftovers, suggesting that everyone had their fill.

If we look underneath the surface of this event, we have a picture of Jesus feeding His Church in the new covenant age. Jesus quoted from Deuteronomy 8:3 when He was tempted by the devil in the wilderness in Matthew. 4:4 when He said, "*It is written, 'MAN SHALL NOT LIVE ON BREAD ALONE, BUT ON EVERY WORD THAT PROCEEDS OUT OF THE MOUTH OF GOD.*" The bread is a reference to *"every word that proceeds from the mouth of God,"* and Jesus, the very Word of God in John 1:1, is delivering it to the pastors (disciples), who will, in turn, give it to the people, His Church, divided into fifties and hundreds. The new covenant church will be fed by God's Word, and it will satisfy every believer. In fact, there will be twelve baskets of leftovers. Twelve refers to the twelve tribes of Israel in the Old Testament and the twelve disciples in the New Testament. In Ephesians 2:20, the twelve apostles will be the church's foundation and will continue to assist Jesus in feeding the new covenant church through sound doctrine.

5. Jesus Walked on the Sea

Now, when evening came, His disciples went down to the sea, and after getting into a boat, they started to cross the sea to Capernaum. It had already become dark, and Jesus had not yet come to them. The sea began to be stirred up because a strong wind was blowing. Then, when they had rowed about three or four miles, they saw Jesus walking on the sea and drawing near to the boat, and they were frightened. But He said to them, "It is I; do not be afraid." So, they were willing to receive Him into the boat, and immediately, the boat was at the land to which they were going. **John 6:16-21**

The west wind often picks up in the evening and catches them in the open water. They were headed directly into it without much progress. The Sea of Galilee is notable for its sudden and severe storms. They had rowed three or three and a half miles, so they were in the middle of the lake. They were terrified to see a figure walking on the water. They thought it was a ghost (Mark 6:49). This occurred in the "fourth watch" of the night, between 3 and 6 o'clock in the morning. Jesus demonstrated that He had supernatural powers to overcome gravity and overpower nature.

He is deity, God in the flesh, and can handle any crisis and come to the believer's aid in any circumstance. In Matthew 28:20, Jesus tells His disciples, *"And lo, I am with you always, even to the end of the age."*

6. Healing a Blind Man

As He passed by, He saw a man blind from birth. And His disciples asked Him, "Rabbi, who sinned, this man or his parents, that he would be born blind?" Jesus answered, "It was neither that this man sinned nor his parents, but it was so that the works of God might be displayed in him." We must work the works of Him who sent Me as long as it is day; night is coming when no one can work. "While I am in the world, I am the Light of the world." When He had said this, He spat on the ground, and made clay of the spittle, and applied the clay to his eyes, and said to him, "Go, wash in the pool of Siloam" (which is translated, Sent). So, he went away and washed and came back seeing. **John 9:1-7**

To most, this passage is about a blind man being healed by Jesus on the Sabbath, but it is much more about healing from sin and the blindness caused by that sinful condition. The new covenant is the means by which every believer can find a victorious life and deliverance from the effects of sin, which places believers in its bondage. Jesus was illustrating the power of the cross by opening the eyes of believers to the mysteries of the kingdom of heaven, which God has reserved for new covenant saints (Matthew 13:11). Spiritual blindness is the by-product of spiritual warfare:

In whose case, the god of this world **has blinded the minds of the unbelieving** *so that they might not see the light of the gospel of the glory of Christ, who is the image of God. For*

> we do not preach ourselves but Christ Jesus as Lord, and ourselves as your bond-servants for Jesus' sake. For God, who said, "Light shall shine out of darkness," is the One who has shone in our hearts to give the Light of the knowledge of the glory of God in the face of Christ. **2 Corinthians 4:4-6**

Not only is the god of this world blinding the minds of all unbelievers to be against Jesus and the gospel, but there is a hardening of the heart that burdens all unconverted Jews during the new covenant age, resulting in a veil over their hearts (2 Corinthians 3:14-16). Whenever the Jew recognizes Jesus as the Messiah, the veil is lifted; therefore, his blindness is resolved in Christ. This warfare is centered on man not seeing *the glory of God in the face of Christ.* When the Light begins to shine in their hearts, the enlightenment of God illuminates the minds of those who seek Him with sincerity. Then, there is a new understanding of the God Who leads one to salvation. A great example of this process is seen in the salvation of the apostle Paul in Acts 9:3-6, when a light shone, and he could hear the Lord speaking directly to his heart amid his blindness. The new covenant provides sight to the blind, as the Lord revealed to Isaiah: *"I will lead the blind by a way they do not know; in paths they do not know, I will guide them. I will make darkness into light before them and rugged places into plains. These are the things I will do, and I will not leave them undone"* (Isaiah 42:16-17).

7. Raising of Lazarus

> So, the sisters sent word to Him, saying, "Lord, behold, he whom You love is sick." But when Jesus heard this, He said, "This sickness is not to end in death, but for the glory of God, so that the Son of God may be glorified by it." **John 11:3-4**

The final of these seven miracles of John's Gospel may be Jesus's greatest: raising Lazarus from the dead after he had been dead for four days. That was vital since the Jewish mind believed that man's spirit remained in the body for three days. This miracle could only be *for the glory of God so that the Son of God may be glorified by it.* The pivotal point of this account is Jesus's words in verses 25-26, *"I am the resurrection and the life; he who believes in Me will live even if he dies, and everyone who lives and believes in Me will never die. Do you believe this?"* What point was He trying to make?

He was speaking about two aspects of the resurrection promised to believers in the new covenant age. The first is a coming resurrection of all believers, dead or alive, at the Rapture of the church: *For the Lord Himself will descend from heaven with a shout, with the voice of the archangel and with the trumpet of God, and* **the dead in Christ will rise first**. *Then we who are alive and remain will be* **caught up** *[Greek –harpazo, Latin - rapturo] together with them in the clouds to meet the Lord in the air, and so we shall always be with the Lord* (1 Thessalonians 4:16-17). The church's Rapture is the next major event on the church calendar.

> *Or do you not know that all of us who have been baptized into Christ Jesus have been baptized into His death? Therefore, we have been buried with Him through baptism into death so that as Christ was raised from the dead through the glory of the Father, so, we too might* **walk in newness of life**. *For if we have become united with Him in the likeness of His death, certainly we shall also be in the likeness of His resurrection, knowing this, that our old self was crucified with Him, in order that our body of sin might be done away with so that we would no longer be slaves to sin; for he who has died is freed from sin. Now, if we have*

died with Christ, we believe that we shall also live with Him, knowing that Christ, having been raised from the dead, is never to die again; death no longer is master over Him. For the death that He died, He died to sin once for all, but the life that He lives, He lives to God. Even so, **consider yourselves to be dead to sin, but alive to God in Christ Jesus.** **Romans 6:3-11**

According to Romans 6, resurrection life also produces a higher quality of life since it answers the problem of sin and sin's control over mankind. Walking in newness of life (verse 4) or resurrection life is the personal identification with Jesus' death and resurrection. Verse 5 tells us that becoming united with Him in His death is the doorway to identification with his resurrection. In Galatians 2:20, *I have been crucified with Christ; and it is no longer I who live,* **but Christ lives in me**; *and the life which I now live in the flesh* **I live by faith in the Son of God**, *who loved me and gave Himself up for me*. Resurrection is Christ's very life within each new covenant believer. When one considers (*logizomai*, meaning to reckon, to recognize as true) himself to be dead, it is death to the self-life, containing the sin nature, and that death sets one free to live for God since one is no longer trying to earn recognition or favor of self. Instead, walking in this newness of life is receiving the free gift of His righteousness and recognizing its value and priority.

In Summary

Although Jesus's public ministry began at His baptism, His miracles, which began at a wedding in Cana, were the means *so that you may believe that Jesus is the Christ, the Son of God, and that believing you may have life in His name.* Jesus changed the water in the water pots to wine to introduce a new covenant, superior to the old covenant, since it *has been enacted on better promises* (Hebrews 8:6). Because the nature of the water was entirely changed to wine, He was also illustrating that *He has made the first obsolete [aphanismos – disappearing or vanishing]* (Hebrews 8:13) superseding the old covenant. Jesus taught, "*Do not think that I came to abolish the Law or the Prophets; I did not come to abolish but to fulfill*" (Matthew 5:17).

The other six miracles in John's Gospel provide further dynamics associated with the new covenant. The healing of the royal official's son appears only in the Gospel of John and illustrates the requirement of believing the promises of God. Abraham's covenant, a covenant of promise, was not made obsolete by the Law of Moses but became essential to a living relationship with God. Healing the paralytic in John 5 at the pool of Bethesda (*Bayith – house, chesed –* mercy, lovingkindness) was intentionally included to symbolize that the new covenant is not about works but, by grace, a gift of God (Ephesians 2:8-9). *The kindness of God leads you to repentance* (Romans 2:4).

The old covenant centered on two elements: the Torah and the temple. The worship and religious activity defined by the Torah took place within the temple. The new covenant centers on the believer's relationship with Jesus, the mediator of the covenant. The food necessary to feed the people would come from the Logos, the Word of God, represented by the bread. Feeding the 5,000 illustrates Jesus giving the bread of the Word to the pastor who feeds the people in groups of fifties and hundreds.

The coverage of Jesus walking on the water is also found in Matthew and Mark. The disciples were afraid, even stating that they were seeing a ghost. Jesus was revealing His deity, that He had complete command over nature and weather, and nothing would keep Him from His commitment in Hebrews 13:5-6, "*I WILL NEVER DESERT YOU, NOR WILL I EVER FORSAKE YOU,*" so that we *confidently say, "THE LORD IS MY HELPER, I WILL NOT BE AFRAID. WHAT WILL MAN DO TO ME?"* *"For nothing will be impossible with God"* (Luke 1:37).

The Jewish mindset of Jesus's day recognized a direct link between sin and suffering. The disciples asked Jesus who was to blame for the man's blindness as if every human affliction can be traced to some active failure by someone. Jesus's answer to the question was telling, *"It was neither that this man sinned, nor his parents; but it was so that the works of God might be displayed in him."* He was saying that human affliction can have more to do with revealing God's glory than identifying someone to blame. Healing this man demonstrated Jesus's ability to heal a birth defect, requiring the ability to create. Man is born with a sin nature and needs a savior, one who can heal him of his sin and its effects.

Lazarus's resurrection is intended to reveal that all believers have a secure future, a resurrection or rapture to meet Jesus in the air to be with him for eternity. In the meantime, Christ believers can experience His life, resurrection life now, as they *become united with Him in the likeness of His death* so that *we too might walk in newness of life.*

Finally

Understanding the framework of the new covenant provides the believer with the greatest opportunity to find the structure of the spiritual life in Christ. The new covenant defines the boundaries of the spiritual man since it identifies God's love and how to function within that love. The spiritual man is *"able to comprehend with all the saints what is the breadth and length and height and depth and to know the love of Christ."* Being *"filled up to all the fullness of God"* is the end result of being rooted and grounded in love, preoccupied with the love of Christ. This rooting in love takes us deep and this grounding establishes a solid foundation in that love. Since God is love (1 John 4:8, 16), everything He does is defined by that love; He cannot do anything outside of that love. Once the believer sees the details of his life as the ultimate by-product of God's love, he discovers the spiritual man.

Chapter 6
Introducing Christianity to the Jews

I also say to you that you are Peter, and upon this rock, I will build My church [ekklesia – called out ones], and the gates of Hades will not overpower it. I will give you the keys of the kingdom of heaven, and whatever you bind on earth shall have been bound in heaven, and whatever you loose on earth shall have been loosed in heaven." **Matthew 16:18-19**

Jesus's public ministry began at His baptism, followed immediately by His temptation in the wilderness. While still ministering in Galilee, He introduced the principle of kingdom life, proper behavior in the kingdom of heaven. It meant a radical change in the laws given at Sinai, those commandments that focused on the public activities of the believer. The Sermon on the Mount was intended to focus attention on the private, inward life. In the beginning, Jesus centered on the inward convictions that would result in blessings of the kingdom.

In the above passage, Jesus told Peter that he would be the one given the keys to the kingdom of heaven to introduce the church age at Pentecost. The church would define the spiritual kingdom Jesus came to proclaim, empowered by the Holy Spirit, the Spirit of truth, who would guide the believer into all the truth (John 16:13). The church would represent *whatever you bind on earth shall have been bound in heaven, and whatever you loose on earth shall have been loosed in heaven.* When Jesus gave this power to the apostles, he meant that whatever they forbade in the church should have divine authority; whatever they permitted or commanded should also have divine authority, that is, should be bound or loosed in heaven. Believers would be guided in the church by the Holy Spirit and the truth of the teaching of Christ.

Raised from the Dead

"Men of Israel, listen to these words: Jesus the Nazarene, a man attested to you by God with miracles and wonders and signs which God performed through Him in your midst, just as you yourselves know— this Man, delivered over by the predetermined plan and foreknowledge of God, you nailed to a cross by the hands of godless men [Romans] *and put Him to death. But God raised Him up again,* **putting an end to the agony of death since it was impossible for Him to be held in its power.** Acts 2:22-24

Just as Peter had stood up among the 120 in the upper room in Acts 1:15, waiting for Pentecost after Jesus's ascension, Peter is now proclaiming to the large gathering in Jerusalem the fulfillment of prophecies of the Messiah's death and resurrection. Jesus had proven His identity through many signs and wonders performed in the midst of many. His life was the fulfillment of the *predetermined plan and foreknowledge of God.* He had demonstrated this plan by overcoming death. In Hebrews 2:9, *But we do see Him who was made for a little while lower than the angels, namely, Jesus, because of the suffering of death crowned with glory and honor, so that by the grace of God He might taste death for everyone.* His victory over death was not just for Him but *for everyone.* He was providing deliverance to believers *who, through fear of death, were subject to slavery all their lives* (Hebrews 2:15).

Return to your Rest

The cords of death [mawet – death occurring by both natural and violent means] *encompassed me, and the terrors of Sheol came upon me; I found distress and sorrow.*

Then I called upon the name of the Lord: "O Lord, I beseech You, save my life!" Gracious is the Lord and righteous; Yes, our God is compassionate. The Lord preserves the simple; I was brought low, and He saved me. **Return to your rest**, *O my soul, for the Lord has dealt bountifully with you. For You have rescued my soul from death, my eyes from tears, my feet from stumbling. I shall walk before the Lord in the land of the living. I believed when I said, "I am greatly afflicted." I said in my alarm, "All men are liars."* **Psalm 116:3-11**

We are not sure who wrote the above psalm, but it expresses praise and service to God because the author had been delivered from impending death and his days had been lengthened out upon the earth. King David wrote many Psalms (i.e., Psalms 18, 22, and 38) about his fears of death, asking God for deliverance and reminding himself that *the Lord has dealt bountifully with* my soul. Many are prophetic of the coming Messiah and the rest He will bring from all enemies, including death itself. When the writer says, *I shall walk before the Lord in the land of the living,* he was speaking of a total belief that he would live *before the Lord*, as in His presence, in His service, and enjoying communion with Him. *"Come to Me, all who are weary and heavy-laden, and I will give you rest* (Matthew 11:28).

The Jewish mindset at the time of Jesus was a weariness of being controlled by other countries, some more severe than others. There had been 400 years of silence, no prophet speaking to the people since their return from Babylonian captivity. They were tired of having to submit themselves to rulers who sometimes did not allow them to freely worship the God of Abraham, Isaac, and Jacob. The Old Testament gave many prophesies of the coming Messiah who would establish His kingdom and His rule. However, they had no concept that Messiah would come twice or that He would die for the sins of the world.

Abraham, Isaac, & Jacob

On that day, some Sadducees (who say there is no resurrection) came to Jesus and questioned Him, asking, "Teacher, Moses said, 'IF A MAN DIES HAVING NO CHILDREN, HIS BROTHER AS NEXT OF KIN SHALL MARRY HIS WIFE, AND RAISE UP CHILDREN FOR HIS BROTHER.' Now there were seven brothers with us, and the first married and died, and having no children left his wife to his brother; so also the second, and the third, down to the seventh. Last of all, the woman died. In the resurrection, therefore, whose wife of the seven will she be? For they all had married her." But Jesus answered and said to them, "You are mistaken, not understanding the Scriptures nor the power of God. For in the resurrection, they neither marry nor are given in marriage but are like angels in heaven. But regarding the resurrection of the dead, have you not read what was spoken to you by God: 'I AM THE GOD OF ABRAHAM, AND THE GOD OF ISAAC, AND THE GOD OF JACOB'? [Exodus 3:6]. He is not the God of the dead but of the living." When the crowds heard this, they were astonished at His teaching. **Matthew 22:23-33**

Jesus made it a point to quote a Scripture from the five books of Moses since the Sadducees only recognized Mose's writings as authority. There were other verses He could have quoted. It was because all classes regarded the Pentateuch as the fundamental source of the Hebrew Religion and all the succeeding books of the Old Testament as developments of it. Our Lord would show that even there, the doctrine of the Resurrection was taught. He selected this passage as being not a bare annunciation of the doctrine in question but as expressive of that glorious truth out of which the Resurrection springs. The Resurrection means that, although physically dead, Abraham, Isaac, and Jacob are alive and well, living in the presence of the Almighty.

Introducing the Holy Spirit

> *"Brethren, I may confidently say to you regarding the patriarch David that he both died and was buried, and his tomb is with us to this day. And so, because he was a prophet and knew that GOD HAD SWORN TO HIM WITH AN OATH TO SEAT one OF HIS DESCENDANTS ON HIS THRONE,* **he looked ahead and spoke of the resurrection of the Christ***, that HE WAS NEITHER ABANDONED TO HADES NOR DID His flesh SUFFER DECAY [Psalm 16:10]. This Jesus, God raised up again, to which we are all witnesses. Therefore, having been exalted to the right hand of God and having received from the Father the promise of the Holy Spirit, He has poured forth this which you both see and hear.*
> **Acts 2:29-33**

In John 7:37-39, Jesus referenced the Holy Spirit on the eighth day of the Feast of Tabernacles, or Shemini Atzeret, in Jerusalem when He said, "*If anyone is thirsty, let him come to Me and drink. He who believes in Me, as the Scripture said, 'From his innermost being will flow rivers of living water.*" John tells us in Verse 39 that Jesus spoke about the Holy Spirit, *whom those who believed in Him would receive.* The Spirit would come after Jesus was glorified. "*And behold, I am sending forth the promise of My Father upon you, but you are to stay in the city until you are clothed with power from on high*" (Luke 24:49).

The Right Hand of the Lord

The sound of joyful shouting and salvation is in the tents of the righteous; **the right hand of the Lord does valiantly. The right hand of the Lord is exalted; the right hand of the Lord does valiantly.** *I will not die but live and tell of the works of the Lord. The Lord has disciplined me severely, but He has not given me over to death. Open to me the gates of righteousness; I shall enter through them, I shall give thanks to the Lord. This is the gate of the Lord; the righteous will enter through it. I shall give thanks to You, for You have answered me, and You have become my salvation.* **Psalm 118:15-21**

When Peter confirms that Jesus had been exalted to the right hand of God, he is speaking of the full approval and authority of God, that Jesus has been given full authority to bring victory over sin and death. *"Your right hand, O Lord, is majestic in power, Your right hand, O Lord, shatters the enemy"* (Exodus 15:6). David recognized that his consistency was directly related to his willingness to set the Lord continually before his face *because He is at my right hand, I will not be shaken* (Psalm 16:8). The right hand of God represents the manifestation of God's power to fulfill all of His promises. The Holy Spirit symbolizes the right hand of God within each believer.

Repent & be Baptized

Therefore, let all the house of Israel [both northern and southern kingdoms] *know for certain that God has made Him both Lord and Christ—this Jesus whom you crucified." Now, when they heard this, they were pierced to the heart* [katanusso – deeply moved] *and said to Peter and the rest of the apostles, "Brethren, what shall we do?" Peter said to them, "Repent* [metanoeo – change the mind, implies pious *sorrow for unbelief and a turning to God], and each of you be baptized in the name of Jesus Christ for the forgiveness of your sins, and you will receive the gift of the Holy Spirit.* **Acts 2:36-38**

Peter's declaration of the Lordship of Christ was a call to action on behalf of those who heard Peter speak since they were deeply moved. Peter defined that response as repent and be baptized. According to Robertson's Word Pictures, *metanoeesate*, first aorist active imperative means. "Change your mind and your life." "Turn right around, and do it now." "You crucified this Jesus. Now crown him in your hearts as Lord and Christ." "And let each one of you be baptized." Note the change of grammatical number from plural to singular and the change of person from second person to third person. This change marks a break in the thought here that the English translation is not preserved. The first thing to do is make a radical and complete change of heart and life. Then let EACH ONE be baptized after this change has taken place, and the act of baptism be performed "in the name of Jesus Christ."

Knowing Him

More than that, I count all things to be loss in view of the surpassing value of knowing [gno sis – knowledge by experience rather than intuition] Christ Jesus my Lord, for whom I have suffered the loss of all things, and count them but rubbish so that I may gain Christ, and may be found in Him, not having a righteousness of my own derived from the Law [self-righteousness], but that which is through faith in Christ, the righteousness which comes from God on the basis of faith, that I may know Him and the power of His resurrection and the fellowship of His sufferings, being conformed to His death; in order that I may attain to the resurrection from the dead. **Philippians 3:8-11**

The Apostle Paul, a former devout Pharisee, recognizes in the above passage that the real treasure of this relationship "in Christ" is the experience of knowing Him beyond the Law of Moses he had previously treasured. The Law was the avenue that allowed him to succeed as a Pharisee and Jewish leader since he could perform to earn recognition. He understood that all his abilities and accomplishments through the Law were rubbish and an impediment to knowing Jesus Christ as Lord. This word *gnosis* emphasizes understanding rather than sensory perception and embraces every organ and mode of knowledge (i.e., seeing, hearing, experience, etc.). This type of knowledge implies verification by the eye or other objective observation. Ultimately, it speaks of the deepest kind of relationship, a connection to the righteousness that comes from God based on faith.

Out of Faith into Faith

Paul further explains in Romans 4:4-5 that the righteousness of God cannot be earned but must be received as a gift based on faith. *Now, to the one who works, his wage is not credited as a favor but as what is due. But to the one who does not work but believes in Him who justifies the ungodly, his faith is credited as righteousness.* God justifies or declares the believer righteous; man's role is to accept God's standards of living. God's righteousness produces a life defined by integrity and blameless conduct. According to Romans 1:17, *For in it* [the gospel], *the righteousness of God is revealed from faith to faith; as it is written, "BUT THE RIGHTEOUS man SHALL LIVE BY FAITH."* The original Greek could be better translated as "by or out of faith into faith." When the believer exercises his faith in a given situation, it leads to another opportunity to trust God.

that if you confess with your mouth Jesus as Lord, and believe in your heart that God raised Him from the dead, you will be saved; for with the heart a person believes, resulting in righteousness, and with the mouth he confesses, resulting in salvation. **Romans 10:9-10**

Chapter 7
Free at Last

These were famous words uttered by Martin Luther King in his speech at the Lincoln Memorial on August 28, 1963, in his "I Have a Dream" speech. He concluded it with:

"And when this happens, when we allow freedom to ring, when we let it ring from every village and every hamlet, from every state and every city, we will be able to speed up that day when all of God's children, black men and white men, Jews, and Gentiles, Protestants, and Catholics, will be able to join hands and sing in the words of the old Negro spiritual, 'Free at last! Free at last! Thank God Almighty, we are free at last!'"

The freedom that MLK was referencing involved the issue of his day: civil rights. The reconstruction of American society since the Civil War has been slow and painful, yet King saw hope for the future, and that hope was in God. Believers' freedom in their relationship with Christ can transform lives and set people free from their failures and shortcomings. Paul saw it clearly when he spoke in Romans 8:2: *For the law of the Spirit of life in Christ Jesus has set you free* [eleutheroo – liberated from the power and punishment of sin] *from the law of sin and of death.*

Luther on Liberty

In anticipation of his trial before Emperor Charles V and Pope Leo X, Martin Luther wrote a treatise entitled "Concerning Christian Liberty." In it, he addresses the idea of two sides of Christian liberty. He said:

A Christian man is the most free lord of all, and subject to none; a Christian man is the most dutiful servant of all and subject to every one. Although these statements appear contradictory yet, when they are found to agree together, they will make excellently for my purpose. They are both the statements of Paul himself, who says, "Though I be free from all men, yet have I made myself servant unto all" (1 Corinthians 9:19), and "Owe no man anything, but to love one another" (Romans 13:8). Now love is by its own nature dutiful and obedient to the beloved object. Thus, even Christ, though Lord of all things, was yet made of a woman made under the law, at once free and a servant, at once in the form of God and in the form of a servant.

Luther saw clearly that the freedom purchased on behalf of each believer by Jesus Christ gives us liberty and servitude simultaneously, freedom from sin and man's control, including the church, while enslaving him to the perfect plan of God and the righteous life that servitude provides. Paul discusses this subject in detail in Romans 6, encouraging each Christian to a deeper sense of freedom through a deeper commitment to His life and will.

Slaves of Righteousness

What, then? Shall we sin because we are not under law but under grace? May it never be! Do you not know that when you present yourselves to someone as slaves [doulos - one who is in a permanent relation of servitude to another, his will being altogether consumed in the will of the other] *for obedience* [hupakouo -to listen to something, hearken with stealth, stillness, or attention in order to yield], *you are slaves of the one whom you obey, either of sin* [hamartia - missing the true end and scope of our lives, which is God] *resulting in death or of obedience resulting in righteousness [dikaiosune – that which is just or right, conformity to all God's commands]? But thanks be to God that though you were slaves of sin, you became obedient from the heart to that form of teaching to which you were committed, and* **having been freed from sin**, *you became slaves of righteousness. I am speaking in human terms because of the weakness of your flesh. For just as you presented your members as slaves to impurity and to lawlessness [anomia – violation of the Law], resulting in further lawlessness, so now present your members as slaves to righteousness, resulting in sanctification. For when you were slaves of sin, you were free in regard to righteousness. Therefore, what benefit were you then deriving from the things of which you are now ashamed? For the outcome of those things is death. But now,* **having been freed from sin and enslaved to God**, *you derive your benefit, resulting in sanctification [hagiosmos – separation unto God], and the outcome, eternal life. For the wages of sin is death, but the free gift of God is eternal life in Christ Jesus our Lord.* **Romans 6:15-23**

We are slaves to that which we obey. Sin leads to death; obedience produces practical righteousness. As believers, the new nature and God's grace provide the foundation for a spiritual life; external rules cannot accomplish what is truly spiritual. The disciples in Rome gave proof of the justice of Paul's argument by walking in the truth. Having been set free from the slavery of sin, they had become the slaves of righteousness, and this did not end in itself; practical righteousness developed as the whole being was set apart for God, with increasing understanding. In obedience, the fruit was sanctification; a spiritual capacity was developed as they were separated from evil to gain a deeper knowledge of God. Sin produces no fruit but ultimately leads to death. Having been set free from sin and now servants to God, this is the true righteousness of obedience, like that of Christ Himself. They had already received their fruit in holiness, and the end result would be eternal life. *For the wages of sin is death, but the free gift of God is eternal life in Christ Jesus our Lord* (Romans 6:23).

Paul's subject is judicial righteousness before God, and he connects his doctrine with John's First Letter, which, on the other hand, addresses the doctrine of propitiation and acceptance when speaking of the impartation of life. The appeal is beautiful to a man in true freedom, liberty of grace, being dead to sin. He is set wholly free by death. To whom will he now yield himself? For now, he is free.

Married to the Law

Or do you not know, brethren (for I am speaking to those who know the law), that the law has jurisdiction over a person as long as he lives? For the married woman is bound by law to her husband while he is living; but if her husband dies, she is released from the law concerning the husband. So then, if while her husband is living, she is joined to another man, she shall be called an adulteress; but if her husband dies, she is free from the law, so that she is not an adulteress though she is joined to another man. Therefore, my brethren, you also were made to die to the Law through the body of Christ, so that you might be joined to another, to Him who was raised from the dead, in order that we might bear fruit for God. For while we were in the flesh, the sinful passions, which were aroused by the Law, were at work in the members of our body to bear fruit for death. But now we have been released [katargeo – freed, the Law rendered inactive] *from the Law, having died to that by which we were bound, so that we serve in newness of the Spirit and not in oldness of the letter.* **Romans 7:1-6**

The Apostle introduces a subject that caused him difficulty: his struggle with his sin nature. Later in the passage, Paul confesses, *For I know that nothing good dwells in me, that is, in my flesh; for the willing is present in me, but the doing of the good is not* (Romans 7:18-19). He has explained above that the victory comes from a recognition of "Who" the believer is married to, the husband, a reference to the Law of Moses or Christ. He clarifies that this change in perspective results from dying to the husband, namely the Law, thereby being free from its requirements. Otherwise, the believer married to the Law of Moses must keep it in its entirety. *For whoever keeps the whole law and yet stumbles in one point `has become guilty of all* (James 2:10). Paul is teaching that the believer cannot be married to the Law and to Christ at the same time.

The aorist, passive, indicative verb, *katargeo*, means that, through Christ's death and resurrection, the believer receives the benefit of this eternal work of God and not through his own efforts. Instead, the believer considers himself dead to the Law but alive to God. *Nevertheless, knowing that a man is not justified by the works of the Law but through faith in Christ Jesus, even we have believed in Christ Jesus, so that we may be justified by faith in Christ and not by the works of the Law; since by the works of the Law no flesh will be justified* (Galatians 2:16).

Spiritual life is a proper perspective and not a series of actions.

Truly Free as a Son

So, Jesus was saying to those Jews who had believed Him, "If you continue [meno – remaining steadfast] in My word, then you are truly disciples of Mine; and you will know the truth, and the truth will make you free." They answered Him, "We are Abraham's descendants and have never yet been enslaved to anyone; how is it that You say, 'You will become free'?" Jesus answered them, "Truly, truly, I say to you, everyone who commits sin is the slave of sin. The slave does not remain in the house forever; the son does remain forever. So, if the Son sets you free, you will be truly free. **John 8:31-36**

When Jesus said, *the truth will make* [or set] *you free*, what did He mean? When one considers that Jesus came *full of grace and truth* (John 1:14) and that grace and truth were realized or subsist in Jesus Christ (John 1:17), we come to understand that grace and truth are inextricably linked and manifested in the person of Christ. In Psalm 57:3, *God will send forth His loving kindness* [hesed – grace] *and His truth.* Truth is wrapped up in the person of Jesus Christ. In addition, the Word of God is characterized as truth in many places, including Jesus's words in John 17:17: *Sanctify them in the truth; Your word is truth*. The conclusion is that the disciple is the one who remains steadfast in receiving and meditating on the Word of God and is set free. When the believer occupies himself with the truth of God's Word and God's Son, he is freed from the slavery of sin, *you will be truly free.*

Paul adds to this conversation in Romans 8:14-15 when he says *For all who are being led by the Spirit of God, these are sons of God. For you have not received a spirit of slavery leading to fear again, but you have received a spirit of adoption as sons by which we cry out, "Abba! Father!"* When the believer sees himself as an adopted son, he becomes more than willing to be led by the Holy Spirit. The son needs no longer to fear of being a slave to sin.

Enslaved No Longer

It was for freedom that Christ set us free; therefore, keep standing firm [steko – steadfast in the faith] *and do not be subject again to a yoke of slavery.* **Galatians 5:1**

For you were called to freedom, brethren; only do not turn your freedom into an opportunity for the flesh, but through love, serve one another. For the whole Law is fulfilled in one word, in the statement, "YOU SHALL LOVE YOUR NEIGHBOR AS YOURSELF." **Galatians 5:13-14**

There are many things that can enslave the believer in this life, many not so obvious. Paul encourages the believers in Galatia to *remain steadfast,* to persevere as a way of life, so that he may avoid the pitfalls associated with worldly forces that seek to lure the believer away from their devotion to Christ. Paul further states that freedom is experienced when the believer occupies himself with his concern and care for others in loving your neighbor as yourself.

Things We Leave Behind

Michael Card writes about one of these subtle enemies of freedom that everyone should be concerned with and the victory that comes from a devoted life:

Things We Leave Behind
Michael Card

There sits Simon, so foolishly wise
Proudly, he's tending his nets
And Jesus calls, and the boats drift away
And all that he owns, he forgets

But more than the nets he abandoned that day
He found that his pride was soon drifting away
And it's hard to imagine the freedom we find
From the things we leave behind

Matthew was mindful of taking the tax
And pressing the people to pay
But hearing the call, he responded in faith
And followed the Light and the Way

And leaving the people so puzzled; he found
The greed in his heart was no longer around
And it's hard to imagine the freedom we find
From the things we leave behind

Every heart needs to be set free
From possessions that hold it so tight
'Cause freedom's not found in the things that we own
It's the power to do what is right
With Jesus, our only possession
And giving becomes our delight
And we can't imagine the freedom we find
From the things we leave behind

We show a love for the world in our lives
By worshipping goods, we possess
And Jesus says, "Lay all our treasures aside
And love God above all the rest."

'Cause when we say no to the things of the world
We open our hearts to the love of the Lord
And it's hard to imagine the freedom we find
From the things we leave behind

Chapter 8
Work Out Your Salvation

The Apostle Paul wrote five different letters (Prison Epistles) from a Roman prison during the early 60's AD: Ephesians, Philippians, Colossians, Philemon and Laodiceans (this letter did not survive). It is interesting to note that Paul spent a short time in a Philippian jail (see Acts 16:19-40) and now writes to the church from prison. This church had supported him on multiple occasions, so he had a special affinity for them. The church saw him as an ambassador of Christ, but he uttered the oracles of God with great authority. They treated him with great praise. Paul wanted them to develop the same measure of convictions that he had, and it began with an understanding of the work of God inside each believer. In Philippians 1:6, *For I am confident of this very thing, that He who began a good work in you will perfect it until the day of Christ Jesus.* God will complete His work.

> *So then, my beloved, just as you have always obeyed [hupakouo – taken heed], not as in my presence only, but now much more in my absence, work out [katergazomai – work intensely, carry out to complete perfection] your salvation with fear [phobos – reverence, respect] and trembling [tromos – dread]; for it is God who is at work [energeo – operative] in you, both to will [thelo – to determine] and to work [energeo – accomplish] for His good pleasure.* **Philippians 2:12-13**

The previous verses in Philippians 2 speak of the humility of Christ. His attitude does *nothing from selfishness or empty conceit, but with humility of mind, regards one another as more important than himself (verse 3).* This is the mind that became a servant, even unto death (verse 8). As a result, He has become the one exalted above every name. His greatness is measured by His humility and service to His Father. *So then, my beloved* introduces this vital message that they should recognize that working out of one's salvation is the result of what God has worked in. Whether in their presence or not, Paul wanted them to place their confidence in the work of Christ and not in themselves: *I can do all things through Him who strengthens me* (Philippians 4:13). Isaiah 26:12 tells us that the Lord performs all our works when we walk with Him: *Lord, You will establish peace for us, since You have also performed for us all our works.*

God's Workmanship

For by grace, you have been saved [sozo – spiritual deliverance] *through faith; and that not of yourselves, it is the gift of God; not as a result of works* [ergon – labor, human effort], *so that no one may boast. For we are His workmanship* [poiema – something made, a workpiece], *created in Christ Jesus for good works, which God prepared beforehand so that we would walk in them* [peripateo – a manner of life]. **Ephesians 2:8-10**

Paul saw the work of salvation more clearly than any other New Testament writer. It was God's work, not man's effort, to keep specific rules and regulations or create a work on behalf of God as a holy offering that would result in God's favor. Instead, Paul states that man is the object of God's work, His workmanship so that the believer might walk in His works, as demonstrated by Jesus Christ and His death, burial, and resurrection. When the believer is led by the Holy Spirit (Romans 8:14), they will walk in maturity and fulfill the Spirit's leading to accomplish God's work, empowered by the Spirit. It is evident that when God created in six days, He completed all His work so that He could rest (Hebrews 4:10). In the same way,

Christ's work as the slain Lamb was complete before the foundation of the world (Revelation 13:8). The working out occurred during His physical life 2,000 years ago.

Some of Moses's last words are found in Deuteronomy 5:33 when he said, *"You shall walk in all* [*kol* – entire, every, all] *the way* [*derek* the path that is traveled] *which the Lord your God has commanded you, that you may live* [*hayah* – be alive] *and that it may be well with you, and that you may prolong your days in the land which you will possess."* The Lord promised that the one who walked in all the ways of the Lord is alive and will be blessed. The Apostle John spoke similar words in 1 John 2:5-6 where the one true believer (the one in Him) abides or remains in Him, he walks in the same manner as Jesus walked, and God's love is perfected in him: *but whoever keeps His word, in him the love of God has truly been perfected. By this, we know that we are in Him: the one who says he abides in Him ought himself to walk in the same manner as He walked.*

The Potter's Hand

The word which came to Jeremiah from the Lord saying, "Arise and go down to the potter's house, and there I will announce My words to you." Then I went down to the potter's house, and there he was, making something on the wheel. But the vessel that he was making of clay was spoiled in the hand of the potter, so he remade it into another vessel, as it pleased the potter to make. Then the word of the Lord came to me saying, "Can I not, O house of Israel, deal with you as this potter does?" declares the Lord. "Behold, like the clay in the potter's hand, so are you in My hand, O house of Israel. **Jeremiah 18:1-6**

The above passage speaks of the method the Lord uses to work within the people of the house of Israel. He is like a potter, molding, shaping, and remaking the clay, a man's heart that needs the work that only He can perform. Jeremiah had stated previously that man's heart is deceitful and desperately sick in its natural state (Jeremiah 17:9). God's work is to transform the heart and the mind of each believer, as Paul presents in Romans 12:2, *And do not be conformed to this world, but be transformed by the renewing of your mind, so that you may prove what the will of God is, that which is good and acceptable and perfect*. This work connects man's heart and mind to God's good, acceptable, and perfect will. In the new covenant age, this work is accomplished by the Holy Spirit, who conforms the believer to the image of Christ (Romans 8:29). It includes the enlightening of the heart to come to know *what is the hope of His calling, what are the riches of the glory of His inheritance in the saints, and what is the surpassing greatness of His power toward us who believe* (Ephesians 1:18-19).

Reasonings

For though we walk in the flesh, we do not war according to the flesh, for the weapons of our warfare are not of the flesh, but divinely powerful for the destruction of fortresses. We are destroying speculations [reasonings] and every lofty thing raised up against the knowledge of God, and we are taking every thought captive to the obedience of Christ. **2 Corinthians 10:3-5**

There is great spiritual warfare surrounding a believer's decisions to honor God in his life. He tends to determine for himself what he should do in his attempts to honor God. The battle Paul speaks of centers on man's thoughts. In his book, "Spiritual Authority," Watchman Nee observes from the above passage the following:

Paul mentions that we must destroy reasonings and every high thing that lifts itself up against the knowledge of God. Man likes to build reasons as strongholds around his thought, yet these reasons must be destroyed and thought taken captive. Reasons are to be cast aside, but thought is to be brought back. In spiritual warfare, the strongholds need to be stormed before the thought can be taken captive. If reasons are not cast aside, there is no possibility of bringing man's thoughts into obedience to Christ.

Man tends to try to solve all his problems and challenges by reason and his ability to map out a conclusion to any difficulty, utilizing his cognitive skills. The spiritual man recognizes that he must follow a different pathway. Once the believer has found obedience to divine authority apart from reason, deferring the decision process to the Divine will opens the door to true spirituality (that which is born of the Spirit is spiritual – John 3:6) and provides a victory over the strength of sin. When man relies on his own ability apart from God, he restricts himself to the natural. But when he allows the Holy Spirit to take charge, the supernatural becomes possible. Consider the following:

There is a story in Judaism's oral tradition about a rabbi named Yehoshua who went on a journey with the prophet Elijah in an effort to understand God's mysterious ways. On the first night of the journey, the pair stayed at the rundown home of a kind elderly couple. Much to Yehoshua's surprise, Elijah prayed that the couple's cow would die immediately. The next day, the two men approached the home of a wealthy man and asked for some food, but the man refused to give them even a morsel. Yehoshua was surprised again when Elijah prayed that the weak foundations of the man's home never collapse. The rest of the journey was filled with more of the same; Elijah prayed for good things to happen to bad people and for bad things to happen to good people.

At the end of the journey, Elijah explained the purpose of his prayers to his very perplexed companion. At the home of the elderly couple, Elijah foresaw that the wife would die the next day. He prayed that the couple's cow be taken instead. At the home of the miserly man, Elijah saw that there was a treasure buried under his home. He prayed that the foundation stays intact so that the man would never find it. Elijah explained all of his prayers similarly. On the surface, none of it made sense, but when Elijah explained the unseen context of each scenario, everything made perfect sense.

One Shepherd

> "My servant David will be king over them, and they will all have one shepherd, and they will walk in My ordinances and keep My statutes and observe them. "They will live on the land that I gave to Jacob, My servant, in which your fathers lived; and they will live on it, they, and their sons and their sons' sons, forever; and David, My servant, will be their prince forever. "I will make a covenant of peace with them; it will be an everlasting covenant with them. And I will place them and multiply them and will set My sanctuary in their midst forever. "My dwelling place also will be with them, and I will be their God, and they will be My people. "And the nations will know that I am the Lord who sanctifies Israel when My sanctuary is in their midst forever."''
> **Ezekiel 37:24-28**

In Ezekiel 37, given to Ezekiel before the final siege of Jerusalem in 587 BC, God gave Ezekiel the prophecy that in future times and not during Ezekiel's time, the Jews would return to their land and become an independent nation again. The fulfillment of this process began on May 14, 1948, with the acceptance of Israel as a nation, but it will not be completed until the Kingdom Age is introduced to the world upon the defeat of the Antichrist and the subsequent elevation of David to his throne. When the people have one shepherd (Jesus Christ, the Messiah), *they will walk in My ordinances and, keep My statutes and observe them.* They will occupy their promised land under a covenant of peace, an everlasting covenant where *I will be their God, and they will be My people.* When He speaks of His dwelling place being with them, He is referencing the indwelling Holy Spirit, who sanctifies the believer to walk in all His ways.

Much of Proverbs is written to address righteousness and distinguish between the righteous, those who conform to God's standards, and the wicked, those who willingly abuse those standards. In Proverbs 10:16-17, *The wages* [pullah – rewards for work] *of the righteous is life, the income* [tebuah – increase, revenue] *of the wicked, punishment. He is on the path of life who heeds* [shamar – protects, guards] *instruction, but he who ignores reproof goes astray.* The righteous one guards and protects God's instructions as a means of the highest quality of life available to him. Proverbs 13:4-6 states that diligence makes one healthy and satisfied. *The soul of the sluggard craves and gets nothing, but the soul of the diligent is made fat* [dashen – good health, satisfied]. *A righteous man* [saddiyq – one who conforms to God's standards] *hates falsehood, but a wicked man acts disgustingly and shamefully. Righteousness* [sedaqah – blameless conduct, integrity] *guards the one whose way is blameless, but wickedness subverts the sinner.*

Believe in Him

Do not work [ergazomai – labor, work] for the food which perishes, but for the food which endures to eternal life, which the Son of Man will give to you, for on Him the Father, God, has set His seal." Therefore, they said to Him, "What shall we do so that we may work the works of God?" Jesus answered and said to them, "This is the work of God, that you believe in Him whom He has sent." **John 6:27-29**

When Jesus said, *Do not work for food that perishes*, He was saying that people should labor for what is eternal and lasts forever. In Matthew 4:4, *Man does not live on bread alone but on every word that proceeds out of the mouth of God*. Physical food is temporary, but spiritual food leads to eternal life. The Son of Man will provide this spiritual food, that is, Christ (John 6:35). God the Father Himself acknowledged Jesus's claim that He is true heavenly *food*. The people recognized that Jesus was saying that God had a work for them. They would do God's requirement if He would inform them what it was. They believed that they could please God by performing good deeds. Jesus's response was a significant correction to their understanding. They could not please God by doing good works. There is only one work of God, that is, one thing God requires. They need to put their trust in the One sent by the Father. Man cannot please God by doing good works for salvation. God demands that people recognize their inability to save themselves and freely receive His gift on the basis of faith alone.

The more the believer walks by faith, the more he will recognize that every work that God does is meant to expand his faith. The working out of what has been worked in is the process of being sanctified in truth. *For their sakes I sanctify Myself, that they themselves also may be sanctified in truth* (John 17:19).

Chapter 9
Perspective

When I was first introduced to studying the Bible, it was in the context of the King James version, and I had a hard time with it. The Old English employed in King James left me searching for meaning in many idioms of speech that the original translators utilized. For example, what does Romans 11:29 mean when it says, *"the gifts and calling of God are without repentance"*? After studying what was behind the various translations, I adopted the New American Standard (NASB) as my primary source because of its attention to both accuracy and readability. By the way, the NASB translates "without repentance" as "irrevocable," and that gives us the right perspective on that verse.

Having the right perspective is critical in properly understanding divine truth. So much of man's troubles are attributable to his lack of understanding and applying truth because his point of view is either wrong or distorted. Distortion can leads him to make many wrong decisions. Proverbs 23:7 tells us that *"as he thinks within himself, so He is."* Having a proper perspective is affected not only by the ability to think clearly but also by the quality of the information being processed. In 2 Corinthians 4:18, *"while we look not at the things which are seen, but at the things which are not seen; for the things which are seen are temporal, but the things which are not seen are eternal."* Divine perspective recognizes that seeing things clearly is not conditioned on sight.

A Story that Illustrates My Point

Once, there were two wealthy Jewish businessmen who lived in Eastern Europe. Both men were involved in real estate and often did business together. One day, the two friends got into a dispute about a small piece of land. Each one claimed to be the owner. Over time, the argument grew into a full-out war. Even though the piece of land in question was practically insignificant in the context of what each man already owned, neither would budge. The two men became bitter enemies.

Eventually, at the insistence of community members, the men agreed to see the local rabbi and let him resolve the dispute. The rabbi listened patiently as each man presented his case. After they had finished speaking, the rabbi asked if he could go and see the land in question. The two men escorted the rabbi to the small piece of land that had caused them both so much anguish.

When they arrived at the site, the rabbi declared that he could not determine which man was the rightful owner. "Do you mind if I ask the land?" the rabbi requested. The two businessmen were bewildered at this strange request, but they agreed for lack of anything else to say. The rabbi pressed his ear to the ground as though he were listening. Then he stood up and nodded knowingly. "The land has resolved this issue for us," the rabbi explained triumphantly. Each man was eager to hear the verdict. "The land told me," said the rabbi, "that you think it belongs to you, and you think it belongs to you. The truth of the matter is, however, that one day soon, both of you will actually belong to it!"

The moral of the story: when you get too attached to the things of this world, your understanding of what really matters is infected. Paul warns us in 2 Timothy 2:3-7 that getting entangled in the affairs of everyday life instead of being focused on the priorities of life will distort the truth:

Suffer hardship with me as a good soldier of Christ Jesus. No soldier in active service entangles himself in the affairs of everyday life so that he may please the one who enlisted him as a soldier. Also, if anyone competes as an athlete, he does not win the prize unless he competes according to the rules. The hard-working farmer ought to be the first to receive his share of the crops. 7 Consider what I say, for the Lord will give you understanding in everything.

With the right perspective, **"the Lord will give you understanding in everything."**

Married to Christ

Or do you not know, brethren (for I am speaking to those who know the law), that the law has jurisdiction over a person as long as he lives? For the married woman is bound by law to her husband while he is living; but if her husband dies, she is released from the law concerning the husband. So then, if while her husband is living, she is joined to another man, she shall be called an adulteress; but if her husband dies, she is free from the law, so that she is not an adulteress though she is joined to another man. Therefore, my brethren, you also were made to die to the Law through the body of Christ, so that you might be joined to another, to Him who was raised from the dead, in order that we might bear fruit for God. For while we were in the flesh, the sinful passions, which were aroused by the Law, were at work in the members of our body to bear fruit for death. But now we have been released [katargeo – freed, the Law rendered inactive] *from the Law, having died to that by which we were bound, so that we serve in newness of the Spirit and not in oldness of the letter.* **Romans 7:1-6**

The Apostle introduces a subject that caused him difficulty: his struggle with his sin nature. Later in the passage, Paul confesses, *For I know that nothing good dwells in me, that is, in my flesh; for the willing is present in me, but the doing of the good is not* (Romans 7:18-19). He explained above that victory comes from recognizing "Who" the believer is married to, the husband, and a reference to the Law of Moses or Christ. He clarifies that this change in perspective results from dying to the husband, the Law, thereby being free from its requirements. Otherwise, the believer married to the Law of Moses must keep it in its entirety. *For whoever keeps the whole law and yet stumbles in one point `has become guilty of all* (James 2:10). Paul is teaching that the believer cannot be married to the Law and to Christ at the same time.

The aorist, passive, indicative verb, *katargeo*, means that, through Christ's death and resurrection, the believer receives the benefit of this eternal work of God and not through his own efforts. Instead, the believer considers himself dead to the Law but alive to God. *Nevertheless, knowing that a man is not justified by the works of the Law but through faith in Christ Jesus, even we have believed in Christ Jesus, so that we may be justified by faith in Christ and not by the works of the Law; since by the works of the Law no flesh will be justified* (Galatians 2:16).

Spiritual life is a proper perspective and not a series of activities.

Signs of the Times

As Christians living in the age between the two comings of Jesus Christ, we need the right perspective. The disciples asked Jesus when He would be coming back and what will be the signs of those times in Matthew 24. The essence of His response was that no one knows when He will return, so be on the alert (vigilant, aware) by keeping watch of what is happening and be ready (prepared) for its eminence. Jesus has been teaching them the right perspective in the last few days. Paul gives us more of those end-times signals in 1 Timothy 4 and 2 Timothy 3.

In Titus 2:11-14, Paul instructed Titus (and us by extension),

> *For the grace of God has appeared, bringing salvation to all men, instructing us to deny ungodliness and worldly desires and to live sensibly, righteously, and godly in the present age,* **looking for the blessed hope and the appearing of the glory of our great God and Savior, Christ Jesus,** *who gave Himself for us to redeem us from every lawless deed, and to purify for Himself a people for His own possession, zealous for good deeds.*

The reference is to His first coming as the grace of God and the Apostle's encouragement to look for His return (second coming) with great anticipation. This perspective will lead His people to be zealous for good deeds and thereby prove to be His possession.

Take a good look at a tapestry from both sides. When it is seen from the intended perspective (above), it looks beautiful, but flip it upside down, and all you see is imperfection. The question is this – from which direction are you seeing your life and your future, from below or from above? The answer to that question may determine the quality of your life in these last days.

Chapter 10
A Hebrew Inheritance

"Go up to a land [eres – earth, used to describe the promised land] flowing with milk and honey [debash – honey, symbolizing the richness and fertility of the land]; for I will not go up in your midst, because you are an obstinate [stubborn] people, and I might destroy you on the way."
Exodus 33:3

An essential element of the covenant God made with Abraham was the inheritance of land promised by God for Abraham and his descendants. Yet, there would be conditions regarding the possession of that land. Before Israel would occupy and possess it, pagan nations needed to be dispossessed of the land. This would not take place for more than 400 years, following Israel's deliverance from Egyptian bondage.

God made a covenant with Israel that they would become his own special people. He promised them an inheritance, namely a land where they could develop into a holy nation. Israel, however, became a people in Egypt before they occupied the land. To become a nation, they had to gain possession of the land. They left Egypt, agreed to the covenant at Sinai, and then proceeded to take Palestine as their possession. However, forty years passed between Sinai and the first successful attempt at conquest.

Iniquity of the Amorites

God said to Abram, "Know for certain that your descendants will be strangers in a land that is not theirs, where they will be enslaved and oppressed for four hundred years. "But I *will also judge the nation whom they will serve, and afterward, they will come out with many possessions. "As for you, you shall go to your fathers in peace; you will be buried at a good old age. "Then, in the fourth generation, they will return here, **for the iniquity of the Amorite is not yet complete."* **Genesis 15:13-16**

Abraham could not possess the land because the sin of the Amorites was not yet complete. Leviticus 18:24-30 teaches that the morality of a people either allows them to occupy a land or causes the land to expel them. Israel possessed Canaan by dispossessing the Amorites due to the sin of its inhabitants, which abounded to the point that God refused to allow them to occupy that land. In such a light, Israel became the means of God's judgment on these nations. Yet, God would use Israel as His instrument of justice only when they willingly submit to His sovereignty and become the inheritance recipients solely under his love. A covenant results in inheritance, but one must come to the inheritance to obtain it. And he must be willing to face all opponents in obtaining the inheritance. Yet, in reality, God defeats the opponents and allows the inheritance to be obtained.

The Land Defiled

*'For the land has become defiled; therefore, I have brought its punishment upon it, so the land has spewed out its inhabitants. 'But as for you, you are to keep My statutes and My judgments and shall not do any of these abominations, neither the native nor the alien who sojourns among you (for the men of the land who have been before you have done all these abominations, and **the land has become defiled**); so that the land will not spew you out, should you defile it, as it has spewed out the nation which has been before you. 'For whoever does any of these abominations,*

those persons who do so shall be cut off from among their people. 'Thus, you are to keep My charge, that you do not practice any of the abominable customs which have been practiced before you, so as not to defile yourselves with them; I am the Lord your God.'" **Leviticus 18:25-30**

Part of a covenant relationship with Yahweh is the people's willingness to live a life consistent with God's people. God had ordained the extermination of the Canaanites, but disobedient Israelites would suffer the same punishment as their predecessors. The land would vomit out its inhabitants to show how detestable these practices are in God's sight. The land designed and consecrated for His people would expel the inhabitants due to their indulgence in the abominations of their immoralities. The iniquity of the Canaanites was now full. The Israelites are exhorted to a pure and holy life on the ground that Yahweh, the Holy One, is their God and that they are His people.

Designated as Sacred

*'You are, therefore, to keep all My statutes and all My ordinances and do them so that the land to which I am bringing you to live will not spew you out. 'Moreover, you shall not follow the customs of the nation which I will drive out before you, for they did all these things, and therefore, I have abhorred them. 'Hence, I have said to you, "You are to possess their land, and I Myself will give it to you **to possess it**, a land flowing with milk and honey." I am the Lord your God, who has separated you from the peoples. 'You are therefore to make a distinction [badal - separate, divide] between the clean animal and the unclean and between the unclean bird and the clean; and you shall not make yourselves detestable by animal or by bird or by anything that creeps on the ground, which I have separated for you*

> *as unclean. 'Thus, you are to be holy [qadosh – designated as sacred] to Me, for I the Lord am holy, and I have set you apart from the peoples to be Mine.* **Leviticus 20:22-26**

Yahweh was about to give the rich and fertile land for them as a possession, whose inhabitants He had driven out because of their abominations, to be their God, who had separated Israel from the nations. For this reason, they were also to separate (make distinctions) between clean and unclean cattle and birds and not defile themselves through unclean animals, with which the earth swarmed and which God had prohibited them from eating or touching when dead because they were defiled. They were designated as sacred since Yahweh was holy, and he had severed them from the nations to belong to Him and be the nation of His possession. They would possess the land in holiness.

Defining Inheritance

The Interpreter's Dictionary of the Bible speaks of inheritance in the Old Testament as:

> *In many instances of biblical usage, the theological meaning of the word goes beyond the legalistic. Apart from any legal processes, it may characterize the bestowal of a merciful God's gift or possession upon his people in fulfillment of a promise or **as a reward for obedience**.*

An inheritance is not something to occupy but, more often, something to possess. When given by God, possession represents the principle of ownership or stewardship requiring accountability to varying degrees. The possession of land, which Israel received by lot from God, was to remain the inalienable property of the families. According to an old-standing custom, the father's property went to his sons, the firstborn receiving a double portion, the other sons single and equal portions. Considering this division, the firstborn, as head of the family, had to provide food, clothing, and other necessities in his house, not only for his mother but also for his sisters until they married. Moses more precisely defined this custom: the father could not deprive his firstborn of his birthright by mere whim, but it might be taken away because of a trespass against the father, as in the case of Reuben.

Righteous Versus Wicked

Cease from anger and forsake wrath; do not fret; it leads only to evildoing. For evildoers will be cut off, but those who wait for the Lord will inherit the land. Yet a little while and, the wicked man will be no more, and you will look carefully for his place, and he will not be there. But the humble will inherit the land and will delight themselves in abundant prosperity. **Psalm 37:8-11**

David was preoccupied with the disparity between God's dealings with the wicked and the righteous. Although we do not know the events that spurned the writing of this psalm, David kept bringing the conversation back to the principle of inheritance of the land. Like Psalm 73, David laments that the wicked are not being dealt with promptly. Humanity desires to see justice when those who cause injustice are not immediately and effectively addressed. Yet David reminds himself that the wicked will be properly confronted in due time. The humble will inherit the land and delight in abundance, a reward for their humility. In the same way, the righteous one who is blessed inherits the land. This inheritance is promised to those who learn to wait for the Lord.

The wicked borrows and does not pay back, but the righteous is gracious and gives. For those blessed by Him will inherit the land, but those cursed by Him will be cut off. **Psalm 37:21-22**

Depart from evil and do good so you will abide forever. For the Lord loves justice and does not forsake His godly ones; they are preserved forever, but the descendants of the wicked will be cut off. The righteous will inherit the land and dwell in it forever. **Psalm 37:27-29**

Wait for the Lord and keep His way, and He will exalt you to inherit the land; when the wicked are cut off, you will see it. **Psalm 37:34**

Rest

"Remember the word which Moses, the servant of the Lord, commanded you, saying, 'The Lord your God gives you rest and will give you this land.' "Your wives, your little ones, and your cattle shall remain in the land which Moses gave you beyond the Jordan, but you shall cross before your brothers in battle array, all your valiant warriors, and shall help them, until the Lord gives your brothers rest, as He gives you, and they also possess the land which the Lord your God is giving them. Then you shall return to your own land and possess that which Moses the servant of the Lord gave you beyond the Jordan toward the sunrise." **Joshua 1:13-15**

Joshua reminds the tribes of Reuben, Gad, and the half-tribe of Manasseh that though they had received their inheritance east of the Jordan, they were committed to fighting with their brothers and assisting in conquering the land west of Jordan from the Canaanites. Both the eastern and western tribes viewed their new homeland as a place of rest from their long wilderness journey. The promise of rest in Canaan is first recorded in

Deuteronomy 3:19-20: *'But your wives and your little ones and your livestock (I know that you have much livestock) shall remain in your cities which I have given you until the Lord gives rest to your fellow countrymen as to you, and they also possess the land which the Lord your God will give them beyond the Jordan. Then you may return every man to his possession, which I have given you.'* Jesus addressed this rest in Matthew 11:28: "*Come to Me, all who are weary and heavy-laden, and I will give you rest.*"

Through Tribulations and Evils

Uriel, the angel assigned to weather according to the Ancient Book of Enoch, had the following conversation with Ezra in 2 Ezdras, chapter 7, written by Ezra and included in the Apocrypha:

"Stand up, Ezra, and hear what I have come to tell you." Suppose there was a great city in a large valley, but the only entrance to it was a very narrow passage through the mountains with fire on the right side and a jagged cliff over deep waters on the left side, and this single path between these two is only wide enough for one man at a time.

Now, if a man was given this city for an inheritance, the only way for the heir to possess it is to go through the danger, right?" I said to him, "Yes, my lord!" He answered and said to me, "So also is Israel's portion. Because of their sakes, God made the world, and when Adam transgressed my commandments, that which had been made was condemned. Because of this, the entrances of this future age are narrow and full of sorrow and travail. They are very few and filled with many perils and pain, but the future world is broad and sure and abundant with eternal fruit. Unless the living pass through the tribulations and evils, they will not receive what has been stored up for them."

The Hebrew's inheritance does not involve a free pass but rather a willingness to stay true to the lifestyle the Lord has ordained for each believer. Although painful and challenging at times, the rewards are immeasurable. The cost is worth it! David recognized this principle in 2 Samuel 24:24: *However, the king said to Araunah, "No, but I will surely buy it from you for a price, for I will not offer burnt offerings to the Lord my God which cost me nothing." So, David bought the threshing floor and the oxen for fifty shekels of silver.*

Chapter 11

From Egypt to Canaan

NATURAL MAN	CARNAL CHRISTIAN	SPIRITUAL CHRISTIAN	REWARDED CHRISTIAN
	Struggle	Maturity	Rest
	Exodus Generation	Second Generation	
	In the Wilderness	Across the Jordan	Receiving the Inheritance
Exodus 1-11	Exo 12 - Deut 34	Joshua 1-11	Joshua 12-22
NON-CHRISTIAN	CARNAL CHRISTIAN	WARFARE	VICTORY
EGYPT	WILDERNESS	CANAAN	
IN THE WORLD	IN THE KINGDOM		AT THE TABLE
1 Corinthians 2:14	1 Corinthians 3:1-3	Romans 12:1-2	2 Cor 5:10; 1 Cor 3:13-14

The best book I've ever read on the subject of the finished work of Christ is "The Reign of the Servant Kings," written by Joseph Dillow. On page 100, he includes the above diagram to illustrate the relationship between the journeys of the children of Israel and the Christian life. This illustration is worth a closer look.

The four columns show the four different states of any person from a New Testament Christian perspective. They include the natural man (unregenerate, unsaved), the carnal Christian (saved but not spiritual, of the flesh), the spiritual Christian, and the rewarded Christian. The diagram compares each of these New Testament conditions to the plight of the Jewish people, from their bondage in Egypt to their eventual possession of the inherited land in Canaan. Scripture is full of biblical illustrations that convey spiritual principles.

Natural Man

In 1 Corinthians 2:14, Paul says, "*But a natural man does not accept the things of the Spirit of God, for they are foolishness to him; and he cannot understand them, because they are spiritually appraised.*" This man is comparable to the Jew still living in bondage in Egypt, as illustrated in the first 11 chapters of Exodus. He has never acknowledged Jesus as Savior and is fully preoccupied with his worldly presence and priorities. The Jews were dealing not only with their bondage to Egypt but also with the plagues that God was bringing against the Egyptians and their land and people. The natural man is subject to his environment and his desires.

Carnal Christian

Paul explains the carnal Christian in 1 Corinthians 3:1-3, "*And I, brethren, could not speak to you as to spiritual men, but as to men of flesh, as to infants in Christ. I gave you milk to drink, not solid food, for you were not yet able to receive it. Indeed, even now, you are not yet able, for you are still fleshly. For since there is jealousy and strife among you, are you not fleshly, and are you not walking like mere men?*"

Carnal Christianity represents a true believer who has yet to find deliverance from the power of the sinfulness of his nature. The powers of his fleshly desires continue to govern his life despite the presence of the Holy Spirit within. His life is defined by continuous struggle, similar to that of the Jews, as represented in Exodus 12 (the introduction of the Passover lamb – a picture of salvation) and Deuteronomy 34 (their wanderings in the wilderness). These are the ones who never make it to the promised land since they believed the bad report of the 10 spies in Numbers 13-14. They never find a home in their faith in God but are always complaining about their situation. They are in the kingdom but unable to find real joy in their salvation, so they continue to wander.

Spiritual Christian

Then, there is the spiritual Christian, who has found deliverance from the power of his nature, the world, and the devil. These are the ones who find their promised land, just as the second-generation Jews did in Joshua 1-11. Romans 12:1-2 says, *"Therefore I urge you, brethren, by the mercies of God, to present your bodies a living and holy sacrifice, acceptable to God, which is your spiritual service of worship. And do not be conformed to this world, but be transformed by the renewing of your mind, so that you may prove what the will of God is, that which is good and acceptable and perfect."*

The spiritual Christian has crossed the Jordan River into the Promised Land and recognizes that the quality of his life is not derived from his circumstances but has allowed the Holy Spirit to lead, direct, and guide his life and decisions. He recognizes the warfare within the world itself and pursues spiritual maturity through his surrender to God's will. He has made himself available to God's purposes. The only thing he lacks is contentment and rest. Rewards is a byproduct of rest.

Rewarded Christian

The final step in the process of complete maturity in Christ is the rewards associated with that reality. These rewards are not only in the next life, but many are for our current existence. In 2 Corinthians 5:10, *"For we must all appear before the judgment seat of Christ, so that each one may be recompensed for his deeds in the body, according to what he has done, whether good or bad."* Then there is 1 Corinthians 3:13-14, *"Each man's work will become evident; for the day will show it because it is to be revealed with fire, and the fire itself will test the quality of each man's work. If any man's work which he has built on it remains, he will receive a reward."*

The Jewish counterpart to this state is found in Joshua 12-22, where the twelve tribes receive their promised lands. The New Testament equivalent to receiving the inheritance of land is faith-rest. Just as New Testament believers are rewarded for their works in heaven, these believers also find the victorious life in their ability to rest in any situation. The Apostle Paul says this in Philippians 4:11-13, *"Not that I speak from want, for I have learned to be content in whatever circumstances I am. I know how to get along with humble means, and I also know how to live in prosperity; in any and every circumstance, I have learned the secret of being filled and going hungry, both of having abundance and suffering need. I can do all things through Him who strengthens me."* The victorious life depends only on God at His banquet table.

References

Charles C. Dillow, Th.D. "The Reign of the Servant Kings". Schoettle Publishing Co.

Chapter 12
Partakers of Christ

When the Lord introduced the Law to Moses, He instituted a covenant centered on the Tabernacle/Temple and the Torah. Religious life would be centered on these two elements. This covenant, also known as the old covenant, would be superseded by the new covenant through Jesus, the Messiah, who would become the Temple (John 2:21) and the fulfillment of the Torah (Matthew 5:17), the Logos, the Word of God (John 1:1). What Jesus accomplished on Calvary when He said, *It is finished*, was much more than the completion of His work on earth. He was the lamb slain before the foundation of the world (Revelation 13:8), the one spoken of to Adam as the seed of the woman who would defeat the works of the enemy (Genesis 3:15).

The Judaism of Jesus' day, as it is today, holds that God gave Jewish leaders the authority to interpret the specifics of the Torah (the Oral Torah) and apply them to the people as they saw fit. Jesus addressed this matter with the Pharisees in Matthew 15, referring to these laws as *the tradition of the elders*. He was confronting these laws when they contradicted the 613 Laws of Moses. Leadership recognized authority the Lord never gave them. This same issue is present in the Roman Catholic Church. When Jesus told Peter, *you are Peter, and upon this rock, I will build My church; and the gates of Hades will not overpower it* (Matthew 16:18), He was not giving the church, through a Pope, authority to make laws and impose them on the people, but instead the Holy Spirit would make those determinations. *But when He, the Spirit of truth, comes, He will guide you into all the truth; for He will not speak on His own initiative, but whatever He hears, He will speak* (John 16:13).

A Time of Reformation

The heavy-handed church-controlled believers' lives with full authority for more than a millennium throughout the Middle Ages, but their authority began to be questioned in the 15th century and then more completely in the 16th century with Martin Luther and other Reformers publishing works that questioned many of the church and papal practices of the day. With the Renaissance came a new freedom for the people, thanks to the advent of the printing press and a humanist movement that emphasized individual rights. It was the perfect breeding ground for major changes to come to the stoic and bureaucratic church, and the Reformers took every advantage of those opportunities with passion, even unto death. The Protestant Reformation would forever change the world. They were introducing personal freedoms to believers through a deeper commitment to the Scriptures and their individual priesthoods. Believers would be reintroduced to their first-century relationship with God.

> *For the Law was given through Moses;* **grace and truth** *were realized through Jesus Christ.* **John 1:17**

> *For* **by grace**, *you have been saved through faith; and that not of yourselves, it is the gift of God; not as a result of works, so that no one may boast.* **Ephesians 2:8-9**

Jesus came to the Jews to introduce a new relationship with God, a new covenant. Unlike the old covenant, this new covenant is unconditional, dependent solely on God and not on man's ability to keep numerous rules and regulations. The religious system introduced through Moses was superseded by a covenant based on grace, a free gift, and faith, man's willingness to place his trust in Jesus Christ, full of grace and truth (John 1:14). Since this new covenant is based on a free gift from God, it cannot fail it is eternal.

The one who believes in Jesus and His accomplishments that Jesus met the requirements of a holy God, the believer's security is eternal; he cannot lose his salvation. The church's struggle is in how man's failure is addressed within a religious system.

Partakers

For we have become partakers [*metochos* – spiritually united to] *of Christ if we hold fast the beginning* [first confidence] *of our assurance* [*hupostasis* – confidence, assurance, guarantee, or proof] *firm until the end.*
Hebrews 3:14

When addressing the challenges associated with human failure, the church is left with three major doctrinal positions that govern the church's responsibility in spiritually addressing human failure. One is Arminianism, which holds that the believer can forfeit his salvation. In this system, the loss of salvation becomes the lever that keeps the believer in a state of fellowship with God. The second is Reformed theology, rooted in Calvinism, which interprets predestination as God choosing those who would be saved, regardless of their free will. Since man is totally depraved, he is not capable of making a choice for God. At salvation, the believer is immediately saved and obeys. The third is defined as being a Partaker of Christ. This position recognizes salvation as eternal (it cannot be lost), and the state of the believer before God is perfect. However, the process of sanctification, which involves becoming spiritually united with Christ, is ongoing and dependent on the believer's free will to maintain fellowship with Christ in his daily walk.

According to Hebrews 3:14, the spiritual unity that comes from a consistent, intimate connection to Christ provides evidence, proof, and assurance of salvation. The ongoing pursuit of God's righteousness in life provides fulfillment and satisfaction. In Matthew 5:6, Jesus said, *"Blessed are those who hunger and thirst for righteousness, for they shall be satisfied."* Unity is driven supernaturally by the Father's love for His Son and Jesus for each follower. Some of His last words to His Father, uttered the night before His crucifixion, are found in John 17:25-26, *"O righteous Father, although the world has not known You, yet I have known You; and these have known that You sent Me; and I have made Your name known to them, and will make it known, so that the love with which You loved Me may be in them, and I in them."*

Partakers of the Holy Spirit

*For in the case of those who have once been enlightened and have tasted of the heavenly gift and have been made **partakers** [metochos – spiritually united to] **of the Holy Spirit**, and have tasted the good word of God and the powers of the age to come, and then have fallen away [parapipto – wander astray], it is impossible to renew them again to repentance since they again crucify to themselves the Son of God and put Him to open shame.* **Hebrews 6:4-6**

Some partake of Him as to be united to Him, in whom He becomes the principle of spiritual life and motion: these have the fruit of the Spirit and communion with Him; they enjoy His personal presence and ongoing fellowship; they have received Him as a spirit of illumination and conviction, of regeneration and sanctification, as the spirit of faith, and as a comforter; and as a spirit of adoption, and the earnest and seal of future glory; but they can never fall away so as to perish.

According to Arminianism, everyone is born with a sin nature and is, therefore, on their way to hell. God enables everyone, at some time in their life, to understand God's gift of salvation. He gives each person the free will to accept or reject the gift. Since its inception, the Catholic Church has employed this principle to maintain discipline among its followers by threatening the loss of salvation, which they teach is achieved through the reception of the sacraments. Arminianism holds that one can lose his salvation when he fails to some degree. There are several troubling verses, including Hebrews 6:4-6, that suggest the loss of salvation occurs when one has *fallen away*. The context of the passages from Hebrews 5:11 through Hebrews 6 refer to believers in Christ who are not maturing in their faith, wandering astray from the path to maturity and away from sound doctrine and faithfulness to the true faith. They've tasted the good word of God and the powers of the age to come, but they've abandoned the right path —the narrow way that leads to life (Matthew 7:14).

Lordship Salvation

Reformed theology prioritizes predestination, that God chooses believers before the foundation of the world for salvation apart from their free will and empowers them with the ability to persevere, to endure until the end. One contemporary proponent of this position was John MacArthur, and according to his book, "The Gospel According to Jesus," he proposes that a true believer has accepted Jesus as both Savior and Lord. This position is commonly known as "Lordship Salvation"; the believer will not continue in sin after salvation. This position also embraces the idea that man's total depravity disqualifies him from being able to choose faith in Jesus freely, so God does it for him. This belief system is becoming increasingly prevalent today.

Abide in Me

"I am the true vine, and My Father is the vinedresser. Every branch in me that does not bear fruit, He removes [airo – take away]; and every branch that bears fruit, He cleans and prunes it so that it may bear more fruit. You are already clean because of the word which I have spoken to you. Abide in Me [dynamic fellowship, not organic union], and I in you. As the branch cannot bear fruit of itself unless it abides in the vine, so neither can you unless you abide in Me. I am the vine, you are the branches; he who abides in Me and I in him, he bears much fruit, for apart from Me you can do nothing. If anyone does not abide in Me, they are thrown away like a branch and wither; and they gather them and cast them into the Fire, where they are burned [divine discipline, loss of rewards]. If you abide in Me, and My words abide in you, ask whatever you wish, and it will be done for you. My Father is glorified by this, **that you bear much fruit***, and so prove to be [ginomai – become] My disciples.* **John 15:1-8**

The above passage, the words of Jesus Himself, provide a framework for a relationship with Christ. As discussed, three possibilities include: 1. The relationship any Christian sustains with Christ (Arminian); 2. The relationship a professing Christian sustains to Christ (Reformed Theology); and 3. A relation that only mature and growing Christians sustain with Christ (Partakers). When viewed closely, it becomes clear that the analogy best describes the Partaker, and a branch "in Me" is not one that is organically connected to the vine but rather a branch that derives its sustenance from Christ and lives in fellowship with Him.

Divine Discipline

The question is raised regarding those who are thrown away like a branch and wither (Verse 6). Does this signify a loss of salvation? Those who fall out of fellowship with Christ will lose touch with the life source and experience divine discipline or the loss of rewards at the Judgment Seat of Christ (1 Corinthians 3:15). In Hebrews 12:8-11:

But if you are without discipline, of which all have become partakers, then you are illegitimate children and not sons. Furthermore, we had earthly fathers to discipline us, and we respected them; shall we not much rather be subject to the Father of spirits and live? For they disciplined us for a short time as seemed best to them, but He disciplines us for our good so that we may share [*metalambano* – partake, share] *His holiness. All discipline for the moment seems not to be joyful but sorrowful; yet to those who have been trained by it, afterward, it yields the peaceful fruit of righteousness.*

The Lord disciplines all of His sons because He loves them. This discipline is intended to reunite us in fellowship with Him and His righteousness. As such, believers are brought into closer fellowship with His holiness through suffering or loss (Philippians 3:10). Fire is typically a reference to judgment, but it rarely refers to hell. The John 15 passage is all about fruit, more fruit, and much fruit. Those who remain in dynamic fellowship with Christ, the vine, will be fruitful to that degree and prove their discipleship. A key to dynamic fellowship is staying in the fight: *For a righteous man falls seven times and rises again, but the wicked stumble in time of calamity* (Proverbs 24:16).

Faith & Assurance

Now faith is the assurance [hupostasis - guarantee] *of things hoped for, the conviction* [elegchos – certain persuasion] *of things not seen.* **Hebrews 11:1**

Benjamin (B.B.) Warfield, a professor of Reformed theology at Princeton Theological Seminary during the late 19th and early 20th centuries and a highly regarded theologian, made the following statement about faith and assurance:

That is to say, with respect to belief, it is a mental recognition of what is before the mind as objectively true and real, and, therefore, depends upon the evidence that a thing is true and real and is determined by this evidence; it is the response of the mind to this evidence and cannot arise apart from it. ***It is, therefore, impossible that belief should be the product of a volition****; volitions look to the future and represent our desires; beliefs look to the present and represent our findings.*

He was saying that faith is not the creation of one's will and desire to act. Faith happens when future promises become present realities. Warfield further states:

Evidence cannot produce belief, faith, except in a mind open to this evidence and capable of responding to it. A mathematical demonstration is demonstrative proof of the proposition demonstrated. But even such a demonstration cannot produce conviction in a mind incapable of following the demonstration.

Faith is not a mechanical result of the presentation of evidence. Good evidence can be refused because of the subjective nature or condition of the mind to which it is addressed. This is the ground of responsibility for belief or faith: *"It is not merely a question of evidence but of subjectivity, and subjectivity is the other name for personality."*

Spiritually Appraised

The biblical solution is acknowledging that the natural man is incapable of this faith because it is spiritually discerned, a gift from God. This gift comes to the man whose heart is open to be illuminated and, therefore, capacity created. Man chooses to accept or reject the evidence provided by creation and found in the truth of Scripture and the gospel. Saving faith, instead of mere mental assent, depends on trust, a reliance upon the evidence. It also perceives a personal God and His love for mankind, as demonstrated at Calvary by Jesus Christ when mankind was His enemy. The nature of this love (agape) is both unconditional and self-sacrificing.

> *The Spirit Himself testifies with our spirit that we are children of God.* **Romans 8:16**

Assurance is a byproduct of the Holy Spirit's ongoing fellowship and communion with the child of God, which produces confidence in the believer's salvation. The Partaker looks outward to Christ and the Holy Spirit, knowing that inwardly, there is no evidence of the perfect position that God provides, based on faith and as a free gift. The Partaker's works represent a co-laboring with Christ in His work. The Arminian will always struggle since his failure could mean forfeiture of security. The warning passages of Scripture address his position, so he works to regain his salvation. The Reformed theology believer relies on his works as evidence of his salvation.

Rewards

So, He said, "A nobleman went to a distant country to receive a kingdom for himself and then return. And he called

ten of his slaves, and gave them ten minas and said to them, 'Do business with this until I come back.' But his citizens hated him and sent a delegation after him, saying, 'We do not want this man to reign over us.' When he returned after receiving the kingdom, he ordered that these slaves, to whom he had given the money, be called to him so that he might know what business they had done. The first appeared, saying, 'Master, your mina has made ten minas more.' And he said to him, **'Well done, good slave, because you have been faithful in a very little thing, you are to be in authority over ten cities.'** *The second came, saying, 'Your mina, master, has made five minas.' And he said to him also,* **'And you are to be over five cities**.*' Another came, saying, 'Master, here is your mina, which I kept put away in a handkerchief, for I was afraid of you because you are an exacting man; you take up what you did not lay down and reap what you did not sow.' He said to him,* **'By your own words, I will judge you, you worthless slave. Did you know that I am an exacting man, taking up what I did not lay down and reaping what I did not sow?** *Then why did you not put my money in the bank, and having come, I would have collected it with interest?' Then he said to the bystanders, 'Take the mina away from him and give it to the one who has the ten minas.' And they said to him, 'Master, he has ten minas already.'* **I tell you that to everyone who has, more shall be given, but from the one who does not have, even what he does have shall be taken away**. *But these enemies of mine, who did not want me to reign over them, bring them here and slay them in my presence."*
Luke 19:12-27

The above parable was given by Jesus to address the principle of rewards in the kingdom of heaven. It helps each believer understand what the Lord requires of them in this life. The nobleman represents Jesus Himself, who leaves the earth after His First Coming for heaven, later to return in His Second Coming. He would leave ten slaves, representing ten disciples, with ten minas (about three months' wages) to manage. Ten is the number for natural order; there were ten commandments that man must recognize as laws that define natural life. Their rejection by the citizens speaks of the reception of Christianity by the world during the Church Age. During His absence, the disciples should carry on the business of life with the provision given. Unlike the Parable of the Talents in Matthew 25, each disciple is given the same amount to begin with.

Each believer is given a measure of faith (Romans 12:3), and Jesus will reward each believer at the Judgment Seat of Christ (1 Corinthians 3:11-15) according to *the quality of each man's work*. At this judgment, the quality of these works will be tested by fire, and those works that survive the fire, represented by gold, silver, or precious stones, will receive a reward. The others, represented by wood, hay, and straw, speak of human effort and will not be rewarded. The first servant was faithful in *a very little thing* and was rewarded by reigning with Christ over ten cities (2 Timothy 2:12). The second is rewarded with five cities, while the third receives no reward, *saved, yet so as through fire* (1 Corinthians 3:15). Each is rewarded based on faithfulness to the will of God. How each believer spends the time God has given him on this earth determines his reward.

> *But, beloved, we are convinced of better things concerning you and things that accompany salvation, though we are speaking in this way. For God is not unjust so as to forget your work and the love which you have shown toward His name, in having ministered and in still ministering to the*

*saints. And we desire that each one of you show the same diligence **so as to realize the full assurance of hope until the end**, so that you will not be sluggish but imitators of those who, through faith and patience, inherit the promises.*
Hebrews 6:9-12

References

Dillow, Joseph C. "The Reign of the Servant Kings." Schoettle Publishing Co.

Chapter 13
Possessing Your Inheritance

Whatever you do, do your work heartily, as for the Lord rather than for men, knowing that from the Lord you will receive the reward of the inheritance [kleronomia – inheritance, possession]. It is the Lord Christ whom you serve. **Colossians 3:23-24**

Like the Old Testament usages, the words for inheritance in the New Testament primarily refer to spiritual obedience as a condition for receiving an inheritance. Becoming an heir can come through a family relationship, through faith, or some form of obedience or merit. Nearly every occurrence of *kleronomos* – inherit includes either the presence or absence of some work or character quality as a condition of obtaining or forfeiting the particular possession. The account of the Rich Young Ruler below provides insight:

Rich Young Ruler

And someone came to Him and said, "Teacher [didaskolos – instructor, master], what good thing shall I do that I may obtain [echo – implies continued possession] eternal life?" And He said to him, "Why are you asking Me about what is good? There is only One who is good, but if you wish to enter into life, keep the commandments." Then he said to Him, "Which ones?" And Jesus said, "YOU SHALL NOT COMMIT MURDER; YOU SHALL NOT COMMIT ADULTERY; YOU SHALL NOT STEAL; YOU SHALL NOT BEAR FALSE WITNESS; HONOR YOUR FATHER AND MOTHER; and YOU SHALL LOVE YOUR NEIGHBOR AS YOURSELF."

zhe young man said to Him, "All these things I have kept; what am I still lacking?" Jesus said to him, "If you wish to be complete [teleios - finished, the end goal], *go and sell your possessions and give to the poor, and you will have treasure in heaven; and come, follow Me." But when the young man heard this statement, he went away grieving, for he was one who owned much property. And Jesus said to His disciples, "Truly I say to you, it is hard* [duskolos – with difficulty] *for a rich man to enter the kingdom of heaven. Again, I say to you, it is easier for a camel to go through the eye of a needle than for a rich man to enter the kingdom of God." When the disciples heard this, they were very astonished and said, "Then who can be saved?" And looking at them, Jesus said to them, "With people, this is impossible, but with God, all things are possible."*
Matthew 19:16-26

Mark 10:17 tells us: *As He was setting out on a journey, a man ran up to Him and knelt before Him and asked Him, "Good Teacher, what shall I do to inherit eternal life?"* This young man, wealthy and most likely a leader in the Synagogue, approached Jesus as *Good Teacher,* kneeling before Him. His question: *what shall I do to inherit eternal life?* It appears he was a good man, sincerely asking the Master a very serious question, not intending to trap Him as the Pharisees did repeatedly, but desiring to be instructed in the right path to eternal life. Jesus' first response sets the man straight on what is good: the only one who is good is God. (According to the Talmud, "There is nothing else that is good but the Law.") He then reminded the young man to *"keep the commandments,"* that is, all 613 commandments. When questioned, *"Which ones?"* Jesus quoted those commandments related to one's relationship with others (6, 7, 8, 9, and 5), summarized by *YOU SHALL LOVE YOUR NEIGHBOR AS YOURSELF.* When he told Jesus that he believed the ruler had honored those commands, he still felt something was lacking. Keeping the Law did not bring any believer to inherit the Kingdom.

This ruler was not asking how he could earn salvation. Instead, he wondered how he could be assured of entering Messiah's Kingdom and his inheritance. Jesus was teaching him that the goodness of the Law of Moses was not sufficient to accomplish this. It would take a more profound commitment, represented by giving up his possessions. When Jesus addressed His disciples, He told them *So then, none of you can be My disciple who does not give up all his own possessions* (Luke 14:33). Jesus also disclosed that there is a spiritual energy that works against those who are rich, who have many possessions. The *eye of a needle* is an entrance to a fortified city that a camel could pass through by getting on its knees, signifying humility, that it is very difficult for a rich man to humble himself before God so as to receive his inheritance in eternity. *"With people, this is impossible, but with God, all things are possible."*

In the Wilderness

Do not harden your hearts, as at Meribah, As in the day of Massah in the wilderness, "When your fathers tested Me, they tried Me, though they had seen My work. "For forty years, I loathed that generation and said they are a people who err in their heart, and they do not know My ways. "Therefore, I swore in My anger, truly they shall not enter into My rest." **Psalm 95:8-11**

For who provoked Him when they had heard? Indeed, did not all those who came out of Egypt led by Moses? And with whom was He angry for forty years? Was it not with those who sinned, whose bodies fell in the wilderness? And to whom did He swear that they would not enter His rest, but to those who were disobedient [apeitheo – disobedient, not to allow oneself to be persuaded]? So, we see that they could not enter because of unbelief [apistos – faithlessness, distrust, unbelief]. **Hebrews 3:16-19**

These passages address the Hebrew people and their forty years in the wilderness before entering the Promised Land. The trip from Mount Sinai, where they received the Law of Moses, to the outskirts of the Promised Land (Kadesh barnea) took only 11 days (Deuteronomy 1:2). Moses was instructed to choose twelve spies, one from each tribe to investigate the lands beyond the Jordan River and send back a report. *We went into the land where you sent us, and it certainly does flow with milk and honey, and this is its fruit. "Nevertheless, the people who live in the land are strong, and the cities are fortified and very large; and moreover, we saw the descendants of Anak there* (Numbers 13:27-28). Apart from Joshua and Caleb, the spies discouraged the people from wanting to enter the Promised Land immediately. They would not accept Caleb's encouragement, *"We should by all means go up and take possession of it, for we will surely overcome it"* (Verse 30). Their unbelief turned to disobedience.

Finding Rest

Therefore, let us fear if, while a promise remains of entering His rest, any one of you may seem to have come short of it. For indeed we have had good news preached to us, just as they also; but the word they heard did not profit them, because it was not united by faith in those who heard. For we who have believed enter that rest. **Hebrews 4:1-3**

If rest is the ultimate prize in a believer's relationship with God, it is faith that not only opens the door to salvation but is the vessel that takes him to his promised land. These Hebrews had established their relationship with God through the Law of Moses, but their lack of faith and willingness to unite faith with what they heard, they failed to find the rest God had promised. RT Kendall, pastor of Westminster Chapel in London for 25 years, observed:

> It would be a serious mistake to dismiss the children of Israel in the wilderness by writing them off as unregenerate from the start. To say that such people were never saved is to fly in the face of the memorable fact that they kept the Passover. They obeyed Moses, who gave an unprecedented, if not strange command to sprinkle blood on either side and over the doors (Exodus 12:7). But they did it... If obeying Moses's command to sprinkle blood on the night of the Passover was not a type of saving faith, I do not know what is. These people were saved. We shall see them in heaven, even if it turns out they were saved so as by fire (1 Corinthians 3:15).

Sealed With the Holy Spirit

> In Him, you also, after listening to the message of truth, the gospel of your salvation—having also believed, you were **sealed** [sphragizo – seal, a mark of protection and ownership] **in Him with the Holy Spirit of promise**, who is given as a pledge [arrabon – first installment] of our inheritance, with a view to the redemption of God's own possession, to the praise of His glory. **Ephesians 1:13-14**

The Greek word *sphragizo* is used to describe a stone being fastened with a seal to prevent it from being removed from its position. The seal was engraved with a mark or distinctive design identifying the owner. It was often made from soft wax using a signet ring, leaving an impression on the wax to identify the owner. When one exercises faith to believe in who Jesus is and what He accomplished for each believer, the Holy Spirit is his seal and guarantee of protection and identity. According to Ephesians 4:30, the sealing is *with a view to the day of redemption* (Wuest), while the transformational work of sanctification takes place in the believer's life. These verses represent one of the strongest arguments that salvation cannot be lost but is eternal. In the same way, Paul warns the believer *Do not grieve* [*lupeo* – afflict with sorrow] *the Holy Spirit of God.* This sealing provides room to fail and recover; it can never be broken!

As the first installment of our inheritance, the Holy Spirit secures a legal claim upon something that is not entirely paid for. He represents an advance payment on the fulfillment of the contract. In Romans 8:23, *And not only this but also we ourselves,* **having the first fruits of the Spirit***, even we ourselves groan within ourselves, waiting eagerly for our adoption as sons, the redemption of our body.* God has legally and morally obligated Himself to the believer's salvation, sanctification, and glorification. It is confirmed when Paul spoke these words in 1 Corinthians 6:19-20 *Or do you not know that your body is a temple of the Holy Spirit who is in you, whom you have from God, and that you are not your own? For you have been bought with a price; therefore, glorify God in your body.* Communion with Christ is the glorification of God in the body.

Spiritually Preserved

Blessed be the God and Father of our Lord Jesus Christ, who, according to His great mercy, has caused us to be born again to a living hope through the resurrection of Jesus Christ from the dead, to obtain an inheritance which is imperishable and undefiled and will not fade away, reserved in heaven for you, who are protected [*phroureo* – spiritually preserved] *by the power of God through faith* [*pistis* – faithfulness] *for a salvation ready to be revealed in the last time.* **1 Peter 1:3-5**

The inheritance spoken of by Peter is not related to one's justification but faithfulness in one's relationship to God through the Holy Spirit. Paul tells us that the filling of the Holy Spirit is produced by one who avoids a life defined by debauchery: *And do not get drunk with wine, for that is dissipation* [*asotia – debauchery*], *but be filled with the Spirit* (Ephesians 5:18). This filling defines a quality of life that believers can access when they allow the Holy Spirit to control their lives by faith in the details of life. Jesus's words in Matthew 19:29-30 explain this principle: *And everyone who has left houses or brothers or sisters or father or mother or children or farms for My name's sake will receive many times as much and will inherit eternal life. But many who are first will be last, and the last, first.*

References

Dillow, Joseph C. "The Reign of the Servant Kings." Schoettle Publishing Co.

Chapter 14
Approaching God: Duty or Identity

According to the American Heritage Dictionary, "duty" can be defined as "An act or a course of action that is required of one by position, social custom, law, or religion," while "identity" means: 1. The set of characteristics by which a person or thing is definitively recognizable or known, and 2. The awareness that an individual or group has of being a distinct, persisting entity. Judaism and Christianity are identifiable by the inward as well as outward characteristics of their followers. The transformation of both the true Jew and the Christ-follower takes place in the heart. Duty can take the believer only so far; identity represents the transformation of the entire man.

> *"Now, Israel, what does the Lord your God require [saal – ask, beg, inquire] from you, but to fear [yare - not simple fear, but reverence, whereby one recognizes the power and position of the individual revered and renders him proper respect] the Lord your God, to walk [halak – basic idea of movement] in all His ways and love Him, and to serve [abad – work, labor] the Lord your God* **with all your heart** *and with all your soul, and to keep the Lord's commandments and His statutes which I am commanding you today for your good? "Behold, to the Lord your God belong heaven and the highest heavens, the earth and all that is in it. "Yet* **on your fathers did the Lord set His affection to love them**, *and He chose their descendants after them, even you above all peoples, as it is this day. "So,* **circumcise your heart** *[mul – remove the hardness of heart to love God]***, and stiffen your neck no longer**. *"For the Lord your God is the God of gods and the Lord of lords, the great, the mighty, and* **the**

awesome God who does not show partiality nor take a bribe. "He executes justice for the orphan and the widow and shows His love for the alien by giving him food and clothing. "So, show your love for the alien, for you were aliens in the land of Egypt. "You shall fear the Lord your God; you shall serve Him and cling to Him, and you shall swear by His name. "**He is your praise, and He is your God**, who has done these great and awesome things for you which your eyes have seen. "Your fathers went down to Egypt seventy persons in all, and now the Lord your God has made you as numerous as the stars of heaven. **Deuteronomy 10:12-22**

In the Mosaic law, God has commanded many things, most of which are related to external observances that can be enforced. But love and veneration cannot be enforced, even by God himself. They must be organic. So, even under the law of ordinances, where so much requires immediate obedience under an almighty God, His ultimate requirements are the internal qualities of reverence and love manifested by loyalty to His character and commandments. These qualities are not the result of divine demands producing outward conformity but rather an inward transformation – a circumcision of the heart.

Circumcision of the Heart

"Circumcise yourselves to the Lord and remove the foreskins of your heart, men of Judah and inhabitants of Jerusalem, or else My wrath will go forth like fire and burn with none to quench it because of the evil of your deeds." **Jeremiah 4:4**

The physical circumcision was an outward sign of the old covenant, but the inward life required the believer's cooperation by a willful personal acceptance of the Lord's personal love and affection and *stiffening your neck no longer*. He is a just God who *does not show partiality nor take a bribe*.

Since He loves the orphan and the widow, He asks the believer to show that same kind of love. The inward transformation is exhibited by the believer's reverence, service, and deep inward commitment to His purposes.

"Moreover, the Lord your God will circumcise your heart and the heart of your descendants, to love the Lord your God with all your heart and with all your soul, so that you may live" (Deuteronomy 30:6). The promise that the LORD your God will circumcise your hearts means that God will graciously grant the nation a new will to obey Him and replace their former spiritual insensitivity and stubbornness. After returning to the promised land with a new heart, they will remain committed to the Lord and, therefore, will experience abundant life. Loving Him wholeheartedly, they would not fall back into apostasy as they had done before. A new heart is an essential feature of the new covenant, which will not be fulfilled for Israel as a nation until the return of Jesus Christ. In Romans 2:29, *he is a Jew who is one inwardly; and circumcision is that of the heart, in the Spirit, not in the letter; whose praise is not from men but from God*. When circumcision of the heart is real, *"He is your praise, and He is your God.*

A Heart of Flesh

"For I will take you from the nations, gather you from all the lands, and bring you into your own land. "Then I will sprinkle clean water on you, and you will be clean; I will cleanse you from all your filthiness and from all your idols. "Moreover, I will give you a new heart and put a new spirit within you, and I will remove the heart of stone from your flesh and give

you a heart of flesh. "I will put My Spirit within you and cause you to walk in My statutes, and you will be careful to observe My ordinances. "You will live in the land that I gave to your forefathers, so you will be My people, and I will be your God. "Moreover, I will save you from all your uncleanness, and I will call for the grain and multiply it, and I will not bring a famine on you. "I will multiply the fruit of the tree and the produce of the field so that you will not receive again the disgrace of famine among the nations. "Then you will remember your evil ways and your deeds that were not good, and you will loathe yourselves in your own sight for your iniquities and your abominations. "I am not doing this for your sake," declares the Lord God, "let it be known to you. Be ashamed and confounded for your ways, O house of Israel!" **Ezekiel 36:24-32**

In the above vision, Ezekiel sees Israel in the Kingdom Age, guided by the Holy Spirit and possessing a heart of flesh (not stone) to bring her into her own land. These new realities of faith will *cause you to walk in My statutes, and you will be careful to observe My ordinances. "Moreover, I will save you from all your uncleanness* and not allow famines to affect your fruitfulness. The culmination of Israel's restoration will not simply be an undoing of Israel's sin to bring her to a state of neutrality but will involve the positive implanting of a new nature in Israel's people, making them righteous. Jeremiah referred to this work of God as the new covenant. These spiritual benefits apply to the Church Age, also defined by the new covenant. *The good man out of the **good treasure of his heart brings forth what is good**, and the evil man out of the evil treasure brings forth what is evil; for his mouth speaks from that which fills his heart* (Luke 6:45). The good man sees the greatness of his God and the power of the new covenant, so he understands that evil comes from *the evil treasure*.

Walk Humbly with God

With what shall I come to the Lord and bow myself before the God on high? Shall I come to Him with burnt offerings, with yearling calves? Does the Lord take delight in thousands of rams, In ten thousand rivers of oil? Shall I present my firstborn for my rebellious acts, the fruit of my body for the sin of my soul? He has told you, O man, what is good; and what does the Lord require [darash – continued, simple action] *of you but to do justice* [render justice faithfully]*, to love kindness, and to walk humbly with your God?* **Micah 6:6-8**

To access the Lord, the religious man looks for religious activities, including burnt offerings or even *my firstborn* (*the fruit of my body for the sin of my soul*), as some means of penance. But the Lord continuously requires rendering justice faithfully, loving to be kind, and walking humbly with the Lord. Jesus referred to this principle when addressing the scribes and Pharisees in Matthew 23:23: *"Woe to you, scribes and Pharisees, hypocrites! For you tithe mint and dill and cummin, and have neglected the weightier* [more important] *provisions of the law: justice and mercy and faithfulness; but these are the things you should have done without neglecting the others."* According to Jesus, there are matters of the Law of Moses that are more important than others, like tithing. He refers to them as justice – doing justice, mercy – showing kindness, and faithfulness – walking humbly with God.

These three are evidence of a man who approaches God as his identity.

Obey My Voice

"For I did not speak to your fathers or command them in the day that I brought them out of the land of Egypt, concerning

burnt offerings and sacrifices. "But this is what I commanded them, saying, 'Obey [shama – hear, listen to] My voice, and I will be your God, and you will be My people; and you will walk in all the way which I command you, that it may be well with you.' "Yet they did not obey [shama] or incline [natah – stretch out, extend] their ear, but walked in their own counsels and in the stubbornness of their evil heart, and went backward and not forward. "Since the day that your fathers came out of the land of Egypt until this day, I have sent you all My servants the prophets, daily rising early and sending them. "Yet they did not listen to Me or incline their ear, but stiffened their neck; they did more evil than their fathers. **Jeremiah 7:22-26**

The essence of obedience to God is the desire to listen closely, to incline one's ear to His voice to carry out His desires. This passage represents the fullness of the old covenant, which states that if the people would pay close attention to what God was saying, He would be their God, and they, in turn, would be His people. In so doing, they would walk in all His ways, *that it may be well with you*. Since the people *walked in their own counsels and the stubbornness of their evil hearts,* they would not be able to obey *and went backward, not forward.* They would not listen to God or His servants, and the evil of their hearts continuously grew. Jeremiah understood that knowing God is by experience and that the quality of man's life is directly related to experiencing Him in the details of life:

Thus says the Lord, "Let not a wise man boast of his wisdom, and let not the mighty man boast of his might, let not a rich man boast of his riches; but let him who boasts boast of this, that he understands and knows [yada – know by observing or reflecting, know by experience] Me, that I am the Lord

> *who exercises lovingkindness, justice, and righteousness on earth; for I delight in these things," declares the Lord.* **Jeremiah 9:23-24**

By His Doing

The work of Christ on the cross changed everything. It took the old covenant to a new level, a new covenant where the ability of God by His Holy Spirit is available to each believer to empower him to fulfill God's purpose for each one. It means that man's natural abilities, weaknesses, or strengths are no longer restrictions or limitations to walking with a holy God in this present world. In Christ, God's wisdom, righteousness, sanctification, and redemption belong to each believer by faith in the One who is wisdom, righteousness, sanctification, and redemption. As a result, his only boast is in the Lord, as Paul comments below:

> *For consider your calling, brethren, that there were not many wise according to the flesh, not many mighty, not many noble; but God has chosen the foolish things of the world to shame the wise, and God has chosen the weak things of the world to shame the things which are strong, and the base things of the world and the despised God has chosen, the things that are, so that He may nullify the things that are, so that no man may boast before God. But* **by His doing,** *you are in Christ Jesus,* **who became to us wisdom from God, and righteousness and sanctification, and redemption,** *so that, just as it is written, "LET HIM WHO BOASTS, BOAST IN THE LORD."* **1 Corinthians 1:26-31**

Since every believer is "in Christ" and has all that he needs, why compare oneself with others? It is the Lord who has done it all! The spiritual blessings that we need are not abstractions that elude our grasp; they are all in a Person, Jesus Christ. He is our wisdom, our righteousness, our sanctification, and our redemption. The emphasis is that God demonstrates His wisdom through the righteousness, sanctification, and redemption that we have in Christ. Each of these theological words carries a special meaning for Christians. Righteousness relates to our standing before God. We are justified: God declares us righteous in Jesus Christ. We are also sanctified, set apart from the world to belong to God and to serve Him. Redemption emphasizes the fact that we are set free because Jesus Christ paid the price for us on the cross. This will lead to complete redemption when Christ returns. So, in one sense, we have the three tenses of salvation given here: we have been saved from the penalty of sin (righteousness); we are being saved from the power of sin (sanctification), and we shall be saved from the presence of sin (redemption). In Christ, the believer's identity, past, present, and future, are complete and resident in each one.

He is our Peace

*For **He Himself is our peace**, who made both groups into one and broke down the barrier of the dividing wall, by abolishing in His flesh the enmity, which is the Law of commandments contained in ordinances, so that in Himself He might make the two into one new man, thus establishing peace.* **Ephesians 2:14-15**

There is an evident allusion here to Isaiah 57:19 (*"Peace, peace to him who is far and to him who is near"*). This "peace" is the union of worship and feelings between the Jews and the Gentiles. Formerly, they were alienated and separated from each other. They had different objects of worship, religious rites, and views and feelings. The Jews regarded the Gentiles with hatred, and the Gentiles viewed the Jews with scorn. Now, says Paul, they are at peace. They worship the same God. They have the same

Savior. They depend on the same atonement. They have the same hope. They look forward to the same heaven. They belong to the same redeemed family. Reconciliation has not only taken place with God but with each other." They all share the same identity: Jesus Christ the Lord.

> *He made Him who knew no sin to be sin on our behalf so that we might become the righteousness of God in Him.*
> **2 Corinthians 5:21**

Chapter 15
Living in Absolutes

According to Martin Luther, leader of the Reformation, "I shall never be a heretic; I may err in dispute, but I do not wish to decide anything finally; on the other hand, I am not bound by the opinions of men." This means that if the truth is not absolute, it is not the truth at all. Aristotle states, "The high-minded man must care more for the truth than for what people think." According to him, if we consider ourselves to be wise individuals, our concern should be to find the truth, not to submit to opinions. Truth is objective, originating outside of oneself, and provides certainty since it can be applied to all people at all times.

There are absolute realities and standards that define what is true and what is not. Actions can be determined to be either right or wrong by how they measure up to those absolute standards. If there are no absolutes, no reality, chaos ensues. If the law of gravity were not absolute, no one would have clarity about any dynamics of life. Laws of science and physics would be irrelevant, and commerce would be impossible. What a chaotic world it would be. Thankfully, two plus two does equal four. There is absolute truth, and it can be found and understood.

In the Truth

Sanctify them in the truth; Your word [*logos* – word as the expression of intelligent discourse] *is truth* [*aletheia* – reality clearly lying before our eyes as opposed to a mere appearance, without reality]. **John 17:17**

The night before His crucifixion, Jesus prayed to His Father for His disciples. He knew He would be leaving them behind after His ascension. *I have given them Your word, and the world has hated them because they are not of the world, even as I am not of the world. I do not ask You to take them out of the world but to keep them from the evil one* (John 17:14-15). Truth would set them apart for their divine purpose: to populate the world with the truth of the Gospel. Truth is reality from God's perspective without distortions or falsehoods. It is a concept beyond the Word of God since it includes the personification of the person of Christ (John 1:14, John 14:6). This means it goes beyond what became canon of Scripture but includes those things revealed by the Holy Spirit, the Spirit of truth, who guides [*hodegeo* – leads the way] the believer *into all the truth; for He will not speak on His own initiative, but whatever He hears, He will speak, and He will disclose to you what is to come* (John 16:13).

The Mind of God

For the word [*logos* – divine revelation or declaration, revealed truth] *of God is living and active* [operative] *and sharper than any two-edged sword, and piercing as far as the division of soul and spirit, of both joints and marrow and able to judge the thoughts and intentions of the heart. And there is no creature hidden from His sight, but all things are open and laid bare to the eyes of Him with whom we have to do.* **Hebrews 4:12-13**

Since the church had grown its roots in the Gentile world, the Jewish concepts and mindset that were a central theme of the New Testament writers did not deal with Hellenistic concepts of the Apostle John's day, including the principle of *Logos*. It means *word* or *reason* in Greek, and the mind of the typical Greek saw life through the lens of the world as a place of order and reason. Logos created and managed this order, which was understood to be the mind of God. This same mind of God dwelling inside man allows him to think rationally. John addressed this mindset by defining that mind as Jesus Christ and that this mind has become a man. Also, the Greek mind (as defined by Plato) conceived of two worlds: the material world in which we live and the immaterial and unseen world. It was the unseen world, the real world, while the material realm was made up of shadows and copies, not real. Jesus is the incarnation of not only the mind of God but also reality! The life of Jesus is a window into the mind of God and His priorities and realities.

According to Hebrews 4:12, the *logos*, the revealed mind of God to man through what God says and who Jesus is, is living and operative and assists the believer in distinguishing that which is of the Spirit or spiritual from that which is of the soul and natural. It can even discern or judge *the thoughts and intentions of the heart.* No one is excluded from its reach.

On the Last Day

He who rejects Me and does not receive My sayings [rhema – the doctrines and promises of God as revealed and taught in the Bible] *has one who judges him; the word* [logos – declaration] *I spoke is what will judge him at the last day.* **John 12:48**

Jesus addressed both the *rhema* and the *logos,* saying they would be the judge on *the last day*, the great white throne judgment. What Jesus said and declared as truth would judge everyone. Deuteronomy 17:12 says, *"The man who acts presumptuously **by not listening to the priest** who stands there to serve the Lord your God, nor to the judge, that man shall die; thus, you shall purge the evil from Israel*. Man is fully accountable to what

God says (*logos*) and what the Holy Spirit utters to the heart (*rhema*).

The *rhema* of God is also referred to as the sword of the Spirit. Ephesians 6:17: *And take THE HELMET OF SALVATION, and the sword of the Spirit, which is the word of God.* A Roman soldier would take his sword in hand, his only offensive weapon; hence, it is "the sword given by the Spirit." *Rhema* refers to the preached Word or an utterance of God occasioned by the Holy Spirit in the heart. Vines Dictionary defines *logos* as reasoned speech and *rhema* as an utterance.

The significance of rhema (as distinct from logos) is exemplified in the injunction to take "the sword of the Spirit, which is the word of God," Eph 6:17; here, the reference is not to the whole Bible as such, but to the individual Scripture which the Spirit brings to our remembrance for use in time of need, a prerequisite.

Enoch and the Scriptures

Written more than 1,000 years before Abraham, the book of Enoch teaches that the righteous are to live their lives according to a series of books (the Scriptures) that will be given to them. Further, these books will judge them, the Book of Enoch not included. In Enoch 104:11-13:

But when they write down truthfully all my words in their languages and do not change or abridge anything from my words, but write them down truthfully, all that I first testified concerning them, then, I know another mystery, that books will be given to the righteous and the wise to become a cause of joy and uprightness and much wisdom. These books will be given to them, and they will believe and rejoice in them, and then all the righteous who have learned the paths of uprightness from them will be rewarded.

All Scripture is given to man through men moved by the Holy Spirit *for teaching, for reproof, for correction, for training in righteousness; so that the man of God may be adequate, equipped for every good work* (2 Timothy 3:16-17). Paul understood that the church would be set apart *by the washing of water with the word [rhema]* (Ephesians 5:26). As the Holy Spirit reveals the deeper truths and meaning of God's doctrines and promises, the church experiences spiritual cleansing. *He saved us, not on the basis of deeds which we have done in righteousness, but according to His mercy,* **by the washing of regeneration and renewing by the Holy Spirit***, whom He poured out upon us richly through Jesus Christ our Savior, so that being justified by His grace, we would be made heirs according to the hope of eternal life* (Titus 3:5-7).

Treasure His Words

My son, if you will receive my words [emer – what God says] and treasure [sapan – conceal something of great value] my commandments within you, Make your ear attentive to wisdom, incline your heart to understanding; For if you cry for discernment, lift your voice for understanding; If you seek her as silver and search for her as for hidden treasures; Then you will discern the fear of the Lord and discover the knowledge of God. For the Lord gives wisdom [chokmah – wisdom, skill, shrewdness]; from His mouth come knowledge and understanding. He stores up sound wisdom for the upright; He is a shield to those who walk in integrity [tom – integrity, completeness], Guarding the paths of justice, and He preserves the way [derek – the path traveled] of His godly ones. Then you will discern righteousness and justice and equity and every good course [every course of action of which goodness is the characteristic]. **Proverbs 2:1-9**

Solomon was given a clear insight into the role and purpose of what God says and how each should receive them as something to be treasured and, therefore, concealed and hidden. When the believer comes to appreciate the fear (reverence) of the Lord, he is given wisdom that God has stored up for the upright. Wisdom keeps company with all the other virtues: prudence, knowledge, and discretion (Proverbs 8:12). It is expressed as a technical capability (Exodus 28:3; 31:3,6; 1 Kings 7:14). It becomes evident in a wise woman (2 Samuel 20:22) who fears the Lord or in a wise king (1 Kings 2:6). Wisdom is also personified as a woman who seeks whoever will come and listen to her, thus receiving a blessing (Proverbs 1:20; 2:2; 3:13,19). The Holy Spirit gives men of good reputation His wisdom (Acts 6:3).

Handling Change

Learning to handle change and diversity are key ingredients in living a godly life. I was a teenager during the 1960s, a decade of major social change in America. The traditional approach to most aspects of society, including religion and government, was being questioned. It appears we are in a similar place today. The rate of change is increasing significantly as well. For the believer, God ordains change in his life as a means of being conformed to the image of Christ (Romans 8:29). *But we all, with unveiled face, beholding as in a mirror the glory of the Lord, are being transformed* [*metamorphoo* – transfigured, change one's form] *into the same image from glory to glory, just as from the Lord, the Spirit* (2 Corinthians 3:18). In this context, welcoming change is a good thing. The believer is being transfigured, made into a different form. It is the evidence that God is at work.

"The Times They Are a-Changin'" is a song written by Bob Dylan and released as the title track of his 1964 album of the same name. Dylan wrote the song as a deliberate attempt to create an anthem of change for the time; it was influenced by the Irish and Scottish ballads: ' Come All Ye Bold Highway Men' and 'Come All Ye Tender Hearted Maidens.' He once said, "This was definitely a song with a purpose. I wanted to write a big song with short, concise verses that piled up on each other in a hypnotic way."

Come gather 'round, people, wherever you roam
And admit that the waters around you have grown
And accept it that soon you'll be drenched to the bone
If your time to you is worth saving
And you better start swimmin' or you'll sink like a stone
For the times, they are a-changin'

Come writers and critics who prophesize with your pen
And keep your eyes wide, the chance won't come again
And don't speak too soon, for the wheel's still in spin
And there's no tellin' who that it's namin'
For the loser now will be later to win
For the times, they are a-changin'

Come, senators, congressmen, please heed the call
Don't stand in the doorway, don't block up the hall
For he that gets hurt will be he who has stalled
The battle outside ragin'
Will soon shake your windows and rattle your walls
For the times, they are a-changin'

Come mothers and fathers throughout the land
And don't criticize what you can't understand
Your sons and your daughters are beyond your command
Your old road is rapidly agin'
Please get out of the new one if you can't lend your hand
For the times, they are a-changin'

> The line, it is drawn, the curse, it is cast
> The slow one now will later be fast
> As the present now will later be past
> The order is rapidly fadin'
> And the first one now will later be last
> For the times, they are a-changin'

God warned the Northern and Southern Kingdoms that *the words of My mouth would judge them:* "*O Ephraim* [Northern Kingdom], *what shall I do to you? O Judah* [Southern Kingdom], *what shall I do to you? For your faithfulness is like a morning cloud, and like the early dew, it goes away. Therefore, I have hewn* [hasab - cut down by blows] *them by the prophets, I have slain them* **by the words of My mouth**, *and your judgments are like light that goes forth. For I desire mercy and not sacrifice, and the knowledge* [data – learning, insight] *of God more than burnt offerings* (Hosea 6:4-6). He was teaching them that their religious activities did not accomplish God's work in their lives, but His words spoken through the prophets were His agents of change in their lives. Change can be a scary thing, but when it is the byproduct of one's pursuit of God, it is a great thing.

Luther's Psalm

God is our refuge [mahseh – shelter from danger] *and strength* [oz – power], *a very present help in trouble. Therefore, we will not fear, though the earth should change and though the mountains slip into the heart of the sea; Though its waters roar and foam, though the mountains quake at its swelling pride. Selah. There is a river whose streams make glad the city of God, the holy dwelling places of the Most High. God is in the midst of her;* **she will not be moved**; *God will help her when morning dawns. The nations made an uproar; the kingdoms tottered; He raised His voice, the earth melted. The Lord of hosts is with us; the God of*

Jacob is our stronghold [misgab – a naturally fortified place]. Selah. Come, behold the works of the Lord, Who has wrought desolations in the earth? He makes wars to cease to the end of the earth; He breaks the bow and cuts the spear in two; He burns the chariots with fire. "Cease striving and know that I am God; I will be exalted among the nations; I will be exalted in the earth." The Lord of hosts is with us; the God of Jacob is our stronghold. **Psalm 46:1-11**

This psalm has been called Luther's Psalm. He was accustomed to singing it in times of trouble. When the times were dark, when the enemies of truth appeared to triumph when disaster seemed to come over the cause in which he was engaged. The friends of the Reformation were dispirited, disheartened, and sad; he was accustomed to saying to his fellow laborers, "Come, let us sing the 46th Psalm." The essence of the psalm's message: no matter what happens, the believer is safe. The God who brings peace to His people while destroying the enemy's weapons is in total charge. That is the absolute truth.

Steve Green wrote a wonderful song entitled "The Mission." The chorus of that song is profound:

To love the Lord thy God is the heartbeat of our mission
The spring from which our service overflows
Across the street or around the world, the mission's still the same
Proclaim and live the truth in Jesus's name

Chapter 16
Priesthood of the Believer

The age of the Reformation bears a strong resemblance to the first century. Both are rich beyond any other period in great and good men, essential facts, and permanent results. Both contain the ripe fruits of preceding and the fruitful germs of succeeding ages. They are turning points in the history of mankind. They are felt in their effects to this day and will be felt to the end of time. They refashioned the world from the innermost depths of the human soul in its contact with the infinite Being. A providential concurrence of events and tendencies of thought ushered them in. Moses and the Prophets prepared the way for Christianity, the dispersion of the Jews, the conquests of Alexander the Great, the language and literature of Greece, the arms and laws of Rome, the decay of idolatry, the spread of skepticism, the aspirations after a new revelation, the hopes of a coming Messiah. The Reformation was preceded and necessitated by the corruptions of the papacy, the decline of monasticism and scholastic theology, the growth of mysticism, the revival of letters, the resurrection of the Greek and Roman classics, the invention of the printing press, the discovery of a new world, the publication of the Greek Testament, the general spirit of enquiry, the striving after national independence and personal freedom. In both centuries we hear the creative voice of the Almighty calling light out of darkness.
Schaff's History of the Church

Sola scriptura (Scripture alone) is upheld by Lutheran and Reformed theologies and asserts that scripture must govern over church traditions and interpretations which are themselves held to be subject to scripture. All church traditions, creeds, and teachings must be in unity with the teachings of scripture as the divinely inspired Word of God.

Sola fide (faith alone) is summarized in the Thirty-nine Articles of the Anglican church, specifically Article XI "Of the Justification of Man:"

"We are accounted righteous before God, only for the merit of our Lord and Savior Jesus Christ by faith, and not for our own works or deservings. Wherefore, that we are justified by faith only is a most wholesome doctrine, and very full of comfort…"

Sola gratia (grace alone) specifically excludes the merit done by a person as part of achieving salvation. *Sola gratia* is the teaching that salvation comes by divine grace or "unmerited favor" only, not as something merited by the sinner.

Solus Christus (Christ only) excludes the priestly class as necessary for sacraments. Solus Christus is the teaching that Christ is the only mediator between God and man, and that there is salvation through no other. The new covenant believer is also part of a holy and royal priesthood (1 Peter 2:5, 9).

Soli Deo gloria, (glory to God alone) stands in opposition to the veneration perceived by many to be present in the Roman Catholic Church of Mary the mother of Jesus, the saints, or angels. *Soli Deo gloria* is the teaching that all glory is to be due to God alone since salvation is accomplished solely through His will and action.

Three Fundamentals

One of the most important principles derived from the Protestant Reformation is the priesthood of the believer. Martin Luther wanted Christians to understand that, in God's eyes, the people were not second-class citizens as compared to the clergy or the nobility. Instead, new covenant believers are all saints, kings, and priests. There are three fundamental principles of the Protestant Reformation: the supremacy of the Scriptures over tradition, the supremacy of faith over works, and the supremacy of the Christian people over an exclusive priesthood. The first may be called the objective, the second the subjective, the third the social or ecclesiastical principle.

While Martin Luther did not use the exact phrase "priesthood of all believers," he infers a general priesthood in Christendom in his 1520 "To the Christian Nobility of the German Nation." He said all Christians "*are truly of the spiritual estate, and there is no difference among them, save of office alone.*" When Paul says that believers are part of one body, one Lord, by one Spirit, one baptism, and called in one hope of your calling (Ephesians 4:4-6), he means that there is no distinction, that we are all one in Christ (Galatians 3:28). Luther continues, *"It is faith that makes men priests, faith that unites them to Christ, and gives them the indwelling of the Holy Spirit, whereby they become filled with all holy grace and heavenly power. The inward anointing - this oil, better than any that ever came from the horn of bishop or pope - gives them not the name only, but the nature, the purity, the power of priests; and this anointing have all they received who are believers in Christ.*"

A Royal Priesthood

"But you are a CHOSEN RACE, a royal PRIESTHOOD, a HOLY NATION, a PEOPLE FOR God's OWN POSSESSION, so that you may proclaim the excellencies of Him who has called you out of darkness into His marvelous light; for you once were NOT A PEOPLE, but now you are THE PEOPLE OF GOD;

you had NOT RECEIVED MERCY, but now you have RECEIVED MERCY." **1 Peter 2:9-10**

Peter acknowledges that as chosen ones (Ephesians 1:4), the believer is automatically part of *"a royal priesthood"* and a holy nation, meaning that he has been set apart for a divine purpose as *"a people for God's own possession."* This divine purpose is *"so that you may proclaim the excellencies of Him who has called you out of darkness into His marvelous light,"* and this empowerment only happens to the one who has accepted his position as a priest by receiving His mercy. The new covenant believer-priest recognizes that he belongs to God and derives his accountability from that position. New Testament believers have been commissioned into God's army of servant priests.

Philip Schaff, in his History of the Church, says,

The Roman church is an exclusive hierarchy and assigns to the laity the position of passive obedience. The bishops are the teaching and ruling church; they alone constitute a council or synod and have the exclusive power of legislation and administration. Laymen have no voice in spiritual matters, they cannot even read the Bible without the permission of the priest, who holds the keys of heaven and hell. This principle [the priesthood of the believer], *consistently carried out, raises the laity to active co-operation in the government and administration of the church; it gives them a voice and vote in the election of the pastor; it makes every member of the congregation useful, according to his peculiar gift, for the general good.*

This principle is the source of religious and civil liberty which flourishes most in Protestant countries. Religious liberty is the mother of civil liberty. The universal priesthood of Christians leads legitimately to the universal kingship of free, self-governing citizens, whether under a monarchy or under a republic.

> *"Unless I am convinced by the testimony of the Scriptures or by clear reason (for I do not trust either in the pope or in councils alone, since it is well known that they have often erred and contradicted themselves), I am bound by the Scriptures I have quoted, and my conscience is captive to the Word of God. I cannot and will not recant anything, since it is neither safe nor right to go against conscience. May God help me. Amen."* **Martin Luther**

Spiritual Sacrifices

As part of a holy nation, the believer-priest has been set apart for God's purposes. In 1 Peter 2:5, *"you also, as living stones, are being built up as a spiritual house for a holy priesthood, to offer up spiritual sacrifices acceptable to God through Jesus Christ."* The old covenant priest was charged with the job of offering animal sacrifices on behalf of the people in the tabernacle/temple to atone for sins. The new covenant priesthood begins with the offering of self to God, which is our spiritual service of worship (Romans 12:1). From this place, he then can become, like Paul, a spiritual sacrifice to others through faith in the High Priest, Jesus Christ. In Philippians 2:17, *"But even if I am being poured out as a drink offering upon the sacrifice and service of your faith, I rejoice and share my joy with you all."* The impartation of God's life is realized when man sees the sacrifice of the Lord through the investment of the priesthood into others.

The old covenant priest was not only responsible for animal sacrifices, but he also burned the incense (a picture of prayer) on the altar of incense, signifying Jesus as our intercessor (Hebrews 7:25), he cleaned and trimmed the lamps of the golden lampstand, which references Jesus as the Light of the world (John 8:12), and he put the bread of the Presence on the table every Sabbath, pointing to Jesus as the Bread of life (John 6:35). In the same way, the new covenant priest is a minister to others through prayer (1 Timothy 2:1-2), declaring the light of the gospel (1 Corinthians 9:16), and encouraging others in the bread of God's Word (Matthew 4:4). And just as the old covenant priest was anointed with oil to fulfill his office, so the new covenant priest is anointed with God's power through the Holy Spirit (1 Corinthians 2:4-5).

Missions

Jesus speaks to the Apostle John about this new covenant priesthood in Revelation 1:6, *"and He has made us to be a kingdom, priests to His God and Father — to Him be the glory and the dominion forever and ever. Amen"*. The ultimate purpose of the priesthood is that God gets the glory and is recognized as the ultimate authority over man and all things (dominion). Beyond the new covenant offices of apostle, evangelist, and pastor-teacher that resemble the office of priest, maybe the greatest example of the new covenant believer-priest is the missionary. Christian missions employ believers of all shapes and sizes in missionary work all over the world in fulfillment of Acts 1:8. They sacrifice their own lives to serve the Lord as soul winners, teachers, and other efforts intended to meet human needs by sharing the gospel, praying for the greatest needs of the people and imparting life through the Word of God. In reality, a missionary is anyone who lays down his/her life to follow God's will in serving human needs, no matter the place.

Chapter 17
The Eighth Day

Numbers have essential meanings in Scripture. For example, four represents the world (four corners), five speaks about grace, six is the number for man, and seven references perfection or completion. But what about the number eight?

The number eight is very significant in that it is used 73 times in the Bible. It is the symbol of resurrection and regeneration. In Bible numerology, eight means a **new beginning**; it denotes "a new order or creation, and man's true 'born again' event when he is **resurrected from the dead into eternal life**." The first historical reference is to Noah and his family as *"eight persons were brought safely through the water"* (1 Peter 3:20). Those eight persons experienced a true new beginning once the flood receded. God instituted another as a sign of the covenant He made with Abraham in Genesis 17:12, that each child would be circumcised on the eighth day. This covenant with Abraham represented a new relationship with God.

Plumpness

The Hebrew word *shemoneh* is translated as eight or eighth and is derived most likely from the root word meaning plumpness as if a surplus above the "perfect" seven. Of course, the first mention of seven is found in Genesis 1 with the creation story, in reference to seven days as a week. Metaphorically, the eighth day takes us above and beyond the seventh day, the day of rest.

Two other Old Testament references to the number eight include 1 Samuel 17:12-14 indicating King David as the youngest of eight children, the eighth child, and the one who would become known as "a man after My (God's) heart." In 2 Chronicles 34:1-3, Josiah, one of only three good kings, became king when he was eight years old. In verse 3, Scripture says, *"For **in the eighth year** of his reign while he was still a youth, he began to seek the God of his father David."* A new beginning took place in Josiah's heart in his eighth year. It says he began to purge the images of other gods from Judah and Jerusalem. Both David and Josiah changed the course of history.

Shemini Atzeret

In Leviticus 23:33-36, the Lord institutes the Feast of Tabernacles (Sukkot) to be celebrated for seven days in fabricated booths as a reminder of the nation's exodus from Egypt. In verse 36: *"For seven days you shall present an offering by fire to the Lord. **On the eighth day**, you shall have a holy convocation and present an offering by fire to the Lord; it is an assembly. You shall do no laborious work."* This eighth day of Sukkot is also known as **Shemini Atzeret** and is a separate—yet connected—a holy day devoted to the spiritual aspects of the festival of Sukkot. Part of its duality as a holy day is that it is simultaneously considered connected to both Sukkot and also a separate festival in its own right. It is referred to as "the great day of the feast." John's gospel cites a particular event that occurred on that day in John 7:37-39:

> *"Now, on the last day, **the great day of the feast**, Jesus stood and cried out, saying, "If anyone is thirsty, let him come to Me and drink. He who believes in Me, as the Scripture said, 'From his innermost being will flow rivers of living water.'" **But this He spoke of the Spirit**, whom those who believed in Him were to receive; for the Spirit was not*

yet given because Jesus was not yet glorified. This connection between the eighth day and the Holy Spirit is significant.

The Fountain of Living Water

Jesus is believed to have been born on the first day of Sukkot, so His dedication, covered by Luke in chapter 2:22-23, was on Shemini Atzeret. In John 8:2, Jesus entered the temple on that day and addressed the woman caught in the act of adultery. When Jesus was writing with his finger on the ground after His statement, *"He who is without sin among you, let him be the first to throw a stone at her,"* He may have been writing their names as a statement of judgment, in fulfillment of Jeremiah 17:13, *O Lord, the hope of Israel, all who forsake You will be put to shame.* **Those who turn away on earth will be written down** *because they have forsaken the fountain of living water, even the Lord.*

> ***After eight days,*** *His disciples were again inside, and Thomas with them. Jesus came, the doors having been shut, and stood in their midst and said, "Peace be with you." Then He said to Thomas, "Reach here with your finger, and see My hands, and reach here your hand and put it into My side, and do not be unbelieving, but believing." Thomas answered and said to Him, "My Lord and my God!" Jesus said to him, "Because you have seen Me, have you believed? Blessed are they who did not see and yet believed."* **John 20:26-29**

Eight days after the resurrection, an important event is covered by the Gospel of John. Thomas had not been present during an earlier meeting of the disciples with the risen Lord. Thomas had expressed doubt after others told him, "We have seen the Lord." Jesus went out of His way to address those doubts by allowing Thomas to touch His wounds as proof that He was real.

This is the moment when Thomas became a believer when he said, *"My Lord and my God!"* It was the eighth day when Thomas finally recognized His resurrection. Jesus then addresses those who follow, that our "come to Jesus" moment is to be realized based on faith when we are taken beyond the physical realm into the spiritual realm.

Anointing

A Hebrew word closely related to *shemoneh* is *shemen* and is translated "anointing" in the King James version. In Isaiah 61:1, *"The Spirit of the Lord God is upon me because* **the Lord has anointed me** *to bring good news to the afflicted; He has sent me to bind up the brokenhearted, to proclaim liberty to captives and freedom to prisoners."* This is a clear reference to Jesus as Messiah and quoted by Him in Luke 4:18 as being fulfilled *"in their hearing"* (verse 21). The Holy Spirit is the source of His anointing and will become that for the New Testament believer also at Pentecost.

It is commonly accepted that the Law was given to Moses on the Feast of Shavuot, otherwise known as Pentecost. This means that the old covenant and the new covenant were given on the same day, some 1,500 years apart. When the Holy Spirit came upon believers in Jesus as Messiah in Acts 2, it was the completion of the old work and the new beginning of a better covenant (Hebrews 8:6). Like **Shemini Atzeret**, it is connected to the old covenant, yet it is its own separate celebration, bringing in an anointing to the believer by the Holy Spirit not experienced by Old Testament believers. This eighth day is really a brand-new week in God's sovereign plan to take us to the Second Coming of Messiah.

Prophecy Fulfilled

One final point is vital to consider. The seven major Jewish festivals are prophetically fulfilled in the two comings of Messiah, the ones occurring in the spring (the former rain) pointing to His first coming and the last three, which all happen in the fall (the latter rain), point to His second coming. Specifically, Rosh Hashanah is also the Feast of Trumpets and is fulfilled by the rapture of the church, Yom Kippur (the Day of Atonement) looks to the Great Tribulation, and Sukkot, the Feast of Tabernacles is a picture of the Kingdom age. If those connections are accurate, then the eighth day of Sukkot brings us to the end of human history, and the new beginning is eternity itself, a higher quality of life. Amen!

Chapter 18
Quality of Life and the Land of the Living

I would have despaired unless I had believed that I would see the goodness of the Lord in the land of the living. **Psalm 27:13**

I shall walk before the Lord in the land of the living. **Psalm 116:9**

I cried out to You, O Lord; I said, "You are my refuge, my portion in the land of the living." **Psalm 142:5**

In each of the above verses, the psalmist refers to the quality of life available to the one who finds his life within a personal relationship, in communion with God. There is a clear sense of walking in His presence and the provision for life that this relationship brings to the believer. It speaks of a purity of heart that allows him to see the Lord (Matthew 5:8).

Hezekiah's Prayer

A writing of Hezekiah, king of Judah, after his illness and recovery: I said, "In the middle [prime] of my life, I am to enter the gates of Sheol [the grave]; I am to be deprived of the rest of my years." I said, "I will not see the Lord, the Lord in the land of the living; I will look on man no more among the inhabitants of the world. "Like a shepherd's tent, my dwelling [body] is pulled up and removed from me. As a weaver, I rolled up my life. He cuts me off from the loom; from day until night, You make an end of me. "I composed my soul until morning. Like a lion—so He breaks all my bones, from day until night, You make an end of me. "Like a swallow, like a crane, so I twitter; I moan like a dove; my eyes look wistfully to the heights. O Lord, I am oppressed; be my security." **Isaiah 38:9-14**

After God healed him, Hezekiah wrote a song to express his thanks to God. He was facing death in the prime of his life. The Aramaic translation found in the Targum of verse 11 could be: *I shall not see the Lord's Lord in the land of the living; or the Lord's Christ in the flesh.* By death, he would be cut off like a cloth being cut from a weaver's loom. He had hoped he would get well, but he got worse. His illness was as if God were a lion breaking all his bones, a figure of speech depicting his deep inner anguish. His cries of pain were like the sound of a swallow or crane, and his mourning was like the sound of a dove. Hezekiah had gazed directly at death, yet he found the Lord as his deliverance. God allows some to view death from both sides of the grave.

Hope for the Living

For I have taken all this to my heart and explain it that righteous men, wise men, and their deeds are in the hand of God. Man does not know whether it will be love or hatred; anything awaits him. It is the same for all. There is one fate for the righteous and for the wicked; for the good, for the clean and for the unclean; for the man who offers a sacrifice and for the one who does not sacrifice. As the good man is, so is the sinner; as the swearer is, so is the one who is afraid to swear. This is an evil in all that is done under the sun, that there is one fate for all men. Furthermore, the hearts of the sons of men are full of evil, and insanity is in their hearts throughout their lives. Afterwards, they go to the dead. For whoever is joined with all the living, there is hope [bittahon

– trust]; surely, a live dog is better than a dead lion. For the living know they will die, but the dead do not know anything, nor have they any longer a reward, for their memory is forgotten. Indeed, their love, their hate, and their zeal have already perished, and they will no longer have a share in all that is done under the sun. **Ecclesiastes 9:1-6**

Solomon states that all people share the same fate or common destiny. However, there are variations as to the nature of that fate. Fate relates to *love or hatred,* adversity or prosperity. Everyone experiences both love and hate; there is one fate for the righteous and the wicked. This applies to the good and the bad, those who are ritually clean as well as those who are ritually unclean. The same destiny befalls everyone; this common fate causes people to be *full of evil*. Solomon added that not only does everybody share this same destiny of adversity or prosperity during life, but they also share the same ultimate fate after life; they all join the dead.

However, even though all people, both righteous and wicked, are subject to the same adversity or prosperity and ultimately join in death, they should not despair of life. Life has advantages over death. Comparing the lot of a live dog with that of a dead lion, Solomon affirmed that it is better to be alive and dishonored. The living, at least, are self-aware and have hope, things they can look forward to enjoying. But the dead have no consciousness or hope of reward or enjoyment. Their passions, love, hate, and jealousy are non-existent. Thus, the living have opportunities and capacities for fruitful labor, but the dead do not. Life has value beyond itself.

Body, Soul, & Spirit

According to the Bible, man is a conglomeration of 3 parts: body, soul, and spirit. Each part has a life of its own. The biological life (*bios*) includes all appetites of the physical body, while the soul (*pseuche*) speaks of the life of the mind and self. Since the fall of Adam, man has been born with a living body and soul. The third part is the spirit [*pneuma*], and although present at man's first birth (Genesis 2:7), it is dead or dormant because of the fall until the second birth, the regeneration of the believer. God always intended that there would be a hierarchy so that man would find his highest quality of life. When the spirit of man is allowed to exercise priority over the soul and body, he finds order and not chaos. *For the flesh sets its desire against the Spirit, and the Spirit against the flesh; for these are in opposition to one another, so that you may not do the things that you please. But if you are led by the Spirit, you are not under the Law* (Galatians 5:17-18).

When the appetites of the body take control (i.e., addictions), man is a slave to these appetites, and his quality of life is compromised. In the same way, when his mind is in charge, he is subject to all kinds of obsessive behaviors. *All a man's labor is for his mouth, yet the appetite is not satisfied. For what advantage does the wise man have over the fool? What advantage does the poor man have, knowing how to walk before the living? What the eyes see is better than what the soul desires. This, too, is futility and a striving after wind* (Ecclesiastes 6:7-9). When the Lord puts things in their proper place, man finds His presence and fullness of joy in his salvation.

Arguing with God

"Be silent before me so that I may speak; then let come on me what may. "Why should I take my flesh in my teeth and

put my life in my hands? "Though He slay me, I will hope in Him. Nevertheless, I will argue my ways before Him. "This also will be my salvation, for a godless man may not come before His presence. "Listen carefully to my speech, and let my declaration fill your ears. "Behold now, I have prepared my case; I know that I will be vindicated. "Who will contend with me? For then, I would be silent and die. **Job 13:13-19**

Amid Job's trial, he wrestled with God in light of the reason and purpose for his struggles. In Job 13:3, *"But I would speak to the Almighty, and I desire to argue* [yakach - refers to the clarification of people's moral standing, which may involve arguments being made for them or against them] *with God."* He was anxious to hear from God, but only after he could express his heart in the matter. *"This also will be my salvation, for a godless man may not come before His presence.* Job understood that his relationship with God defined his quality of life. *"Though He slay me, I will hope in Him."* He also knew that the Lord was willing to hear his case. Job was not afraid to argue with God.

Waiting for My Change

"Man, who is born of woman, is short-lived and full of turmoil. "Like a flower, he comes forth and withers. He also flees like a shadow and does not remain. "You also open Your eyes on him and bring him into judgment with Yourself. "Who can make the clean out of the unclean? No one! **"Since his days are determined, the number of his months is with You, and his limits You have set so that he cannot pass.** *"Turn Your gaze from him that he may rest until he fulfills his day like a hired man. "For there is hope for a tree, when it is cut down, that it will sprout again, and its shoots will not fail. "Though its roots grow old in the ground and its stump dies in the dry soil, At the scent of water, it will*

*flourish and put forth sprigs like a plant. "But man dies and lies prostrate. Man expires, and where is he? "As water evaporates from the sea, and a river becomes parched and dried up, So, man lies down and does not rise. Until the heavens are no longer, he will not awake nor be aroused out of his sleep. "Oh, that You would hide me in Sheol, That You would conceal me until Your wrath returns to You, that You would set a limit for me and remember me! "If a man dies, will he live again? All the days of my struggle, **I will wait until my change comes**."* **Job 14:1-14**

Job had a clear understanding of the master plan of God for each life, both in terms of its length and its boundaries. Paul had similar insights in Acts 17:26-27, *and He made from one man every nation of mankind to live on all the face of the earth, having determined their appointed times and the boundaries of their habitation, that they would seek God*. The uniqueness of man and his ordained life on earth is not to be repeated, as is true of the tree that is cut down, *that it will sprout again, and its shoots will not fail.* Man is different. At his death, *So man lies down and does not rise.* His death represents the end of something meaningful but also the beginning of something greater. *All the days of my struggle, I will wait until my change comes.*

The Finality of Death

"You will call, and I will answer You; You will long for the work of Your hands. "For now, You number my steps; You do not observe my sin. "My transgression is sealed up in a bag, and You wrap up my iniquity. "But the falling mountain crumbles away, and the rock moves from its place; Water wears away stones, its torrents wash away the dust of the earth; so, You destroy man's [enos – emphasizing man's frailty] *hope. "You forever overpower him, and he departs;*

You change his appearance and send him away. "His sons achieve honor, but he does not know it, or they become insignificant, but he does not perceive it. "But his body pains him, and he mourns only for himself." **Job 14:15-22**

Job affirmed his certainty that God would summon him to court, for He would be longing to see Job, *the work of Your hands*. Job said that when God spoke, he would answer Him. And yet, when God did speak, Job could not answer even one of His questions. Though counting his steps, God would no longer record his sin, for his offenses would be *sealed up in a bag*. This is the message of the gospel.

Though Job anticipated that death would release him from life's deepest struggles, he had no hope of correcting any wrong steps before his demise. Like a crumbling mountain, like stones worn down by water, and like soil washed away by rainstorms, the hope of man in his frailty disappears. At death, God forcibly overcomes him, changes his appearance, and sends him away from all he knew and possessed in this life. What view does a man have of his future generations after death? He views his own life according to its pains.

Now My Eye Sees You

And Job again took up his discourse and said, "Oh that I were as in months gone by, as in the days when God watched over me; when His lamp shone over my head, and by His light, I walked through darkness; as I was in the prime of my days when the friendship of God was over my tent; when the Almighty was yet with me, and my children were around me; **Job 29:1-5**

As Job considers his past as he sensed the presence of God and His ongoing care, *when God watched over me,* he still did not understand the purpose of this trial in light of the counsel of his "friends." Contemplating all the good things he had done. It did not make sense. In verses 14-15, *"I put on righteousness, and it clothed me; my justice was like a robe and a turban. "I was eyes to the blind and feet to the lame.* Why would God want to destroy his life in so many ways?

The answer came later, in chapter 42, when he told God, *"I know that You can do all things and that no purpose of Yours can be thwarted. 'Who is this that hides counsel without knowledge?' "Therefore, I have declared that which I did not understand, things too wonderful for me, which I did not know." 'Hear, now, and I will speak; I will ask You, and You instruct me.' "I have heard of You by the hearing of the ear, but now my eye sees You; Therefore, I retract, and I repent in dust and ashes"* (Job 42:2-6). His sight was now allowing him to recognize *the goodness of the Lord in the land of the living.* The Lord's plan for Job's life was perfect!

Inherit a Blessing

To sum up, all of you be harmonious, sympathetic, brotherly, kindhearted, and humble in spirit, not returning evil for evil or insult for insult, but giving a blessing instead, for you were called for the very purpose that you might inherit a blessing. For "THE ONE WHO DESIRES LIFE, TO LOVE AND SEE GOOD DAYS, MUST KEEP HIS TONGUE FROM EVIL AND HIS LIPS FROM SPEAKING DECEIT. "HE MUST TURN AWAY FROM EVIL AND DO GOOD; HE MUST SEEK PEACE AND PURSUE IT. "FOR THE EYES OF THE LORD ARE TOWARD THE RIGHTEOUS, AND HIS EARS ATTEND TO THEIR PRAYER, BUT THE FACE OF THE LORD IS AGAINST THOSE WHO DO EVIL." Who is there to harm you if you prove zealous for what is good? But even if you should suffer for the sake of righteousness, you are blessed. AND DO NOT FEAR THEIR INTIMIDATION, AND DO NOT BE TROUBLED, but sanctify Christ as Lord in your hearts, always being ready to make a defense to everyone who asks you to give an account for the hope that is in you, yet with gentleness and reverence. **1 Peter 3:8-15**

Peter's conclusion to the whole matter was to *sanctify Christ as Lord in your hearts, always being ready to make a defense to everyone who asks you to give an account for the hope in you, yet with gentleness and reverence.* When Jesus is set apart, made holy in the heart as Lord and Master, the believer's quality of life is confirmed by a readiness to defend the faith by expressing to others the hope and confident expectation of His return and his eternal future. The value and quality of life are recognized in the way it is lived, as giving a blessing instead of pursuing one. When the believer stops performing to earn something and instead finds his joy in serving others as the Lord Himself would be doing, he is no longer concerned with perfection. His perfection is found in the Lord Jesus Christ. *I shall walk before the Lord in the land of the living.*

An Enigma

For now, we see in a mirror dimly [en ainigma – obscurely, an enigma], but then face to face; now I know in part, but then I will know fully just as I also have been fully known. But now faith, hope, love, abide these three; but the greatest of these is love. **1 Corinthians 13:12-13**

While in the land of the living, man cannot see things as they are, but rather, in obscurity, abstract, as inaccurate reflections of reality. Functioning in this physical realm, he must rely on faith, hope, and love. These are the elements that provide clarity when things are not transparent or discernable. Faith (trust) looks back 2,000 years to Jesus's first coming, and hope (confident expectation) looks ahead to His second coming. Agape (unconditional) love is the overriding factor that holds everything together. God is love, and the love of Christ motivates the believer. Faith and hope will no longer be present in eternity, but love remains as the eternal consequence of spiritual life. Love bears all things, believes all things, hopes all things, endures (*hupomeno* – remains steadfast in) all things (1 Corinthians 13:7).

Chapter 19
Mountains

I was listening to a message about the Mount of Transfiguration, and it came to me that many major events in the Bible take place on a mountain. What is the significance of the mountain? Mountains certainly suggest strength and stability. In Psalm 30:7, *"O Lord, by Your favor You have made my mountain to stand strong."* They can also speak about the depth of our difficulties in Matthew 17:20.

When I think of mountain experiences, Abraham's offering on Mount Moriah comes immediately to mind. This event was monumental not only in Abraham's life but also in the Jewish nation as a whole since they purposed to locate Solomon's temple at the same exact location. In Genesis 22, God tested Abraham by commanding him to take his son, Isaac, and offer him as a burnt offering. Abraham was willing to obey and even had the knife ready to strike when the Lord stopped him; Abraham proved his faith. Mountain experiences can represent God's testing. Hebrews 11:17-19 tells us, *By faith Abraham, when he was tested, offered up Isaac, and he who had received the promises was offering up his only begotten son; it was he to whom it was said, "IN ISAAC YOUR DESCENDANTS SHALL BE CALLED." He considered that God is able to raise people even from the dead, from which he also received him back as a type.*

And how about what took place on Sinai? God had delivered the nation of Israel from bondage in Egypt and led them to Mount Sinai to receive His Law. He called Moses to meet with Him on the mountain to receive the two tablets and many other commandments. These instructions included the following: *"'And you shall be to Me a kingdom of priests and a holy nation.' These are the words that you shall speak to the sons of Israel" (Exodus 19:6). If the people would follow His commands, they would become His possession in the earth. A brand-new relationship with God was introduced on this mountain at Pentecost.

Who are You Following?

And then there was Mount Carmel (1 Kings 18). Elijah would challenge the people with this question, *"How long will you hesitate between two opinions? If the Lord is God, follow Him; but if Baal, follow him"* (1 Kings 18:21). Their first response was no response so Elijah felt he was alone while 450 prophets represented Baal. To demonstrate whose God would show up, they prepared two altars and prayed to their God for His response. After pouring gallons of water on Elijah's altar, the God of Abraham, Isaac & Jacob showed up big; the wood, offering, and even the stones were completely burnt, and all the water licked up. God was proving His power against any false god. He demonstrated His power against all adversaries on a mountain, and Elijah eliminated the prophets of Baal.

In 1 Kings 19, Elijah was on the run from Ahab and Jezebel after the experience on Mount Carmel and found a mountain (unidentified) to hide in. In verses 11-12, God said, *"'Go forth and stand on the mountain before the Lord.' And behold, the Lord was passing by! And a great and strong wind was rending the mountains and breaking in pieces the rocks before the Lord; but the Lord was not in the wind. And after the wind an earthquake, but the Lord was not in the earthquake. After the earthquake a fire, but the Lord was not in the fire; and after the fire a sound of a gentle blowing* [whisper]." The Lord was teaching Elijah that attention-getting experiences aren't always how He communicates His will. Elijah needed to learn to quiet himself from activities to hear the voice of God and find His will. In Psalm 46:10, *"Cease striving and know that I am God; I will be exalted among the nations, I will be exalted in the earth."*

The Choosing of the Twelve

In Mark 3:13-14, Scripture says, *"And He went up on the mountain and summoned those He Himself wanted, and they came to Him. And He appointed twelve so they would be with Him and that He could send them out to preach."* This mountain is traditionally considered Mount Hatten, located 5 miles west of the Sea of Galilee. The Lord Jesus chose this place to establish His holy relationship with twelve men who would eventually change the world. Jesus promised to empower them through the Holy Spirit to spread the news of a new covenant with God. *When the day of Pentecost had come, they were all together in one place. And suddenly there came from heaven a noise like a violent rushing wind, and it filled the whole house where they were sitting. And there appeared to them tongues as of fire distributing themselves, and they rested on each one of them. And they were all filled with the Holy Spirit and began to speak with other tongues, as the Spirit was giving them utterance* (Acts 2:1-4).

A most incredible event took place on the Mount of Transfiguration. It most likely happened on Mount Tabor and included only three of Jesus's disciples, Peter, James, and John. It was such a profound moment on many levels, demonstrating visibly to the three that Jesus was God incarnate through the shining of His face and garments, the shekinah glory. Then Moses and Elijah appeared and talked with Jesus. The voice of God from heaven spoke, *"This is My beloved Son, with whom I am well-pleased; listen to Him!"* There are many different interpretations of what it all meant. Still, many believe that Moses and Elijah represent the Law and the Prophets, which is an idiom used to identify the entire Old Testament. The Father instructed the disciples to listen closely to all that Jesus was saying, that what Jesus was saying would supersede the Old Testament teaching. Both Peter and John wrote about their experience as a moment when they understood something new. In 2 Peter 1:16-18, *For we did not follow cleverly devised tales when we made known to you the power and coming of our Lord Jesus Christ, but we were eyewitnesses of His majesty. For when He received honor and glory from God the Father, such an utterance as this was made to Him by the Majestic Glory, "This is My beloved Son with whom I am well-pleased"— and we ourselves heard this utterance made from heaven when we were with Him on the holy mountain.*

Final Instructions

Finally, Jesus spent his last moments as the risen Lord on *"the mount called Olivet."* He had some final instructions for His disciples, including Acts 1:8: *"But you will receive power when the Holy Spirit has come upon you, and you shall be My witnesses both in Jerusalem, and in all Judea and Samaria, and even to the remotest part of the earth."* He was then lifted up as they watched until they could see Him no more. There were two men in white clothing (I believe they were angels) who told those in attendance that Jesus would return *"in just the same way as you have watched Him go into heaven"* (verse 11). Many interpret this to mean that Jesus will return to earth at His second coming in the very same place and way, on Mount Olivet. In Zechariah 14:4, *In that day His feet will stand on the Mount of Olives, which is in front of Jerusalem on the east. The Mount of Olives will be split in its middle from east to west by a very large valley so that half of the mountain will move toward the north and the other half toward the south.* Mount Olivet connects His first coming to His second coming.

God established His holy city on Mount Zion as a place of strength and protection. It will become the center of human life for 1,000 years in the Kingdom Age when Jesus will reign from the Holy Mountain. Psalm 125:1-2, *"Those who trust in the Lord are as Mount Zion, which cannot be moved but abides forever. As the mountains surround Jerusalem,* ***so the Lord surrounds His people from this time forth and forever****."*

Each believer can have a mountaintop experience with God when he knows he has heard directly from Him in response to his need for God to come through in some way, through words, encouragement, understanding, or even a miracle. In this way, the Lord demonstrates His faithfulness to the believer as trustworthy.

Chapter 20

The Storehouses

There are several references in the Old Testament to God's storehouses, a place where all the provisions for His creation are stored. Deuteronomy 28:12 identifies *His good storehouse, the heavens*, as the place where He keeps rain for the land as well as the blessings of "all the work of your hand." It's also the place where He will make those who obey Him the head and not the tail (verse 13). When I think of a storehouse, I think about the end of the movie, "Raiders of the Lost Ark," and the massive government warehouse where the Ark was finally stored. It is the place where God fulfills the disciples' prayer to *give us our daily bread* day by day (Luke 11:3). It reminds me of Amazon, which has massive warehouses from which orders are delivered to anyone who requests them and arranges proper payment.

Some of these storehouses contain snow and hail, *which I have reserved for the time of distress, for the day of war or battle* (Job 38:22-23). In Psalm 33:6-8, the psalmist writes, *By the word of the Lord the heavens were made, and by the breath of His mouth all their host. He gathers the waters of the sea together as a heap;* **He lays up the deeps in storehouses**. *Let all the earth fear the Lord; let all the inhabitants of the world stand in awe of Him*. The storehouses are a demonstration of God's omnipotence, His ability to provide for every need and answer every prayer.

Remember the Sabbath Day to Keep it Holy

One of the ways the Lord reminded the Israelites of His faithfulness in providing for them in the wilderness was through the Sabbath celebration. In Exodus 16, God commanded them to do no work on the day of rest, that He would provide *"bread for two days on the sixth day"* (Verse 29). He was teaching them how to trust Him for everything. While traveling through the wilderness, God provided manna (meaning "what is it?") each morning with double the amount on the sixth day. The Law of Moses also instituted the Sabbath year {shemitah year) in Leviticus 25, intended to provide rest and refreshment for the land. God promised that He would provide for them for an entire year, every sixth year, if they would trust Him.

It is interesting to note that the Babylonian captivity of Judah was directly related to their failure to honor the Sabbath year for 490 years (70 x 7). In 2 Chronicles 36:20-21, *Those who had escaped from the sword he carried away to Babylon were servants to him and his sons until the rule of the kingdom of Persia, to fulfill the word of the Lord by the mouth of Jeremiah* **until the land had enjoyed its sabbaths.** *All the days of its desolation, the land rested until seventy years were complete*. The Jews spent 70 years in captivity to allow their lands to rest for 70 years because they did not trust in His storehouses.

Living in God's Security

For the Old Testament Jew, only by listening to obey the Lord's commands would they receive the blessings intended for them from His storehouses. In Deuteronomy 11:13-16, *It shall come about, if you* **listen obediently** *to my commandments which I am commanding you today, to love the Lord your God and to serve Him with all your heart and all your soul, that* **He will give the rain for your land in its season,** *the early* [winter - former] *and late* [spring - latter] *rain, that you may gather in your grain and your new wine and your oil. He will give grass in your fields for your cattle, and you will eat and* **be satisfied.** *Beware that your hearts are not deceived and that you do not turn away to serve and* *worship* other gods. It was always to remind them of the deception of serving and worshipping other gods.

In Leviticus 26:5-6, *You will thus eat your food to the full and* **live securely in your land. "I shall also grant peace in the land so that you may lie down with no one making you tremble.** *I shall also eliminate harmful beasts from the land, and no sword will pass through your land."* God's security and one's satisfaction are for those who can trust Him fully.

Former & Latter Rain

Hosea 6:3 tells us, *So, let us know, let us press on to know the Lord. His going forth is as certain as the dawn, and He will come to us like the rain, like the spring rain watering the earth.* The early/former rain and the latter rain reference Messiah's two comings, the first in the fall and the other in the spring. Many ancient Jewish scrolls reference the Messiah as the "God of Righteousness," Sun of Righteousness," "Unique Teacher of Righteousness," and the "Final Melchizedekian Priest." With these scrolls available to the priests of Jesus's day, His coming should not have taken any of them by surprise.

> *For unto us, a Child is born, unto us a Son is given; and the government will be upon His shoulder. and His name will be called Wonderful, Counselor, Mighty God, Everlasting Father, Prince of Peace. Of the increase of His government and peace, there will be no end, upon the throne of David and over His kingdom, to order it and establish it with judgment and justice from that time forward, even forever. The zeal of the Lord of hosts will perform this.* **Isaiah 9:6-7**

The above passage refers to two Messiahs or one Messiah with two comings: one in the weakness of a Jewish child, while the other is ready to take the throne of David, establishing justice and righteousness for the sake of God's people. The misconceptions of Rabbinic thinking regarding the Messiah are the evidence of a demonic influence that keeps the unregenerate Jew under the veil of the religious system he holds to. In 2 Corinthians 3:16, *whenever a person turns to the Lord* [Jesus as Messiah], *the veil is taken away.*

Seeking the Kingdom

God's provisions, specifically His storehouses, are also available to New Testament believers. In Matthew 6:31-34, Jesus taught, *"Do not worry then, saying, 'What will we eat?' or 'What will we drink?' or 'What will we wear for clothing?' For the Gentiles eagerly seek all these things; for your heavenly Father knows that you need all these things. But* **seek first His kingdom and His righteousness**, *and all these things will be added to you. "So, do not worry about tomorrow, for tomorrow will care for itself. Each day has enough trouble of its own."* He emphasized that our attention should be on spiritual matters, promoting His kingdom and His righteousness, and He will open His storehouses on our behalf. He further speaks about our attitude toward tomorrow. He says tomorrow is not worthy of worry or anxiety because tomorrow has its own storehouses.

Giving

Just as God has storehouses, the temple also has a storehouse, representing the overflow of God's provisions for humanity to support the spiritual work on earth. In Malachi 3:8, the Lord speaks to the people about their attitude toward financing His work by asking them if they understood that not contributing a tithe (10%) to this work was like robbing God. In the same way, bringing *"the whole tithe"* to the storehouse will assuredly result in an overflow of blessings. This principle also applies to the church, as seen in 2 Corinthians 9:6-8, where God employs His grace as the means of providing abundance to all who give with a cheerful heart.

Prayer

"When you pray, you are not to be like the hypocrites; for they love to stand and pray in the synagogues and on the street corners so that they may be seen by men. Truly, I say to you, they have their reward in full. But you, when you pray, go into your inner room, close your door, and pray to your Father who is in secret, and your Father who sees what is done in secret will reward you. "And when you are praying, do not use meaningless repetition as the Gentiles do, for they suppose that they will be heard for their many words. So, do not be like them, for your Father knows what you need before you ask Him." **Matthew 6:5-8**

We pray because God tells us to ask. When we have needs or discern that others require His intervention, He wants us to ask and keep asking (Luke 18:1-8). Our encouragement is to know that God's storehouses are abundant and overflowing. When we ask with the right intentions and motives, God is happy to answer in His perfect timing. Consider Solomon in 1 Kings 3:11-14:

God said to him, "Because you have asked this thing and have not asked for yourself long life, nor have asked riches for yourself, nor have you asked for the life of your enemies, but have asked for yourself discernment to understand justice, behold, I have done according to your words. Behold, I have given you a wise and discerning heart so that there has been no one like you before you, nor shall one like you arise after you. "I have also given you what you have not asked, both riches and honor, so that there will not be any among the kings like you all your days. "If you walk in My ways, keeping My statutes and commandments, as your father David walked, then I will prolong your days."

For it is You who blesses the righteous man, O Lord, **You surround him with favor** *as with a shield.* **Psalm 5:12**

Chapter 21
Determination

> *And when I came to you, brethren, I did not come with superiority of speech or of wisdom, proclaiming to you the testimony of God. For I determined* [krino - judge in one's own mind as to what is right, proper, expedient; to deem, decide, determine, resolve] *to know nothing among you except Jesus Christ and Him crucified.* **1 Corinthians 2:1-2**

Paul's first letter to Corinth addressed many issues the church and its leadership faced, beginning with a problem of factions within the church. He encouraged them *that there be no divisions among you* (1 Corinthians 1:10). Through a deeper conversation about the word of the cross, he highlighted that the wisdom and power of God are not derived from men's efforts or ability but through the Holy Spirit. Paul taught them that *God has chosen the foolish things of the world to shame the wise, and God has chosen the weak things of the world to shame the things which are strong* (1 Corinthians 1:27). Taking the matter further, Paul made a determination, a resolve that his preaching would be defined by the person of *Jesus Christ and Him crucified*. His reasoning: *and my message and my preaching were not in persuasive words of wisdom, but in demonstration of the Spirit and of power, so that your faith would not rest on the wisdom of men, but on the power of God* (1 Corinthians 2:4-5).

A Personal, Crucified Christ

The only subject of teaching concerning which the Apostle had formed a determined resolve in his mind when coming to Corinth was the preaching of Christ and Him as being crucified. Paul did not dwell on the miraculous in the life of Christ, which would have pandered to the Jewish longing for a sign, nor did he put forward elaborate theories of the gospel, which would have been a concession to the Greek's longing for wisdom. Instead, he preached a personal Christ, especially the fact that He had been crucified. He realized the stumbling block that preaching a crucified Christ would have been to both Jews and Greeks.

A Firm, Fixed Intention

But Ruth said, "Do not urge me to leave you or turn back from following you; for where you go, I will go, and where you lodge, I will lodge. Your people shall be my people, and your God, my God. "Where you die, I will die, and there I will be buried. Thus, may the Lord do to me, and worse, if anything, but death parts you and me." When she saw that she was determined [amas – strong, determined, courageous] *to go with her, she said no more to her.* **Ruth 1:16-18**

Meriam Webster defines determination as 1. the resolving of a question by argument or reasoning, 2. the act of deciding definitely and firmly, and 3. a firm or fixed intention to achieve a desired end. In the believer's pursuit of getting to know God, he will be challenged to make serious decisions that dramatically affect his life. Ruth had to decide whether or not she would stay in her home country without a husband or follow Naomi, her mother-in-law, to a country she knew nothing about with no provisions of life in sight. That decision would ultimately affect all of history when she married Boaz and became part of the lineage of the Messiah. Each believer is presented at different times with choices that will affect his life and could change his future.

Daniel's Commitment

But Daniel made up his mind [siym – appoint, commit, determine] that he would not defile himself with the king's choice food or with the wine which he drank, so he sought permission from the commander of the officials that he might not defile himself. Now, God granted Daniel favor and compassion in the sight of the commander of the officials.
Daniel 1:8-9

Young Daniel was presented with a similar decision of importance early on in his time in Babylon under foreign rule. His determination to stay kosher and not eat from the king's table testified to God that he would be faithful amid strong opposition. Later, he would be faced with death in a lion's den if he did not stop praying to His God, the God of Abraham, Isaac, and Jacob. God would use Daniel and his faithfulness to give us clear prophecies related to the end times, complementing God's revelations to the Apostle John on Patmos. They would alter the course of history and confirm God's promises to His people and beyond.

The Son of Comfort

So, then those who were scattered because of the persecution that occurred in connection with Stephen made their way to Phoenicia and Cyprus and Antioch, speaking the word to no one except to Jews alone. But there were some of them, men of Cyprus and Cyrene, who came to Antioch and began speaking to the Greeks also, preaching the Lord Jesus. **And the hand of the Lord was with them**, *and a large number who believed turned to the Lord. The news about them reached the ears of the church at Jerusalem, and they sent* **Barnabas** *[son of consolation, comfort] off to Antioch. Then, when he arrived and witnessed the grace of God, he rejoiced and began to encourage them all with resolute* [*prothesis* – **determination**, *involves purpose, resolve, and design*] *heart to remain true to the Lord, for he was a good man, and full of the Holy Spirit and of faith. And considerable numbers were brought to the Lord. And he left for Tarsus to look for Saul; and when he had found him, he brought him to Antioch. And for an entire year, they met with the church and taught considerable numbers, and the disciples were first called Christians in Antioch. Now, at this time, some prophets came down from Jerusalem to Antioch. One of them, named Agabus, stood up and began to indicate by the Spirit that there would certainly be a great famine all over the world. And this took place in the reign of Claudius. And in the proportion that any of the disciples had means, each of them* **determined** *to send a contribution for the relief of the brethren living in Judea. And this they did, sending it in charge of Barnabas and Saul to the elders.* **Acts 11:19-30**

The above passage gives real insights into the heart of Barnabas. He was a Levite of Cyprus and an early convert to the Christian faith. His original name was Joses, but he derived his unusual title from his remarkable powers of exhorting the people and ministering consolation to the afflicted. He was one of those who gave up all their worldly substance, strength, and influence to support and spread the gospel. He introduced Paul to the disciples on the latter's visit to Jerusalem three years after his conversion, but the apostles were still unsure of Paul's conversion. Paul left Jerusalem and spent the next ten years or so relearning the Scriptures from a new covenant perspective in Tarsus. Afterward, Barnabas brought Paul from Tarsus to Antioch, and they labored together for two years with great success. They attended the Council of Jerusalem. Following a disagreement over the role of

John Mark, they separated, and Barnabas took John Mark with him on an independent missionary tour.

Ministry to the Gentiles

The account refers to Stephen to illustrate another result of his martyrdom. His death helped move the gospel into Samaria and incited Saul to persecute the church more vigorously, and he consequently was converted. It created the environment for spreading the gospel to Gentile lands, including Phoenicia, Cyprus, and Antioch. It would take men of great faith with a determined heart and the power of the Holy Spirit to fulfill God's ultimate plan.

Barnabas is an excellent example of a believer who is fulfilled in the purpose God has called him to do. Determination causes the believer to commit to a cause that is above and beyond him and willing to sacrifice himself for the greater purpose. It opens the door for the Holy Spirit to take charge and empower one to live a higher quality of life, committed to the faith as he has been taught. The first church gatherings were characterized by Acts 2:41-42: *So then, those who had received his word were baptized; and that day, there were added about three thousand souls. They were continually devoting themselves to the apostles' teaching and to fellowship, to the breaking of bread, and to prayer.*

A Settled Mind

Therefore, my beloved brethren, be steadfast [hedraios – settled], immovable, always abounding in the work of the Lord, knowing that your toil is not in vain in the Lord. **1 Corinthians 15:58**

Isaiah understood, "*The steadfast [samak – uphold, sustained] of mind You will keep in perfect peace because he trusts in You"* (Isaiah 26:3). This perfect peace, literally *shalom, shalom*, is the byproduct of the heart and mind that are upheld or sustained by one's willingness to trust in God. In Psalm 57:7, *My heart is steadfast* [kun – fixed], *O God, my heart is steadfast; I will sing, yes, I will sing praises!* A steadfast heart is one fixed and immovable on the precious and magnificent promises of God, leading the believer into becoming a partaker of the divine nature (2 Peter 1:4). The hope of the resurrection and of future glory should stimulate us to great and self-denying efforts in honor of Him who has revealed that doctrine, and who purposes graciously to reward us there. Other people are influenced and excited to make great efforts in hopes of honor, pleasure, or wealth. Christians should be excited to toil and self-denial by the prospect of immortal glory and by the assurance that their hopes are not in vain and will not deceive them.

The Hope of the Gospel

And although you were formerly alienated and hostile in mind, engaged in evil deeds, yet He has now reconciled you in His fleshly body through death, in order to present you before Him holy and blameless and beyond reproach— if indeed you continue in the faith **firmly established and steadfast**, *and not moved away from the hope of the gospel that you have heard, which was proclaimed in all creation under heaven, and of which I, Paul, was made a minister.*
Colossians 1:21-23

Hebrews 6:19-20 tells us that *This hope* [elpis – desire of some good with a confident expectation it will occur] *we have as an anchor of the soul, a hope both sure and steadfast and one which enters within the veil, where Jesus has entered as a forerunner for us, having become a high priest forever according to the order of Melchizedek.* This hope becomes an anchor for the soul as one *continues in the faith,* remaining steadfast and not moved away by outside influences. The enemy wishes to distract the believer by methods that undermine God's promises.

Never Shaken

For he will never be shaken; the righteous will be remembered forever. He will not fear evil tidings [bad news]*; his heart is steadfast, trusting in the Lord. His heart is upheld; he will not fear until he looks with satisfaction on his adversaries. He has given freely to the poor; his righteousness endures forever; His horn will be exalted in honor. The wicked will see it and be vexed; he will gnash his teeth and melt away; the desire of the wicked will perish.* **Psalm 112:6-10**

The one that will never be shaken is never to fear bad news or adversaries who oppress the people of God. This believer gives to the poor, and his heritage will be honored. Like the Jews sang after crossing the Red Sea:

"I will sing to the Lord, for He is highly exalted; the horse and its rider He has hurled into the sea. "The Lord is my strength and song, and He has become my salvation; this is my God, and I will praise Him; my father's God and I will extol Him. "The Lord is a warrior; the Lord is His name. "Pharaoh's chariots and his army He has cast into the sea; and the choicest of his officers are drowned in the Red Sea. "The deeps cover them; they went down into the depths like a stone. "Your right hand, O Lord, is majestic in power, Your right hand, O Lord, shatters the enemy. "And in the greatness of Your excellence, You overthrow those who rise up against You; You send forth Your burning anger, and it consumes them as chaff." **Exodus 15:1-7**

Chapter 22

The Harvest is Plentiful

In Genesis 46:3-4, God told Jacob that the Lord would make him a great nation, promising that He would go with Jacob and his family to Egypt and *"I will surely bring you up again."* God would birth the nation of Israel, beginning with the seventy of Jacob's family, as reported in Genesis 46, as well as Joseph and his family already there, and then deliver them. In Exodus 1, Scripture says that the sons of Israel would be fruitful and increase significantly, multiply, and become exceedingly mighty for a season. However, once the Pharoah who favored Joseph was gone, a new leader would place them in hard labor for hundreds of years.

> *Now, after this, the Lord appointed seventy others and sent them in pairs ahead of Him to every city and place where He Himself was going to come. And He was saying to them, "The harvest is plentiful, but the laborers* [ergates — laborer, worker] *are few; therefore, beseech the Lord of the harvest to send out laborers into His harvest. Go, behold, I send you out as lambs in the midst of wolves. Carry no money belt, no bag, no shoes, and greet no one on the way. Whatever house you enter, first say, 'Peace be to this house.' If a man of peace is there, your peace will rest on him, but if not, it will return to you. Stay in that house, eating and drinking what they give you, for the laborer is worthy of his wages. Do not keep moving from house to house. Whatever city you enter, and they receive you, eat what is set before you; and heal those in it who are sick, and say to them, 'The kingdom of God has come near to you.' But whatever city you enter and they do not receive you, go out into its streets and say, 'Even the dust of your city which clings to our feet we wipe*

off in protest against you; yet be sure of this, that the kingdom of God has come near.' I say to you, it will be more tolerable in that day for Sodom than for that city.
Luke 10:1-12

Seventy

Just as Israel started with seventy, the church also began with seventy laborers, seventy disciples. The number 70 is significant in Scripture. It combines 7, referring to completion, and 10, meaning natural order. Seventy speaks of the completion of natural order. Consider the following:

- 70 holy days – 52 Sabbaths, 7 days of Passover, 1 day of Pentecost, 1 day of Trumpets, 1 Day of Atonement, 8 days of Tabernacles
- 70 descendants of Noah after the flood speaking of 70 nations and languages (Josephus Antiquities)
- 70 members of Jacob's family begin the Hebrew nation in Egypt (Genesis 46)
- 70 elders to stand together with Him [70 members of Sanhedrin]
- 70 years of exile
- 70 names of God according to Midrash (Jewish commentary on Scripture)
- 70 years of life (Psalm 90:10)
- 70 sent out in Luke 10 to preach the Gospel
- 70 weeks of Daniel until the return of Messiah

Laborers

Harvesting is real work, hard work. God is looking for those who are ready and willing to work. The Church Father Hippolytus, Bishop of Rome in the third century, identified the names of the seventy, and they are included at the end of this writing. These were men totally committed to the work at hand. The work to establish the church after Jesus's ascension was placed on these seventy men, along with the apostles. It would be necessary for them to pray for more laborers, not spectators, who are willing to dedicate themselves to this highest purpose. Becoming a follower of Jesus is not a spectator sport, and He intends no personal glory for those who participate.

According to Luke 10, Jesus's instructions included not taking supplies or money since those accepting their message would provide for their basic needs. The seventy had a right to expect to be received by their Jewish brethren as they went to them to declare the presence of the King among them. They were proclaiming the coming of the Prince of Peace. Acts 10:36, *The word which He sent to the sons of Israel, preaching peace through Jesus Christ (He is Lord of all).* If the owner of the house was indeed a son of peace, he would gladly welcome His messengers. *"Peace I leave with you; My peace I give to you; not as the world gives do I give to you. Do not let your heart be troubled, nor let it be fearful"* (John 14:27). The disciple represents His peace and authority, so he goes in that boldness of faith (Matthew 28:20).

Looking for the Kingdom

"'The kingdom of God has come near to you. The evidence that this kingdom is near is found in the miracles and healing of the sick. It is not a physical kingdom but a new reality, the kingdom of heaven coming down to earth and realized by those who recognize its king. In John 3:3, Jesus told Nicodemus, "*Truly, truly, I say to you, unless one is born again, he cannot see the kingdom of God.*"

"For the kingdom of heaven is like a landowner who went out early in the morning to hire laborers for his vineyard. When he had agreed with the laborers for a denarius for the day, he sent them into his vineyard. And he went out about the third hour and saw others standing idle in the marketplace; and to those, he said, 'You also go into the vineyard, and whatever is right I will give you.' And so they went. Again, he went out about the sixth and the ninth hour and did the same thing. And about the eleventh hour, he went out and found others standing around, and he said to them, 'Why have you been standing here idle all day long?' They said to him, 'Because no one hired us.' He said to them, 'You go into the vineyard too.' "When evening came, the owner of the vineyard said to his foreman, 'Call the laborers and pay them their wages, beginning with the last group to the first.' When those hired about the eleventh hour came, each one received a denarius. When those hired first came, they thought they would receive more, but each also received a denarius. When they received it, they grumbled at the landowner, saying, 'These last men have worked only one hour, and you have made them equal to us who have borne the burden and the scorching heat of the day.' But he 'answered and said to one of them, Friend, I am doing you no wrong; did you not agree with me for a denarius? Take what is yours and go, but I wish to give to this last man the same as to you. Is it not lawful for me to do what I wish with what is my own? Or is your eye envious because I am generous?' So, the last shall be first, and the first last."
Matthew 20:1-16

Laborers in the Vineyard

Jesus told this parable in which a landowner went out early in the morning and hired men to work in his vineyard for the day at an agreed price of one denarius, the normal daily pay for a laborer. Later, about the third hour (around 9 A.M.), the landowner encouraged others in the marketplace to work in the vineyard, not for a stipulated wage but for whatever was right. The landowner employed more laborers during the sixth hour (about noon), the ninth hour (3 P.M.), and even some during the eleventh hour (5 P.M.) when only one hour was left for labor.

When it came time (evening, i.e., 6 P.M.) for the landowner to pay the workers, he began with those who had worked the shortest amount of time and paid each of them one denarius. When those who worked the entire day came for compensation, they thought they would receive more than a denarius. They had labored all day and borne the burden of the work and the heat of the day. They had agreed, however, to work for a stipulated amount, and that is what they received. The landowner argued that he had the right to do what he chose with his money. He reminded them they should not be envious of his generosity toward those who had labored only briefly.

Through this illustration, Jesus was teaching that the matter of rewards is controlled by God, the "landowner" in the parable. God is the One before whom all accounts will be settled. Many who have prominent places will someday find themselves demoted. Many who often find themselves at the end of the line will be promoted to the head of the line: The last will be first, and the first will be last. The last called were first paid and were equal to the first in compensation; the first were behind the others in time of payment and in the spirit with which they received their wages; they were also treated with less generosity than the others. According to Barnes Notes:

"Many are called into my kingdom; they come and labor as I command them; many of them are comparatively unknown and obscure; yet they are real Christians and shall all receive the proper reward. A few I have chosen for higher stations in the church. I have endowed them with apostolic gifts or with superior talents and suited them for wider usefulness. They may not be as long in the vineyard as others; their race may be sooner run, but I have chosen to honor them in this manner, and I have a right to do it. I injure no one and have a right to do what I will with my own." Thus explained, this parable has no reference to the call of the Gentiles, nor to the call of aged sinners, nor to the call of sinners out of the church at all. It is simply designed to teach that in the church, among the multitudes who will be saved, Christ makes a difference. He makes some more useful than others without regard to the time which they serve, and he will reward them accordingly. **Barnes Notes**

Rejection

"Woe to you, Chorazin! Woe to you, Bethsaida! For if the miracles had been performed in Tyre and Sidon which occurred in you, they would have repented long ago, sitting in sackcloth and ashes. But it will be more tolerable for Tyre and Sidon in the judgment than for you. And you, Capernaum, will not be exalted to heaven, will you? You will be brought down to Hades! "The one who listens to you listens to Me, and the one who rejects you rejects Me, and he who rejects Me rejects the One who sent Me." **Luke 10:13-16**

The traditional site of "Chorazin" (the name of a fish) is at the north end of the Sea of Galilee. "Bethsaida" ("fish town") Julius was its near neighbor. Thus, Jesus presented the contrast between two villages at the north end of the Sea of Galilee and two towns at the south end of the Dead Sea: Sodom and Gomorrah. All four cities do not exist at in present times. Both Chorazin and Bethsaida, representatives for many other similar towns, had received much of Jesus's ministry. Tyre and Sidon, two Phoenician cities on the Mediterranean coast, had suffered severe judgment for rejecting God and His people. Jesus's point was that judgment would come on people disregarding His offer of salvation. At the same time, Jesus was teaching that His laborers will be rejected, but in reality, He is the one being rejected. The laborer learns not to take rejection personally.

Divine Ability

The seventy returned with joy, saying, "Lord, even the demons are subject to us in Your name." And He said to them, "I was watching Satan fall from heaven like lightning. Behold, I have given you authority to tread on serpents and scorpions and over all the power of the enemy, and nothing will injure you. Nevertheless, do not rejoice in this, that the spirits are subject to you, but rejoice that your names are recorded in heaven." **Luke 10:17-20**

When the laborer is commissioned into the plan of God, he is empowered to fulfill that plan with divine ability and God's power to overcome any obstacles, even Satan and his demons. It is divine authority. Yet the source of his joy is the reality that his home is heaven and his reward for the way God used him in His plan. The completion of natural order is the fulfillment of the Church Age (new covenant) and the welcoming of the Kingdom Age.

	The Seventy Disciples according to Hippolytus		
1	James, the Lord's half brother; Bishop of Jerusaem*	36	Hermes, Bishop of Dalmatia
2	Cleopas, Bishop of Jerusalem	37	Patrobulus, Bishop of Puteoli
3	Matthias, took Judas Iscariot's place in Acts 1	38	Hermes, Bishop of Philippi
4	Thaddeus, conveyed the epistle to Abgarus	39	Linus, Bishop of Rome
5	Ananias, baptized Paul, Bishop of Damascus	40	Caius, Bishop of Ephesus
6	Stephen, the first martyr	41	Philogus, Bishop of Sinope
7	Philip, baptized the eunuch	42	Olympus & Rhodion, married in Rome*
8	Prochorus, Bishop of Nicomedia	43	Rhodion, martyred in Rome
9	Nicanor, died when Stephen was martyred	44	Lucius, Bishop of Laodicia in Syria
10	Timon, Bishop of Bostra	45	Jason, Bishop of Tarsus
11	Parmenos, Bishop of Soli	46	Sosipater, Bishop of Iconium
12	Nicolaus, Bishop of Samaria	47	Tertius, Bishop of Iconium
13	Barnabas, Bishop of Milan	48	Erastus, Bishop of Panellas
14	Mark, writer of the Gospel, Bishop of Alexandria	49	Quartus, Bishop of Berytus
15	Luke, wrote Gospel & Acts	50	Apollo, Bishop of Caesarea
16	Silas, Bishop of Corinth	51	Cephas
17	Silvanus, Bishop of Thesalonika	52	Sosthenes, Bishop of Colophonia
18	Crices(Crescens), Bishop of Carchedon in Gaul	53	Tychicus, Bishop of Colophonia
19	Epaenetus, Bishop of Carthage	54	Epaphroditus, Bishop of Andriace
20	Andronicus, Bishop of Pannonia	55	Caesar, Bishop of Dyrrachium
21	Amplias, Bishop of Odyssus	56	Mark, cousin to Barnabas, Bishop of Apollonia
22	Urban, Bishop of Macedonia	57	Justus, Bishop of

			Eleuthreopolis
23	Stachys, bishop of Byzantium	58	Artemas, Bishop of Lystra
24	Barnabas, Bishop of Heraclea	59	Clement, Bishop of Sardinia
25	Phhygellus, Bishop of Ephesus of the party of Simon	60	Onesphorus, Bishop of Corone
26	Hermogenes, of the party of Simon	61	Tychicus, Bishop of Chalcedon
27	Demas, who later became a priest of idols	62	Carpus, Bishop of Berytus in Thrace
28	Apelles, Bishop of Smyrna	63	Evodus, Bishop of Antioch
29	Aristobulus, Bishop of Britain	64	Aristarchus, Bishop of Apamea
30	Narcissus, Bishop of Athens	65	Mark, who is John, Bishop of Bibloupolis
31	Herodian, Bishop of Tarsus	66	Zenas, Bishop of Diospolis
32	Agabus the prophet	67	Philemon, Bishop of Gaza
33	Rufus, Bishop of Thebes	68	Aristarchus
34	Asyncritus, Bishop of Hyrcania	69	Pudes
35	Phlegon, Bishop of Marathon	70	Trophimus, martyred with Paul
* The Scripture indicated James was an unbeliever until after the Resurrection.			
Since #42 contains 2 people, we can conclude James was not one of the original 70.			

Chapter 23
Forevermore

> *For a child will be born to us* [nation of Israel], *a son will be given to us, and the government* [misra – rule, dominion] *will rest on His shoulders; and His name will be called Wonderful* [pele - a wonder, a miracle, a marvel, something unusual or extraordinary]. *Counselor* [yaats – consultant, advisor, Jethro in Exodus 18:19], *Mighty God* [eel gibbor – brave, strong, mighty], *Eternal* [ad - perpetuity, unforeseeable future] *Father, Prince of Peace* [shalom – tranquility, wholesome]. *There will be no end to the increase of His government or of peace on the throne of David and over his kingdom, to establish it and to uphold it with justice and righteousness from then on and* **forevermore** [olam - a very long time]. *The zeal of the Lord of hosts will accomplish this.* **Isaiah 9:6-7**

The above passage, like Isaiah 61:1-2, addresses both of Messiah's comings. His first would be characterized by a newborn child who would have dominion as a king, although not in a physical sense. *Jesus answered, "My kingdom is not of this world"* (John 18:36). It would be His second coming when there *will be no end to the increase of His government or of peace on the throne of David and over his kingdom.* Isaiah also identifies the Messiah's names when He comes, beginning with *Wonderful,* the Hebrew *pele* which speaks not only of marvelous and miraculous but also extraordinary. When God assigns a name, it addresses a characteristic of that individual. Jesus would be extraordinary!

Isaiah also refers to this coming Messiah as *Counselor, Mighty God, Eternal Father*, and *Prince of Peace. Counselor* describes a consultant or advisor as opposed to an authoritarian or dictator. *Eel gibbor* specifies that He will be a God of great strength and might; it is a name given to God in Isaiah 10:21 and Jeremiah 32:18. *Eternal Father* and *Prince of Peace* indicate His fatherhood and that He would bring peace and wholeness as a prince. The promises would be *justice and righteousness from then on and* **forevermore.** What is forevermore?

Time & Eternity

It should be noted that there is no general word for time in Hebrew, and there are no special terms for the past, present, future, and eternity. The Hebrew words *ad* and *olam* (a very long time) should be compared, with special attention given to the nineteen times when these words were used together. Justice and righteousness describe His kingdom *from then on and forevermore*. *Olam* usually refers to looking forward but often expresses the idea of looking backward. It can also refer to a particular span of time. Forevermore does not only reference eternity.

> *Before the mountains were born or You gave birth to the earth and the world, even from everlasting to everlasting, You are God.* **Psalm 90:2**

And this brings us to the meaning of the word eternity. Eternity is a term used to express the concept of something that has no end and/or no beginning. God has no beginning or end, but He cannot be wholly defined by eternity, especially as a measure of time. (God is eternal, but eternity does not equal God. Similarly, God is all-powerful, but power does not equal God.) Eternity is one of God's attributes, but having created time, He is greater than time and exists outside of it.

Completed Before it Begins

"Remember the former things long past [olam – long time past, of old], for I am God, and there is no other; I am God, and there is no one like Me, **Declaring the end from the beginning***, and from ancient times, things which have not been done, saying, 'My purpose will be established, and I will accomplish all My good pleasure'; Calling a bird of prey from the east, the man of My purpose from a far country. Truly, I have spoken; truly, I will bring it to pass. I have planned it; surely, I will do it.* **Isaiah 46:9-11**

The Lord, through Isaiah, is reminding the Hebrews that God has been consistently dealing with His people as His commitment to be their God. *"Listen to Me, O house of Jacob, and all the remnant of the house of Israel, you who have been borne by Me from birth and have been carried from the womb; Even to your old age I will be the same, and even to your graying years I will bear you! I have done it, and I will carry you, and I will bear you, and I will deliver you* (Isaiah 46:3-4). From the vantage point of eternity, God sees everything as completed before it begins. Time is no obstacle to the plans and purposes of God. *I know that everything God does will remain forever; there is nothing to add to it, and there is nothing to take from it, for God has so worked that men should fear Him* (Ecclesiastes 3:14). The Father of Time & Eternity is fully equipped to fulfill every good pleasure.

Dwelling in Eternity

For thus says the high and exalted One Who lives forever [sakan – dwells in eternity], whose name is Holy, "I dwell on a high and holy place, and also with the contrite and lowly of spirit in order to revive the spirit of the lowly and to revive the heart of the contrite. **Isaiah 57:15**

When man was created, he was made in the image of God (Genesis 1:26). Just as God is three dimensional (Father, Son, & Holy Spirit), so he created man as body, soul, and spirit. The entire material world follows this same pattern. Space is defined by height, width, and depth, while matter exists in either gas, solid, or liquid. Since time is linear, it can be referred to as past, present, or future. The material world, patterned after a three-dimensional God, is also three-dimensional. As a spirit, God dwells outside of time, in eternity, but enters time and space *with the contrite and lowly of spirit.* The condition of man's heart determines his connection to God.

Opportune Time

There is an appointed time [zepan – opportune] for everything. And there is a time for every event under heaven. **Ecclesiastes 3:1**

In Ecclesiastes 3, Solomon introduces a discussion of time when he says, "*There is an appointed* [opportune] *time for everything* [actions & events]. *And there is a time* [as a duration] *for every event* [activity – what one desires] *under heaven*". The essence of this verse is that God has given time as a gift to be managed to discern its most significant meaning and find His will amid its details. It also brings up the idea of seasons of life when conditions or events govern different periods of life: *A time to kill and a time to heal, a time to tear down, and a time to build up. A time to weep and a time to laugh, a time to mourn, and a time to dance* (verses 2-4). The summary of the passage is found in verse 11, where God has made everything beautiful or appropriate in its time. The highest quality of life is found when man seeks God's daily purpose.

Make the Days Count

As for the days of our life, they contain seventy years, or if due to strength, eighty years, yet their pride is but labor and sorrow; for **soon it is gone, and we fly away**. *Who understands the power of Your anger and Your fury, according to the fear [yirah – reverence, acknowledging God's good intentions] that is due You? So,* **teach us to number [manah – make it count] our days**, *that we may present to You a heart of wisdom.* **Psalm 90:10-12**

Moses recognized that his length of days on earth is numbered, and the quality of that life revolves around his ability to number his days, meaning that each day has great value in and of itself, so he focuses his attention on the current day; it has value unto itself. When prioritizing each day in this way, he finds the wisdom of God intended for that day. **For a thousand years in Your sight are like yesterday** *when it passes by or as a watch in the night. You have swept them away like a flood; they fall asleep; in the morning, they are like grass which sprouts anew. In the morning, it flourishes and sprouts anew; toward evening, it fades and withers away* (Psalm 90:4-6). Each day is an integral part of God's larger plan for each life. *God saw all that He had made, and behold,* **it was very good** (Genesis 1:31).

In the Present Moment

*I am the Alpha and the Omega," says the Lord God, "***who is and who was and who is to come, the Almighty**.*"* **Revelation 1:8**

Just like Jesus was crucified between two thieves, the present is also being stolen from the believer by the past and the future. Too many are driven either by the failures of the past or the unknowns of the future, and this robs them of the joy in the relationship God has intended. You see, He told Moses in Exodus 3 that His name is *"I Am that I Am,"* which means He is the God of the present moment and therefore every moment. Jesus acknowledged that His name is also "I Am" when he told the Jewish leadership that *"before Abraham was born, I am"* (John 8:58). Ultimately, God meets each of us in the present moment, learning that to *"cease striving and know that I am God"* (Psalm 46:10) is our place of rest. Jesus taught His disciples to *"seek first His kingdom and His righteousness"* and *"do not worry about tomorrow"* (Matthew 6:33-34), meaning His presence is in the present moment.

> *He has weakened my strength in the way* [the course he was pursuing]; *He has shortened my days. I say, "O my God, do not take me away in the midst of my days;* **Your years are throughout all generations.** *"Of old You founded the earth, and the heavens are the work of Your hands. "Even they will perish, but You endure, and all of them will wear out like a garment; like clothing, You will change them, and they will be changed. "But You are the same* [God does not change], *and Your years will not come to an end. "The children of Your servants will continue, and their descendants will be established* [kun – make firm, prepare] *before You."*
> **Psalm 102:23-28**

Psalm 102 is entitled A Prayer for an Afflicted Man. He laments his weakened state due to his experiences, yet he understands that the Lord's endurance and immutability (He does not change) will carry the day. "But **be glad and rejoice forever in what I create**; *for behold, I create Jerusalem for rejoicing and her people for gladness* (Isaiah 65:18). God's people, both old covenant and new covenant, will find their rest in the Father of Time & Eternity, forevermore.

Chapter 24
Death and Resurrection

What is the opposite of death? For most, the answer would be life. In 1 Corinthians 15, Paul answers the question by addressing resurrection, both the physical and spiritual. Resurrection cancels death, removing its sting, 1 Corinthians 15:55-57, "O DEATH, WHERE IS YOUR VICTORY? O DEATH, WHERE IS YOUR STING?" *The sting of death is sin, and the power of sin is the law; but thanks be to God, who gives us the victory through our Lord Jesus Christ.* Jesus's physical death and resurrection were the culmination of the last two weeks of his physical life when he raised Lazarus from the dead and declared in John 11:25-26, "*I am the resurrection and the life; he who believes in Me will live even if he dies, and everyone who lives and believes in Me will never die. Do you believe this?*" Christ's resurrection is available to anyone who believes in Him.

> *And so, Simon Peter also came, following him, and entered the tomb; and he saw the linen wrappings lying there, and the face-cloth which had been on His head, not lying with the linen wrappings, but rolled up in a place by itself. So, the other disciple who had first come to the tomb then also entered, and he saw and believed. For as yet, they did not understand the Scripture, that He must rise again from the dead.* **John 20:6-9**

The above reference speaks of two pieces of linen found in the empty tomb, one wrapping his body and the other covering his head. I've done some research on the subject of the Shroud of Turin, and I believe there is sufficient evidence to recognize it as the actual linen referenced by John. There is also the Sedarium of Odiero (Spain), a cloth that matches the description of the head covering found in the tomb. Significant scientific research has been performed on both artifacts; they represent physical evidence of Christ's death, burial, and resurrection. Peter and the others needed to see the empty tomb with the grave clothes to believe. Their understanding of all that took place would follow.

Three Days

Jesus answered them, "Destroy this temple, and in three days I will raise it up." The Jews then said, "It took forty-six years to build this temple, and will You raise it up in three days?" But He was speaking of the temple of His body. So, when He was raised from the dead, His disciples remembered that He said this, and they believed the Scripture and the word which Jesus had spoken.
John 2:19-22

From the beginning of His public ministry, Jesus taught that He would suffer and die before being raised from the dead. He always connected His death to his resurrection; although they are separate events, they must be seen together. In the above passage, He indicates that He will be dead three days and be raised again. Jesus addresses this same idea in Matthew 12:40-42, where He uses Jonah, who spent three days in *the belly of the sea monster,* as a prophecy of the Son of Man, who will *be three days and three nights in the heart of the earth*.

Our current understanding of the events of that week does not support Jesus being buried for three full days and nights, but a closer look at other ancient documents (Dead Sea Scrolls) specifies that Passover was on Nissan 14, Tuesday dusk to Wednesday dusk. The Sabbath referenced was not the weekly seventh-day Sabbath, but the high holy Sabbath of Unleavened Bread on Wednesday-Thursday. If the Last Supper/Passover occurred on Tuesday evening, and His trial and crucifixion all happened before Wednesday dusk, then Jesus was in the tomb all day Thursday, Friday, and Saturday, confirming Jesus's words. The disciples would be fully aware of these matters.

"God Forbid It"

> *From that time, Jesus began to show His disciples that He must go to Jerusalem, and suffer many things from the elders and chief priests and scribes, and be killed and be raised up on the third day. Peter took Him aside and began to rebuke Him, saying, "God forbid it, Lord! This shall never happen to You." But He turned and said to Peter, "Get behind Me, Satan! You are a stumbling block to Me, for you are not setting your mind on God's interests, but man's."*
> **Matthew 16:21-23**

Although Jesus reiterated the Father's plan that He would suffer and die to be raised from the dead, Peter and the others had great difficulty accepting it. In the above exchange, Peter tells Him that he forbids it as if he knew what was best. Jesus had to rebuke Peter as a mouthpiece of Satan since he was evaluating the circumstance from man's viewpoint rather than God's perfect plan. Even after seeing the Transfiguration of Jesus with Moses and Elijah and His Father speaking from heaven, Jesus still reminded them of His suffering to come. *"But I say to you that Elijah already came, and they did not recognize him but did to him whatever they wished. So, also the Son of Man is going to suffer at their hands"* (Matthew 17:12).

Firstborn From the Dead

He is also head of the body, the church, and He is the beginning, the firstborn from the dead so that He Himself will come to have first place in everything. For it was the Father's good pleasure for all the fullness to dwell in Him, and through Him to reconcile all things to Himself, having made peace through the blood of His cross; through Him, I say, whether things on earth or things in heaven. **Colossians 1:18-20**

The Apostle Paul understood the implications of Christ's death and resurrection like no other and wrote extensively about them in 1 Corinthians 15. In the above passage, he identifies Jesus as **the firstborn from the dead**, *so He Himself will come to have first place in everything.* It was His precious blood from His suffering and crucifixion that accomplished peace for all mankind and released us from sin for all who would believe. According to Revelation 1:5, *and from Jesus Christ, the faithful witness,* **the firstborn of the dead**, *and the ruler of the kings of the earth. To Him who loves us and released us from our sins by His blood.* Jesus has the keys of death and of Hades, meaning He has full authority over death (Revelation 1:18). His victory over death is full and complete.

Your Faith is Worthless

Now, if Christ is preached, that He has been raised from the dead, how do some among you say that there is no resurrection of the dead? But if there is no resurrection of the dead, not even Christ has been raised; and if Christ has not been raised, then our preaching is vain, your faith also is vain. Moreover, we are even found to be false witnesses of God because we testified against God that He raised Christ, whom He did not raise, if in fact the dead are not raised. For if the dead are not raised, not even Christ has

been raised; and if Christ has not been raised, your faith is worthless; you are still in your sins. Then those also who have fallen asleep in Christ have perished. If we have hoped in Christ in this life only, we are of all men most to be pitied.
1 Corinthians 15:12-19

The culture in which Paul wrote to the Corinthians, although under Roman rule, was heavily Hellenistic, significantly influenced by Greek philosophy that man is not resurrected from the dead. The Sadducees also taught this error. Paul argued that it is not a rational conclusion if Jesus actually rose from the dead. Since Paul met the risen Lord on the way to Damascus, he knew that Christ's resurrection is real and central to everything the Christian believes; otherwise, *your faith is worthless; you are still in your sins*. The assurance of Christ's resurrection means that believers will also be raised. *If we have hoped in Christ in this life only, we are of all men most to be pitied* [full of misery]. As Paul wrote in his first letter to them, it would be foolishness to the world.

Death is Abolished

But now Christ has been raised from the dead, the first fruits [the first of the ripe fruits] *of those who are asleep* [dead]. *For since by a man came death, by a man also came the resurrection of the dead. For as in Adam all die, so also* **in Christ all will be made alive**. *But each in his own order: Christ the first fruits, after that those who are Christ's at His coming, then comes the end, when He hands over the kingdom to God the Father, when He has abolished all rule and all authority and power. For He must reign until He has put all His enemies under His feet.* **The last enemy that will be abolished is death**. *For HE HAS PUT ALL THINGS IN SUBJECTION UNDER HIS FEET. But when He says, "All things* *are put in subjection," it is evident that He is excepted [ektos – excluded – Jesus will remain subject to the Father] who put all things in subjection to Him. When all things are subjected to Him, then the Son Himself also will be subjected to the One who subjected all things to Him, so that God may be all in all. Otherwise, what will those do who are baptized for the dead? If the dead are not raised at all, why are they baptized for them? Why are we also in danger every hour? I affirm, brethren, by the boasting in you which I have in Christ Jesus our Lord, **I die daily**. If, from human motives, I fought with wild beasts at Ephesus, what does it profit me? If the dead are not raised, LET US EAT AND DRINK, FOR TOMORROW WE DIE. Do not be deceived: "Bad company corrupts good morals." Become sober-minded as you ought, and stop sinning; for some have no knowledge of God. I speak this to your shame.* **1 Corinthians 15:20-34**

Christ, the first of the ripe fruits, has prepared the path for all believers to be resurrected and made alive. God has an order, a sequence, in the resurrection. When Jesus Christ returns in the air, He will take His church to heaven after raising from the dead all who have trusted Him and have died in the faith at the rapture (1 Thessalonians 4:16-17). When He returns to the earth in judgment, the lost will experience *the resurrection of judgment* (John 5:29). Nobody in the first resurrection will be lost, but nobody in the second resurrection will be saved.

When Jesus Christ comes to the earth to judge, He will banish sin for a thousand years and establish His kingdom. Believers will reign with Him and share His glory and authority. This kingdom prophesied in the Old Testament, is called the Millennium by many teachers. But even after the Millennium, there will be one final rebellion against God (Revelation 20:7-10) which Jesus Christ will put down by His power. The lost will then be raised, judged, and cast into the lake of fire. Then death itself shall be cast into hell, and the last enemy shall be destroyed. Jesus Christ will have put all things under His feet! He will then turn the kingdom over to the Father, and then the eternal state - the new heavens and new earth will begin.

When Paul says *I die daily*, he was likely referring to the perils and trials which he had endured at Ephesus; and his object was to impress their minds with the firmness of his belief in the certainty of the resurrection, on account of which he suffered so much, and to show them that all their hopes rested also on this same conviction (boasting).

Death Rendered Powerless

Therefore, since the children share in flesh and blood, He Himself likewise also partook of the same, that through death He might render powerless him who had the power of death, that is, the devil, and might free those who through fear of death were subject to slavery all their lives.
Hebrews 2:14-15

Then death and Hades were thrown into the lake of fire. This is the second death, the lake of fire. And if anyone's name was not found written in the book of life, he was thrown into the lake of fire. **Revelation 20:14-15**

But now has been revealed by the appearing of our Savior Christ Jesus, who abolished [katargeo – destroyed] death *and brought life [zoe – life of God]* and immortality *[incorruption] to light through the gospel.* **2 Timothy 1:10**

In Hebrews 2:10, the Author or Captain of our salvation needed to suffer to bring many sons to glory. These sons were once held in servitude by their enemy, Satan. Since they were human, their Captain had to become human and die for them, to rescue them. But by doing so, He was able to destroy...the devil. It does not mean that Satan ceased to exist or to be active. Instead, he used *katageo* as "to render powerless" the power of death over those whom Christ redeems. In speaking of the devil as wielding the power of death, Satan uses people's fear of death to enslave them to his will. Often, people make wrong moral choices out of their intense desire for self-preservation. We are reminded that they were no longer subject to such slavery and that they could face death with the same confidence in God their Captain had. Death and Hades will be *thrown into the lake of fire.*

Life in the Gospel

Paul tells Timothy that the life of God is incorruptible and that it is found in the gospel and brought to light by the death and resurrection of Christ. According to Barnes Notes:

> This is one of the great and glorious achievements of the gospel and one of the things by which it is distinguished from every other system. The word rendered "hath brought to light" - *footizoo* - means to give light, to shine; then to give light to, to shine upon; and then to bring to light, to make known. The sense is that these things were obscure or unknown before and have been disclosed to us by the gospel. It is, of course, not meant that there were NO intimations of these truths before, or that NOTHING was known of them—for the Old Testament shed some light on them; but that they are fully disclosed to man in the gospel. It is there that all ambiguity and doubt are removed and that the evidence is so clearly stated as to leave no doubt

on the subject. The intimations of a future state, among the wisest of the pagans, were certainly very obscure, and their hopes very faint.

Finding Life in Death

Truly, truly, I say to you, unless a grain of wheat falls into the earth and dies, it remains alone; but if it dies, it bears much fruit. He who loves his life loses it, and he who hates his life in this world will keep it to life eternal. If anyone serves Me, he must follow Me; and where I am, there My servant will be also; if anyone serves Me, the Father will honor him. **John 12:24-26**

The wheat analogy illustrates a general paradoxical principle that death is the way to life. In Jesus' case, His death led to glory and life not only for Himself but also for others. He is speaking about the spiritual life found on the other side of death, beyond one's personal interests and priorities. Jesus defines that life as: *He who loves his life loses it, and he who hates his life in this world will keep it to life eternal.* That reality is the premise for service to God and is only possible for those who follow Him. Following Jesus denotes a fellowship of faith and a fellowship of life, sharing in His sufferings not only inwardly but outwardly if necessary. Such outward fellowship with Jesus, however, could not continue without inner moral and spiritual fellowship, without a life resembling His and a self-denying sharing of His cross.

Chapter 25
Judge Not

In John 3:17, Jesus told Nicodemus that *God did not send the Son into the world to judge the world but that the world might be saved through Him* (Jesus). If the world was not judged by God, neither should anyone judge another. This Greek word for judge is *krinoe*, which means to separate, distinguish, or discriminate between good and evil. Spiros Zodhiates says it is *to form and express a judgment or opinion about any person or thing, more commonly unfavorable*. It speaks of *a habit of forming a judgment hastily, harshly, and without an allowance for every palliating circumstance and a habit of "expressing" such an opinion harshly and unnecessarily when formed*. Judging is one of the most destructive activities any believer can participate in. The consequences can be immediate. Antisemitism, like all forms of prejudice, should fall into the category of judging.

Antisemitism

The current war in Israel against Hamas is highlighting the climate around the world regarding the attitudes toward the Jews. Antisemitism is rearing its ugly head all over the world, evidenced by protests and other public displays against Israel's right to defend itself against the horrific evil perpetrated by Hamas against the civilian population near Gaza on October 7, 2023. It is of great importance for the Christian believer to understand the history and nature of this condition.

According to the U.S. State Department, *"Antisemitism is a certain perception of Jews, which may be expressed as hatred toward Jews. Rhetorical and physical manifestations of antisemitism are directed toward Jewish or non-Jewish individuals* and/or their property, toward Jewish community institutions and religious facilities." It exists prevalently not just in nations that are opposed to Israel and its existence but even within the Christian community in America and worldwide.

An article written by Gary Rosenblatt in March 2020 quotes Abraham Foxman, a child survivor of the Holocaust who led the ADL for five decades regarding our current state: *"We're living in an environment today that is more user-friendly to the virus* [of antisemitism],*"* he said, *"a time of incivility, lack of tolerance, no respect for the truth. And with it comes politicization, polarization, frustration, anger, hate—all the elements that fuel the virus."* The comparison to a virus similar to Covid 19 is appropriate since antisemitism can be both highly contagious and deadly.

> "I am the good shepherd; the good shepherd lays down His life for the sheep. He who is a hired hand and not a shepherd, who is not the owner of the sheep, sees the wolf coming and leaves the sheep and flees, and the wolf snatches them and scatters them. He flees because he is a hired hand and is not concerned about the sheep. I am the good shepherd, and I know My own and My own know Me, even as the Father knows Me and I know the Father; and I lay down My life for the sheep. I have other sheep, which are not of this fold; I must bring them also, and they will hear My voice; and they will become one flock with one shepherd. For this reason, the Father loves Me, because I lay down My life so that I may take it again. **No one has taken it away from Me, but I lay it down on My own initiative**. I have authority to lay it down, and I have authority to take it up again. This commandment I received from My Father."
> **John 10:11-18**

The world would blame the Jews for Jesus's death even though Jesus gave up His life willingly. The Roman Emperor Constantine had a Christian conversion experience around 312 AD and declared tolerance for Christianity in 313 AD. The Council of Nicaea took place in 325 AD and he wrote a letter referring to Jews as *polluted wretches* and *to have no fellowship with the perjury of the Jews* and that *we have nothing in common with the usage of these parricides and murderers of our Lord*. Even Martin Luther had strong feelings of antisemitism, as he wrote in *The Jew and Their Lies* (1543):

What shall we Christians do with this damned, rejected race of Jews? Since they live among us, and we know about their lying, blasphemy, and cursing, we cannot tolerate them if we do not wish to share in their lies, curses, and blasphemy. In this way, we cannot quench the inextinguishable fire of divine rage (as the prophets say) nor convert the Jews. We must prayerfully and reverentially practice a merciful severity. Perhaps we may save a few from the fire and the flames. We must not seek vengeance. They are surely being punished a thousand times more than we might wish them. Let me give you my honest advice.

Spiritual Warfare

The devil (Satan) would like nothing more than to see the complete destruction of God's people, including the Jews and the nation of Israel. We see in Scripture that he is the accuser of the brethren (Revelation 12:10), *who accuses them before our God day and night*. Jesus told us that he has come to kill, steal, and destroy (John 10:10). He is a murderer from the beginning (John 8:44), and He is against anyone who recognizes the God of Abraham, Isaac, and Jacob. He accuses even the high priest as he did to Joshua in Zechariah 3:1-2: *Then he showed me Joshua, the high priest standing before the Angel of the Lord, and Satan standing at his* right hand to oppose him. And the Lord said to Satan, "The Lord rebuke you, Satan! The Lord who has chosen Jerusalem rebuke you! Is this not a brand plucked from the fire?" In Revelation 17:6, the great harlot is *drunk with the blood of the saints and with the blood of the witnesses of Jesus.*

> *Now, Joseph was handsome in form and appearance. It came about after these events that his master's wife looked with desire at Joseph, and she said, "Lie with me." But he refused and said to his master's wife, "Behold, with me here, my master does not concern himself with anything in the house, and he has put all that he owns in my charge. "There is no one greater in this house than I, and he has withheld nothing from me except you because you are his wife. How then could I do this great evil **and sin against God?"** As she spoke to Joseph day after day, he did not listen to her to lie beside her or be with her.* **Genesis 39:6-10**

Testament of Joseph

Let's examine Joseph, Jacob's eleventh son, and his trial with Potiphar's wife and her accusation of rape. The challenges of walking with the Lord in difficult circumstances are many times overwhelming. Pharoah's wife was enamored with Joseph, his handsome appearance and his commitment to integrity before his master, Potiphar. She was relentless in her pursuit of getting Joseph to lie with her and betray her husband. The Testament of Joseph (part of the Dead Sea Scrolls) contains the words of Joseph in dealing with this woman.

> *"How often she fawned upon me with words as a holy man, with guile in her talk, praising my chastity before her husband while desiring to destroy me when we were alone. She lauded me openly as chaste, and in secret, she said unto*

me, 'Do not be afraid of my husband; for he is convinced you are chaste, so that even should one tell him concerning us, he would never believe him.' For all these things, I lay upon the ground in sackcloth, and I besought God that the Lord would deliver me from the Egyptian. When she prevailed nothing, she came again to me under the plea of instruction, that she might know the word of the Lord. She said unto me, 'If you want me to abandon my idols, just tell me, and I will persuade my husband to depart from his idols, and we will walk in the law of your Lord.' I said unto her, 'The Lord does not want those who reverence Him to live in uncleanness, nor does He take pleasure in those who commit adultery.' She held her peace, longing to accomplish her evil desire. I gave myself yet more to fasting and prayer that the Lord should deliver me from her." **Testament of Joseph, chpt 4**

According to other chapters in the Testament of Joseph, she threatened to murder her husband, commit suicide, and even tried to drug him by "sprinkling my food with enhancements." Joseph's response to these attempts was, *"Now therefore, know that the God of my father has revealed your wickedness to me by an angel, and I have kept it* [the food] *to convict you, if perhaps you may see it and repent. But that you may learn that the wickedness of the ungodly has no power over those who reverence God in chastity."* She even came to visit him in prison and promised to get him released from jail if he would relinquish to her demands. It shows the lengths that the devil will go to destroy the godly ones.

Righteous Judgment

Therefore, you have no excuse, every one of you who passes judgment, for in that which you judge another, you condemn yourself, for you who judge practice the same things. And we know that the judgment of God rightly falls upon those who practice such things. But do you suppose this, O man, when you pass judgment on those who practice such things and do the same yourself, that you will escape the judgment of God? **Romans 2:1-3**

By the very act of sitting in judgment upon your fellowman, one passes sentence upon himself. As Jesus said in John 7:24, *"Do not judge according to appearance but judge with righteous judgment."* What we are talking about is the importance of knowing the truth and the relevant facts surrounding the situation. This is the only acceptable form of judging. Solomon understood that when he became king of Israel, he needed the ability to discern truth in the midst of unclear circumstances to be able to judge the people righteously. He asked God for wisdom, and God gave it to him.

And He will delight in the fear of the Lord, and **He will not judge by what His eyes see, nor make a decision by what His ears hear**, *But with righteousness, He will judge the poor, and decide with fairness for the afflicted of the earth, and He will strike the earth with the rod of His mouth, and with the breath of His lips, He* will slay *the wicked.*
Isaiah 11:3-4

The above passage addresses the Messiah during the Kingdom Age when He will rule as king over the entire earth. As Jesus said in John 7:24, He will *judge with righteous judgment.* The damage done to anyone without knowing all the facts can be devastating. This environment becomes the devil's playground, where all kinds of accusations are possible. The destruction caused against one being unrighteously judged can ultimately destroy a person's life.

Straightening up, Jesus said to her, "Woman, where are they? Did no one condemn you?" She said, "No one, Lord." And Jesus said, "I do not condemn you, either. Go. From now on, sin no more." **John 8:10-11**

References

Felix Halpern. "Thy Kingdom Come: The Mystery Of Israel's Glory". Destiny Image Publishers

Chapter 26
Session of Christ

This Jesus God raised up again, to which we are all witnesses. Therefore, having been exalted to the right hand of God [place of honor and approval], *and having received from the Father the promise of the Holy Spirit, He has poured forth this which you both see and hear.* **Acts 2:32-33**

Peter spoke these words to the gathering in Jerusalem at Pentecost when 3,000 souls received Jesus as Messiah. He was introducing the period in history known as the Session (sitting) of Christ, the ministry of Jesus between His first and second coming as High Priest, Head of the Church, and mediator of the new covenant. Peter was also confirming his position as king, as prophesied by David in Psalm 110:

The Lord says [ne um - oracle, divine communication between the Father and the Son] *to my Lord: "Sit at My right hand until I make Your enemies a footstool for Your feet." The Lord will stretch forth Your strong scepter from Zion, saying, "Rule* [radah - exercise dominion] *in the midst of Your enemies." Your people will volunteer freely* [nedabah - willingly] *in the day of Your power; in holy array, from the womb of the dawn, Your youth are to You as the dew. The Lord has sworn and will not change His mind, "You are a priest forever according to the order* [dibrah - manner] *of Melchizedek." The Lord is at Your right hand; He will shatter kings in the day of His wrath. He will judge among the nations; He will fill them with corpses; He will shatter the chief men over a broad country. He will drink from the brook by the wayside; therefore, He will lift up His head.*

Psalm 110:1-7

David has been given the privilege of hearing a conversation between Yahweh, the Father, and Messiah, His Son. The right hand of the Father is also the place of authority and dominion. *He will shatter kings in the day of His wrath. He will judge among the nations; He will fill them with corpses; He will shatter the chief men over a broad country.* Stephen saw Him seated at the right hand when he was stoned to death in Acts 7:56: *"and he said, "Behold, I see the heavens opened up and the Son of Man standing at the right hand of God."* The psalm refers to a people who will willingly follow Him, a reference to the church as well as those in the Kingdom Age.

David sees the Messiah as not only a king but also *a priest forever, according to the order of Melchizedek.* Jesus was not of the tribe of Levi, as those of the Aaronic priesthood, but of Judah, as the king of the Jews, thus combining the offices of priest and king. At His baptism, Jesus would reunite the offices of prophet with king and priest, signified by the Holy Spirit and the dove. The order of Melchizedek represents the combining of all three offices in one individual. The Dead Sea Scrolls tell us that there have been nine individuals occupying this position prior to Jesus, starting with Adam and ending with Jacob. Jesus is the tenth and final King of Righteousness.

High Priest

For every high priest taken from among men is appointed for men in things pertaining to God, that he may offer both gifts and sacrifices for sins. He can have compassion for those who are ignorant and going astray since he himself is also subject to weakness. Because of this, he is required as for the people, so also for himself, to offer sacrifices for sins. And no man takes this honor to himself, but he who is called by God, just as Aaron was. So also Christ did not glorify Himself to become High Priest, but it was He who said to Him: "You are My Son, Today I have begotten You." As He also says in another place: "You are a priest forever according to the order of Melchizedek." **Hebrews 5:1-6**

The high priesthood of Christ is a central focus of the Session of Christ. *Every priest stands daily ministering and offering time after time the same sacrifices, which can never take away sins* (Hebrews 10:11). According to The New Unger's Bible Dictionary:

The functions peculiar to the high priest consisted partly of periodically presenting the sin offering for himself (Leviticus 4:3-12) and the congregation, as well as the atoning sacrifice and the burnt offering on the Great Day of Atonement (Leviticus 16). He also consulted the Lord by means of the Urim and Thummim regarding important matters affecting the theocracy and informing the people thereon (Numbers 27:21; 1 Samuel 30:7-8). The high priest had oversight of the rest of the priests and of the entire worship and was at liberty to exercise all the other priestly functions as well.

Intercession

According to F.F. Bruce, *The presence of Messiah at God's right hand means that for His people, there was now a way of access to God more immediate and heart-satisfying than the obsolete temple ritual had ever been able to provide.* As High Priest, *He is able to save forever those who draw near to Him* since He is always interceding for each one (Hebrews 7:25). Intercession is the means by which He intervenes to the Father on behalf of believers for advocacy (1 John 2:1), deliverance (Romans 8:33-34) and care (1 Peter 5:7).

Jesus's sacrifice is the one offering on earth once for all, but the intercession for us in the heavens (Hebrews 7:26) is an ongoing work. This demonstrates God's never-ending love, that we can never be separated from the love of God in Christ (Romans 8:26,34,39). He intercedes for those who come unto God through Him; it is not for the unbeliever (John 17:9). Jesus is both the offeror and the offering. His intercession is founded on His voluntary offering of Himself without spot to God. The virtue of His sacrifice is salvation and forgiveness; His intercession is the avenue into God's favor; it cannot be earned. In Exodus 30:8, *And when Aaron lights the lamps at twilight, he shall burn incense on it, a perpetual incense before the Lord throughout your generations.* Of the intercession of Christ, we may conclude that it is righteous: it is founded upon justice and truth (Hebrews 7:26; 1 John 3:5), compassionate (Hebrews 2:17; 5:8), perpetual (Hebrews, 7:25), and efficacious (1 John 2:1).

Preparing a Place

In My Father's house are many dwelling places; if it were not so, I would have told you, for I go to prepare a place for you. If I go and prepare a place for you, I will come again and receive you to Myself, that where I am, there you may be also. **John 14:2-3**

Jesus gave full assurance to His disciples that there was preparation work in heaven to be accomplished by the Father through the Son so that they would be ready to spend eternity with Him. Jesus would soon be leaving them with the expectation that He would return for all believers in Christ to be with Him always. According to Hebrews 9:28, *so Christ also, having been offered once to bear the sins of many, will appear a second time for salvation without reference to sin to those who eagerly await Him.* The disciples were being encouraged to *await Him eagerly*.

Prayer for Disciples

"I ask on their behalf; I do not ask on behalf of the world, but of those whom You have given Me; for they are Yours, and all things that are Mine are Yours, and Yours are Mine, and I have been glorified in them. I am no longer in the world, and yet they themselves are in the world, and I come to You. Holy Father, keep them in Your name, the name which You have given Me, that they may be one even as We are. While I was with them, I was keeping them in Your name which You have given Me; and I guarded them, and not one of them perished but the son of perdition, so that the Scripture would be fulfilled. "But now I come to You; and these things I speak in the world so that they may have My joy made full in themselves. I have given them Your word, and the world has hated them because they are not of the world, even as I am not of the world. I do not ask You to take them out of the world but to keep them from the evil one. They are not of the world, even as I am not of the world. Sanctify them in the truth; Your word is truth. As You sent Me into the world, I also have sent them into the world. For their sakes, I sanctify Myself, that they themselves also may be sanctified in truth. "I do not ask on behalf of these alone, but for those also who believe in Me through their word; that they may all be one; even as You, Father, are in Me and I in You, that they also may be in Us, so that the world may believe that You sent Me. "The glory which You have given Me I have given to them, that they may be one, just as We are one; I in them and You in Me, that they may be perfected in unity, so that the world may know that You sent Me, and loved them, even as You have loved Me. Father, I desire that they also, whom You have given Me, be with Me where I am,

so that they may see My glory which You have given Me, for You loved Me before the foundation of the world. "
John 17:9-24

Jesus spoke these words the night before His crucifixion. It illustrates His great concern and care for the welfare of not only His disciples but all those who would believe in Him. It is a picture of His intercession, which is taking place every day on behalf of those who believe. Jesus acknowledges that His followers do not belong to Him but to the Father. His prayer was that the Father would keep them in the Father's name or nature so that they would be united in purpose. Jesus wishes that *they may have My joy made full in themselves.* He then emphasizes the role that the Word of God would play in the believer's life: *Sanctify them in the truth; Your word is truth.* It would be the truth of His Words that will unify the believers as the Father and Son are united. The believer's relationship to the Word of God will serve as evidence that the Son of God has appeared to the world on behalf of the Father. Unity is the avenue into His glory, the glory given to the Son and passed on to those who truly believe and follow Him.

Walking Among the Lampstands

Then I turned to see the voice that was speaking with me. And having turned, I saw seven golden lampstands, and in the middle of the lampstands, I saw one like a son of man, clothed in a robe reaching to the feet and girded across His chest with a golden sash. His head and His hair were white like white wool, like snow, and His eyes were like a flame of fire. His feet were like burnished bronze, when it has been made to glow in a furnace, and His voice was like the sound of many waters. In His right hand, He held seven stars, and out of His mouth came a sharp two-edged sword, and His face was like the sun shining in its strength. When I saw Him,

I fell at His feet like a dead man. And He placed His right hand on me, saying, "Do not be afraid; I am the first and the last, and the living One; and I was dead, and behold, I am alive forevermore, and I have the keys of death and of Hades. **Revelation 1:12-18**

John was given an amazing vision of the Son of Man walking among the seven golden candlesticks, speaking of the seven churches of Revelation 2 and 3 and symbolizing the New Testament church. The description of His appearance, similar to that in Daniel 7:13, is of a priest *clothed in a robe reaching to the feet.* The whiteness of His hair corresponds to that of the Ancient of Days, God the Father: God the Son has the same purity and eternity as God the Father, as signified by the whiteness of His head and hair. The eyes, like blazing fire, describe His piercing judgment of sin. This concept is further enhanced by His feet, which were like burnished bronze glowing in a furnace. The bronze altar in the temple was related to sacrifice for sin and divine judgment on it. His voice was compared to the roar of rushing waters. His face glowed with a brilliance like the sun shining. In His right hand, Jesus held seven stars, representing the pastors of the seven churches. Significantly, Christ held them in His right hand, indicating sovereign possession. Speaking of Christ's role as Head of the Church, John saw a sharp double-edged sword coming out of His mouth, a reference to the authority and convicting power of the Word of God.

Head of the Church

And what is the surpassing greatness of His power toward us who believe. These are in accordance with the working of the strength of His might which He brought about in Christ when He raised Him from the dead and seated Him at His right hand in the heavenly places, far above all rule and authority and power and dominion, and every name that is named, not only in this age but also in the one to come. And He put all things in subjection under His feet and gave Him as head over all things to the church, which is His body, the fullness of Him who fills all in all. **Ephesians 1:19-23**

For the ones who recognize Christ as *head over all things to the church,* He gives access to *the surpassing greatness of His power toward us who believe.* Christ's authority over all things is the key to discovering the fullness of Christ, which is found only in His body, the church.

Mediator of the New Covenant

For if the blood of goats and bulls and the ashes of a heifer sprinkling those who have been defiled sanctify for the cleansing of the flesh, how much more will the blood of Christ, who through the eternal Spirit offered Himself without blemish to God, cleanse your conscience from dead works to serve the living God? For this reason, He is the mediator of a new covenant so that, since a death has taken place for the redemption of the transgressions that were committed under the first covenant, those who have been called may receive the promise of the eternal inheritance. **Hebrews 9:13-15**

The blood of Christ provides every believer with eternal redemption through which the blessings of the new covenant are inaugurated, and should affect the way they serve God. First covenant rituals served for the ceremonially unclean and only made them outwardly clean, but the blood of Christ can do much more. His was a sacrifice of infinite value because, through the eternal Spirit, He offered Himself unblemished to God. With this assertion, the writer of Hebrews involves all three Persons of the

Godhead in the sacrifice of Christ, which magnifies the greatness of His redemptive offering. Unblemished describes Christ's perfection.

Such a great accomplishment ought to cleanse our consciences from dead works, which refers to the Levitical rituals that, in contrast with the work of Christ, can never impart spiritual life. Their consciences ought to be perfectly free from any need to engage in religious works and ceremonial rites. When they retain their confidence in the perfect efficacy of the Cross, they will hold fast to their profession and serve the living God within the new covenant environment, *with the promise of eternal inheritance.*

Chapter 27
Spiritual Leadership & Divine Authority

Watchman Nee (1903 – 1972) became a Christian in mainland China in 1920 at seventeen and began writing in the same year. Throughout the nearly thirty years of his ministry, the Lord clearly demonstrated that Watchman Nee was a unique gift from the Lord to His Body for His move in this age. He was responsible for the establishment of more than 4,000 house churches throughout China. In 1952, he was imprisoned for his faith; he remained in prison until he died in 1972. His words remain an abundant source of spiritual revelation and supply to Christians throughout the world.

One of his greatest works was "Spiritual Authority." The truths it promotes are essential to understanding and living the life of Christ in this present world. I highly recommend it to all believers. That book has inspired this writing.

Introducing the Kingdom

Jesus answered, "My kingdom is not of this world. If My kingdom were of this world, then My servants would be fighting so that I would not be handed over to the Jews; but as it is, My kingdom is not of this realm." Therefore, Pilate said to Him, "So You are a king?" Jesus answered, "You say correctly that I am a king. For this, I have been born, and for this, I have come into the world to testify to the truth. Everyone who is of the truth hears My voice." **John 18:36-37**

Before Jesus was baptized onto the scene, John the Baptist was preaching, "*Repent, for **the kingdom of heaven is at hand***" (Matthew 3:2). Jesus took up this same mantle in Matthew 4:17 as he began speaking to the masses and then extended it to His disciples' charge in Matthew 10:7, *"And as you go, preach, saying,* **'The kingdom of heaven is at hand.'"** But what did this all mean? Was Messiah ready to demonstrate his physical authority, or was there some other, more profound meaning of the kingdom of heaven? The answer to this question may be found in the above exchange with Pilate: *My kingdom is not of this realm... For this, I have been born, and for this, I have come into the world to testify to the truth.*

> *Now having been questioned by the Pharisees as to when the kingdom of God was coming, He answered them and said, "The kingdom of God is not coming with signs to be observed; nor will they say, 'Look, here it is!' or, 'There it is!' For behold, the kingdom of God is in your midst* [within you]." **Luke 17:20-21**

The term "within you" is often misunderstood. The Pharisees were rejecting Him as the Messiah and were not believers. It would not make sense for Jesus to have told the Pharisees that the kingdom of God was within them as if it were some sort of spiritual kingdom. It is better to translate the phrase "within you" as "*in your midst*." Some feel that the force of the expression is "within your possession or within your reach." Jesus's point was that He was standing right in their midst. All they needed to do was acknowledge that He was indeed the Messiah who could bring in the kingdom as its king, and they could begin to experience the promised kingdom in a spiritual sense.

In His public ministry, Jesus taught many parables that address the kingdom of heaven or the kingdom of God. In fact, eight of them appear in Matthew 13. He was teaching the dynamics of this kingdom, which all of His disciples and followers need to understand. These principles allow us not only to grasp the conditions of entry but also how to function and thrive within the kingdom.

Submission to Authority

Have this attitude in yourselves which was also in Christ Jesus, who, although He existed in the form of God, did not regard equality with God a thing to be grasped, but emptied Himself, taking the form of a bond-servant, and being made in the likeness of men. Being found in appearance as a man, He humbled Himself by becoming obedient to the point of death, even death on a cross. For this reason, also, God highly exalted Him and bestowed on Him the name which is above every name, so that at the name of Jesus EVERY KNEE WILL BOW, of those who are in heaven and on earth and under the earth, and that every tongue will confess that Jesus Christ is Lord, to the glory of God the Father. **Philippians 2:5-11**

Jesus acknowledged that He was a king to Pilate, yet Paul recognized that His greatest attribute may be humility, submission to authority. This attitude created in Him the capacity to be a bond-servant, to accept even humiliation to fulfill God's will for His life. According to Watchman Nee, "He had to empty Himself of His divinity and then humbled Himself in His humanity." Although He was the Son, He would be treated as a man and willing to accept whatever the Father willed, even when He didn't understand the purpose (Matthew 26:42). According to Hebrews 5:8-9: *Although He was a Son, He learned obedience from the things which He suffered. And having been made perfect, He became to all those who obey [hupakouo – listen with attention to obey] Him the source of eternal salvation.* Watchman Nee further states:

> *The Lord came to this world emptyhanded; He did not bring obedience with Him. He learned obedience through what He suffered and thus became the source of eternal salvation to all who obey Him. By going through suffering after suffering, He learned to be obedient unto death, even death on a cross. When the Lord came forth from the Godhead to become man, He truly became a man – weak and acquainted with suffering. Every suffering He bore ripened into a fruit of obedience. No suffering of any kind was able to stir Him to murmuring or fretfulness.*

Jesus established God's kingdom by perfectly obeying God's authority and absolutely submitting to His rule. This most clearly defines walking in the spiritual kingdom that is ordained for those who recognize Jesus as king. It is the basis for those prepared for spiritual leadership.

Delegated Authority

"We gave you strict orders not to continue teaching in this name, and yet, you have filled Jerusalem with your teaching and intend to bring this man's blood upon us." But Peter and the apostles answered, "We must obey God rather than men… And we are witnesses of these things; and so is the Holy Spirit, whom God has given to those who obey [peitharcheo – submit to authority] Him." **Acts 5:28-29, 32**

In Romans 13:1-7, Christians are instructed to honor governing authorities as having authority established by God. All legitimate authority comes from God as delegated authority and is acknowledged within the kingdom as a means of recognizing God's will. When God's authority is challenged by those delegated in His authority, they must be resisted. The disciples were put in jail by Jewish leadership because they were having great success leading Jewish citizens to receive Jesus as Messiah, and the leaders were *filled with jealousy.* The disciples responded to the leaders' demands to cease evangelical activities: "*We must obey God rather than men.*" Delegated authority is always subject to divine authority.

The Authority of Moses

Then Miriam and Aaron spoke against Moses because of the Cushite woman whom he had married (for he had married a Cushite woman), and they said, "Has the Lord indeed spoken only through Moses? Has He not spoken through us as well?" And the Lord heard it. (Now the man Moses was very humble [anaw – see others as more important], more than any man who was on the face of the earth.) Suddenly, the Lord said to Moses and Aaron and to Miriam, "You three come out to the tent of meeting." So, the three of them came out. Then the Lord came down in a pillar of cloud and stood at the doorway of the tent, and He called Aaron and Miriam. When they had both come forward, He said, "Hear now My words: if there is a prophet among you, I, the Lord, shall make Myself known to him in a vision. I shall speak with him in a dream. "Not so, with My servant Moses, he is faithful in all My household; With him, I speak mouth to mouth, even openly, and not in dark sayings, and he beholds the form of the Lord. Why, then, were you not afraid to speak against My servant, against Moses?"
Numbers 12:1-8

Before Moses was ready to be the man God chose to lead the nation of Israel from bondage by the Egyptians, he had to spend forty years in the land of Midian. What qualified him for this important position? The above passage tells us that Moses had been humbled to become the humblest man on the face of the earth. More than any other characteristic, humility (*anaw*), by force, seeing others as more important, became his most important commodity to fulfill God's purpose for him. It was necessary for him to experience enforced humility in order to experience genuine humility. It would be this foundation that would allow Moses to speak mouth-to-mouth with the Lord. Yet, Miriam and Aaron challenged Moses' authority, some might say for legitimate reasons, but Moses did not defend himself. God had entrusted His delegated authority to Moses in the work, and God would protect him. True spiritual leaders are secure in their positions under divine authority and need not defend themselves.

Challenging God's Man

*So, the anger of the Lord burned against them, and He departed. But when **the cloud had withdrawn from over the tent**, behold, Miriam was leprous, as white as snow. As Aaron turned toward Miriam, behold, she was leprous. Then Aaron said to Moses, "Oh, my lord, I beg you, do not account this sin to us, in which **we have acted foolishly** and in which we have sinned. "Oh, do not let her be like one dead, whose flesh is half eaten away when he comes from his mother's womb!" Moses cried out to the Lord, saying, "O God, heal her, I pray!" But the Lord said to Moses, "If her father had but spit in her face, would she not bear her shame for **seven days**? Let her be shut up for seven days outside the camp, and afterward, she may be received again." So Miriam was shut up outside the camp for seven days, and the people did not move on until Miriam was received again. Afterward,* *however, the people moved out from Hazeroth and camped in the wilderness of Paran.* **Numbers 12:9-16**

God responds to Mirian and Aaron with anger as evidenced by the fact that the cloud (His presence) was withdrawn from over the tent. Yahweh needed to deal immediately and specifically with their attack against God's anointed. Whether legitimate or not, God will deal directly with his delegated authority; man should leave it up to Him. When Miriam was found leprous, Aaron immediately went to Moses to admit their foolish actions and ask God for mercy, and Moses did just that. Yahweh responded that His punishment for her was appropriate – seven days of leprosy outside the camp. God will enforce His authority with justice.

Don't Touch God's Anointed

Now, when Saul returned from pursuing the Philistines, he was told, saying, "Behold, David is in the wilderness of Engedi." Then Saul took three thousand chosen men from all Israel and went to seek David and his men in front of the Rocks of the Wild Goats. He came to the sheepfolds on the way, where there was a cave, and Saul went in to relieve himself. Now, David and his men were sitting in the inner recesses of the cave. The men of David said to him, "Behold, this is the day of which the Lord said to you, 'Behold; I am about to give your enemy into your hand, and you shall do to him as it seems good to you.'" Then David arose and cut off the edge of Saul's robe secretly. It came about afterward that David's conscience bothered him because he had cut off the edge of Saul's robe. So he said to his men, "Far be it from me because of the Lord that I should do this thing to my lord, the Lord's anointed, to stretch out my hand against him, since he is the Lord's anointed." David persuaded his men with these words and did not allow them to rise up against Saul. And Saul arose, left the cave, and went on his way. **1 Samuel 24:1-7**

Another example of true spiritual leadership is found in the life of King David. He had been anointed by God to be king of Israel as a teenager but would not be able to take his throne until after Saul was dead. David recognized that Saul was still God's delegated authority even though Saul continued for many years to try to kill him. As he hid with his men in the cave at Engedi, an opportunity presented itself for him to eliminate his enemy. David was convicted in his conscience after he *cut off the edge of Saul's robe secretly.* He understood that he nor his men had the right to touch the Lord's anointed. After over a decade of being on the run for his life, David eventually became King over Judah at Hebron when he was thirty and then over all Israel at Jerusalem seven years later.

The Word of the Kingdom

In Jesus's day, the Pharisees were dividing the Law of Moses into a hierarchy, with some being greater than others. Yet Jesus had quoted a Scripture from the Law of Moses (Deuteronomy 8:3) in Matthew 4:4 when He stated, "*It is written, 'MAN SHALL NOT LIVE ON BREAD ALONE, BUT ON EVERY WORD THAT PROCEEDS OUT OF THE MOUTH OF GOD.'*" Jesus was teaching the importance of every Word, that all Scripture is necessary food.

In His public ministry, Jesus taught many parables addressing the kingdom of heaven or the kingdom of God. In fact, eight of them appear in Matthew 13. He was teaching the dynamics of this kingdom, which all of His disciples and followers need to understand. These principles allow us to grasp not only the conditions of entry but also how to function and thrive within the kingdom.

The first of the eight parables from Matthew 13 directly references the Word of God, *"the Word of the kingdom."* The King's primary method of communication in the kingdom is the Word. Success in the kingdom is tied to hearing the Word and understanding it. The parable defines that the condition of the heart is the primary criterion that determines success. The seed sown beside the road has no room to establish its roots and, therefore, is easy pickings for the devil. This condition of the heart is determined by how the Word is received. In 1 Thessalonians 2:13, Paul says, *"For this reason we also constantly thank God that when you received the word of God which you heard from us,* **you accepted it not as the word of men,** *but for what it really is, the word of God, which also performs its work in you who believe."* The Word has an intended work (see Isaiah 55:11), and it cannot do its work without having been received from God (the King) with the divine authority accompanying it. According to Hebrews 4:2, the Word must be united by faith to accomplish what God intends.

Reasonings

For as he [a man] *thinks* [*saar* - to calculate or to set a price on] *within himself, so he is* (Proverbs 23:7). So much of the quality of a person's life can be tied to one's thought life. The word translated "think" is that of misers who count the cost of everything that their guests eat or drink. They find no enjoyment in their guests but only worry about the cost of it all. There is intense spiritual warfare surrounding one's thought life. The mindset defines how the believer connects with God. In Romans 8:5- 6, *those who are according to the flesh set their minds* [*phroneo* – mindset, involving the will, affections, and conscience] *on the things of the flesh, but those who are according to the Spirit, the things of the Spirit. For the mind set on the flesh is death, but the mind set on the Spirit is life and peace.* Setting one's mind on things above and not on earthly things propels the believer into the spiritual mind, thus finding life and peace.

> *Now I, Paul, myself urge you by the meekness and gentleness of Christ—I who am meek when face to face with you, but bold toward you when absent! I ask that when I am present, I need not be bold with the confidence with which I propose to be courageous against some who regard us as if we walked according to the flesh. For though we walk in the flesh, we do not war according to the flesh, for the weapons of our warfare are not of the flesh, but divinely powerful for the destruction of fortresses* [ochuroma – any strong arguments in which one trusts]. *We are destroying speculations* [logismos – reasonings hostile to the Christian faith] *and every lofty thing* [hupsoma – a lofty tower or fortress built up proudly by the enemy] *raised up against the knowledge of God, and we are taking every thought captive to the obedience of Christ, and we are ready to punish all disobedience, whenever your obedience is complete.* **2 Corinthians 10:1-6**

According to Watchman Nee: *Paul mentions that we must destroy reasonings and every high thing that lifts itself up against the knowledge of God. Man likes to build reasons as strongholds around his thought, yet these reasons must be destroyed and thought taken captive. Reasons are to be cast aside, but thought is to be brought back. In spiritual warfare, the strongholds need to be stormed before the thought can be taken captive. If reasons are not cast aside, there is no possibility of bringing man's thoughts into obedience to Christ.*

Man has a tendency to try and solve all of his problems and challenges by reason and his ability to map out the conclusion to any difficulty utilizing his cognitive skills. Spiritual leadership follows a different pathway. Once the believer has found obedience to divine authority as his modus operandi (mode of operation), deferring the decision process to the Divine will opens the door to true spirituality (that which is born of the Spirit is spiritual – John 3:6) and provides a victory over the strength of sin. In 1 Peter 1:14-16, *As obedient children, do not be conformed to the former lusts which were yours in your ignorance, but like the Holy One who called you, be holy yourselves also in all your behavior; because it is written, "YOU SHALL BE HOLY, FOR I AM HOLY."* Holiness is a willful decision to be set apart from worldly influences for a life in the kingdom under divine authority.

A Kingdom Which Cannot Be Shaken

See to it that you do not refuse Him who is speaking. For if those did not escape when they refused him who warned them on earth, much less will we escape who turn away from Him who warns from heaven. And His voice shook the earth then, but now He has promised, saying, "YET ONCE MORE I WILL SHAKE NOT ONLY THE EARTH BUT ALSO THE HEAVEN [Jesus Christ]." This expression, "Yet once more," denotes the removing of those things which can be shaken, as of created things, so that those things which cannot be shaken may remain. Therefore, since we receive a kingdom which cannot be shaken, let us show gratitude, by which we may offer to God an acceptable [well-pleasing] *service* [latreuo – to worship God] *with reverence and awe, for our God is a consuming fire.* **Hebrews 12:25-29**

The above passage demonstrates the letter to the Hebrews' final warning concerning a kingdom that cannot be shaken. These warnings can come from earth or heaven. The warfare against the believer is the clash of two kingdoms, and the end result is the shaking away of all created (man-made) things. The administration of this unshakable kingdom allows the believer to experience the blessings of that kingdom, producing a heart of gratitude. The end result is well-pleasing worship of God *with reverence and awe.* These words speak of the fear of the Lord, which brings the believer wisdom (chokmah) and knowledge of the Holy One (Proverbs 9:10). This wisdom represents the knowledge and the ability to make the right choices at the opportune time, a manifestation of spiritual leadership.

References

Watchman Nee. "Spiritual Authority". Christian Fellowship Publishers, Inc.

Chapter 28
No Private Interpretation

But know this first of all, that no prophecy of Scripture is a matter of one's own [private] interpretation [epilúseos - indicates that no prophecy comes from any private source, referring to the exposition of the will and purposes of God by the prophets themselves]. **2 Peter 1:20**

"Whatever I command you, you shall be careful to do; you shall not add to nor take away from it. **Deuteronomy 12:32**

"You shall not add to the word which I am commanding you, nor take away from it, that you may keep the commandments of the Lord your God which I command you. **Deuteronomy 4:2**

Do not add to His words, or He will reprove you, and you will be proved a liar. **Proverbs 30:6**

I testify to everyone who hears the words of the prophecy of this book: if anyone adds to them, God will add to him the plagues which are written in this book; and if anyone takes away from the words of the book of this prophecy, God will take away his part from the tree of life and from the holy city, which are written in this book. **Revelation 22:18-19**

The words of the Lord are pure [tahor – clean, pure, genuine, no mixture of falsehood] words, as silver tried in a furnace on the earth, refined seven times (Psalm 12:6). The purity of God's word is key to its ability. Its purity results from being refined and tested (Psalm 119:140). This is why the above warnings are so important; any additions, subtractions, or private interpretations of the Word of God make the words impure, less effective, or even worthless. Applying the Word of God against Jesus as Satan did in the wilderness can even be evil. In any case, the truth of the Word of God can be trusted without any alterations.

The Tradition of the Elders

Rabbinic Judaism has been the mainstream form of Orthodox Judaism since the 6th century, after the codification of the Babylonian Talmud. Rabbinic Judaism has its roots in the Pharisaic school of Second Temple Judaism. It is based on the belief that Moses at Mount Sinai received both the Written Torah and the Oral Torah from God. The Oral Torah, transmitted orally, explains the Written Torah; the prohibition to do any "creative work" on the Sabbath, which is not clearly defined in the Torah, is given a practical understanding in the Oral Torah, defining what constitutes Sabbath laws. At first, it was forbidden to write down the Oral Torah, but after the destruction of the Second Temple, it was decided to write it down in the form of the Talmud and other rabbinic texts for preservation. The Sadducees, Karaite Judaism, Samaritanism, and the Essenes do not recognize the Oral Torah as having divine authority nor the rabbinic procedures used to interpret Jewish Scripture.

> *Then some Pharisees and scribes came to Jesus from Jerusalem and said, "Why do Your disciples break* **the tradition of the elders***? For they do not wash their hands when they eat bread." And He answered and said to them, "Why do you yourselves transgress the commandment of God for the sake of your tradition? For God said, 'HONOR YOUR FATHER AND MOTHER,' and, 'HE WHO SPEAKS EVIL OF FATHER OR MOTHER IS TO BE PUT TO DEATH.' But you say, 'Whoever says to his father or mother, "Whatever I*

have that would help you has been given to God," he is not to honor his father or his mother.' And by this, you invalidated the word of God for the sake of your tradition. You hypocrites rightly did Isaiah prophesy of you: 'THIS PEOPLE HONORS ME WITH THEIR LIPS, BUT THEIR HEART IS FAR AWAY FROM ME. 'BUT IN VAIN DO THEY WORSHIP ME, TEACHING AS DOCTRINES THE PRECEPTS OF MEN '" [Isaiah 29:13]. **Matthew 15:1-9**

During His three-year public ministry, Jesus consistently confronted the Pharisees and their methods of enforcing the Oral Law as if the Lord had also given it to Moses on Mount Sinai. He referred to this practice as *the tradition of the elders,* and, in some cases, they made it superior to the written Law. Isaiah spoke of this same issue 700 years before Christ (Isaiah 29:13). As quoted above, the Scriptures have multiple warnings about adding to or removing what is written in the Bible. This has been a consistent problem when man does not reverence or properly respect the authority of Scripture from the heart. *They* [the Pharisees] *tie up heavy burdens and lay them on men's shoulders, but they themselves are unwilling to move them with so much as a finger. But they do all their deeds to be noticed by men, for they broaden their phylacteries and lengthen the tassels of their garments* (Matthew 23:4-5). Today's Orthodox Judaism has fallen into this trap. Modern evangelical Christianity is not far behind. When Christians add to the Scriptures, they spoil the purity of God's Word, compromising its ability to enlighten the eyes (Psalm 19:8).

The Holy Spirit and the Kingdom

Throughout the Old Testament, God always spoke through His ordained men by "the Spirit of the Lord." The Spirit of God anointed the prophets to speak to His people with words of encouragement, warnings, and identification of sins committed, including predictions and prophecies of future events and judgments. Ordained offices, including priests, kings, and prophets, were anointed through a ceremony utilizing anointing oil to represent the Holy Spirit, which rested upon them to fulfill their unique offices. Inspiration and divine empowerment came through the Holy Spirit.

On multiple occasions, the Old Testament prophesies the Kingdom Age, when Israel would again occupy its promised land, and the Messiah would rule them. The Pharisees asked Jesus about the kingdom of God in Luke 17:20-21, and His response is enlightening. He tells them that the kingdom cannot be recognized by observable physical signs but that it is "*in your midst.*" The Greek word *entos* literally means *inside;* Jesus introduced the concept that the kingdom of God is a reality that exists inside each one who recognizes the king and is, therefore, of the truth. The Pharisees were never able to grasp this principle. In John 18:36, Jesus told Pilate: "*My kingdom is not of this world. If My kingdom were of this world, then My servants would be fighting so that I would not be handed over to the Jews; but as it is, My kingdom is not of this realm.*" The Messiah's first coming would introduce a "spiritual" kingdom.

This "spiritual" kingdom would require a brand-new approach to God's laws. Instead of the old covenant, i.e., the Law of Moses, written on tablets of stone, the new covenant specifies that God's laws are written on the believer's heart (Hebrews 8:10). Instead of Jewish leaders enforcing these laws externally, the Holy Spirit would be the administrator, from the inside. John 16:8-11 tells the story:

Conviction

And He, when He [the Holy Spirit] comes, will convict [elegcho – convince, persuade, shown to be wrong] the world concerning sin and righteousness and judgment; concerning sin, because they do not believe in Me; and concerning righteousness, because I go to the Father and you no longer see Me; and concerning judgment, because the ruler of this world has been judged. **John 16:8-11**

One of the weaknesses of the old covenant form of justice is how the laws are enforced. Multiple verses throughout the Scriptures establish that God is no respecter of persons and shows no partiality or favoritism to anyone in relation to His justice. *Opening his mouth, Peter said: "I most certainly understand now that God is not one to show partiality"* (Acts 10:34). Yet the woman caught in the act of adultery was brought before Jesus alone (John 8:3) while the Law of Moses (Leviticus 20:10) requires that both participants are subject to death. The Holy Spirit convicts the whole world without partiality; the law of God restores the soul when applied perfectly (Psalm 19:7).

Adultery

You shall not commit adultery. **Exodus 20:14**

In The Complete Word Study Dictionary, Spiros Zodhiates identifies the word translated "commit adultery" (*naap*) as used for the physical act (Ex 20:14; Lev 20:10; Prov 6:32; Jer 5:7; 7:9; 29:23; Hos 4:2; Mal 3:5). In Leviticus 20:10, *'If there is a man who commits adultery with another man's wife, one who commits adultery with his friend's wife, the adulterer and the adulteress shall surely be put to death.* Adultery is intended to speak of a physical act. When the definition of adultery is expanded to include non-sexual interactions, it should be considered a private interpretation.

"You have heard that it was said, 'YOU SHALL NOT COMMIT ADULTERY' [Exodus 20:14]; *but I say to you that everyone who looks at a woman with lust for her has already committed adultery with her in his heart.* **Matthew 5:27-28**

Kingdom Life

Jesus's public ministry began at His baptism, followed immediately by His temptation in the wilderness. While still ministering in Galilee, He introduced the principle of kingdom life, proper behavior in the kingdom of heaven. It meant a radical change in the laws given at Sinai, those commandments that focused on the public activities of the believer. The Sermon on the Mount was intended to focus attention on the private, inward life. In the beginning, Jesus centered on the inward convictions that would result in blessings of the kingdom. Each of these blessings is associated with a godly, internal condition that occupies itself with the Father's attitudes.

"Blessed are the poor [ptoechos – cower like a beggar, utter helplessness] *in spirit, for theirs is the kingdom of heaven." "Blessed are those who mourn* [lament, grieve], *for they shall be comforted." "Blessed are the gentle* [kind], *for they shall inherit the earth." "Blessed are those who hunger* [starved] *and thirst* [desire ardently] *for righteousness, for they shall be satisfied." "Blessed are the merciful* [compassionate], *for they shall receive mercy." "Blessed are the pure* [sincere, transparent] *in heart, for they shall see God." "Blessed are the peacemakers* [bringing peace to others], *for they shall be called sons of God." "Blessed are those who have been persecuted for the sake of righteousness, for theirs is the kingdom of heaven." "Blessed are you when people insult you and persecute you and*

falsely say all kinds of evil against you because of Me."
Matthew 5:3-11

In each of these blessings, the inward condition produces the blessing and defines any resulting activity. Kindness of heart (toward others) results in the believer inheriting the earth. Kingdom life is an inward experience that produces a quality of life that may not be possible under a religious system such as the old covenant. When the heart is not fully engaged in the relationship with God, '*THIS PEOPLE HONORS ME WITH THEIR LIPS, BUT THEIR HEART IS FAR AWAY FROM ME. 'BUT IN VAIN DO THEY WORSHIP ME, TEACHING AS DOCTRINES THE PRECEPTS OF MEN* '" (Matthew 15:8-9). The purity of the Word of God alone is not enough to keep the people in line, as is evidenced by the Old Testament history of the Jews.

The Weakness of the Law

*For what the Law could not do, weak as it was through the flesh, God did: sending His own Son in the likeness of sinful flesh, and as an offering for sin, He condemned sin in the flesh so that the requirement of the Law might be fulfilled in us, who do not walk according to the flesh **but according to the Spirit**.* **Romans 8:3-4**

The Ten Commandments specifically addressed outward actions and the believer's accountability. At the same time, Jesus says that kingdom behavior takes the Law to another level by addressing the heart motive behind the action. *But he is a Jew who is one inwardly; and circumcision is that which is of the heart, by the Spirit, not by the letter; and his praise is not from men, but from God* (Romans 2:29). This higher standard is **only attainable through the power of the Holy Spirit** and not by living under the rule of the Commandments. Paul restates this principle in Titus 2:11-12 when he said *For the grace of God has appeared, bringing salvation to all men, instructing us to deny ungodliness and worldly desires and to live sensibly, righteously, and godly in the present age*. It is the grace of God that teaches us *to live sensibly, righteously, and godly in the present age.*

In Secret

*"Beware of practicing your righteousness before men to be noticed by them; otherwise, you have no reward with your Father who is in heaven. So, when you give to the poor, do not sound a trumpet before you, as the hypocrites do in the synagogues and in the streets so that they may be honored by men. Truly I say to you, they have their reward in full. But when you give to the poor, do not let your left hand know what your right hand is doing, so that your giving will be **in secret**, and your Father who sees what is done in secret will reward you.* **Matthew 6:1-4**

The entire chapter of Matthew 6 addresses the principle of the outward, public life versus the inward, secret life. Jesus mentions not only giving but also prayer, forgiveness, fasting, and wealth and the importance of the godliness of the heart motives behind each activity. *"And when you are praying, do not use meaningless repetition as the Gentiles do, for they suppose that they will be heard for their many words* (Verse 7). Practicing righteous activities publicly makes it self-righteousness; there is no reward since God gets no glory. *"For if you forgive others for their transgressions, your heavenly Father will also forgive you"* (Verse 14). The right heart attitude always produces a godly result. *But store up for yourselves treasures in heaven, where neither moth nor rust destroys, and where thieves do not break in or steal* (Verse 20).

Jesus summarizes the chapter in verses 22-23 when He says, "*The eye is the lamp of the body; so, then, if your eye is clear* [*haploos* — seeing things as they are, no distortions], *your whole body will be full of light. But if your eye is bad* [*poneros* — evil, lack of character], *your whole body will be full of darkness. If then the light that is in you is darkness, how great is the darkness!* The eye speaks of the attitude of the heart. When the heart is properly engaged with God, then understanding will be without distortion.

The Thought Life

For as he [a man] *thinks* [*saar* - to calculate or set a price on] *within himself, so he is.* **Proverbs 23:7**

So much of a person's life quality can be tied to one's thought life. The Hebrew word translated "think" is that of misers who count the cost of everything that their guests eat or drink. They find no enjoyment in their guests but only worry about the cost of it all. There is intense spiritual warfare surrounding one's thought life. The mindset defines how the believer connects with God.

Man's experience as a member of the human race includes both a public persona and a private, personal life measured by his thoughts and motives. To most of the world, we are known by our public persona, activities that define our outward life, but only a few know the person of the heart, the inward life defined by his thoughts. According to Paul in Romans 8:5-6, *For those who are according to the flesh set their minds on the things of the flesh, but those who are according to the Spirit, the things of the Spirit. For the mind set on the flesh is death, but the mind set on the Spirit is* **life and peace**. This **life and peace** principle is referenced in Malachi 2:5 regarding Levi: "*My covenant with him was one of* **life and peace**, *and I gave them to him as an object of reverence; so he* *revered Me and stood in awe of My name*. The heart of this mindset is a reverence for God. Setting one's mind on things above and not on earthly things propels the believer into the spiritual mind, thus finding life and peace.

Human Reason vs. Spiritual Understanding

Man tends to try and solve all of his problems and challenges by reason and his own ability to map out the conclusion to any difficulty utilizing his cognitive skills. Spiritual leadership follows a different pathway. Once the believer has found obedience to divine authority as his mode of operation, deferring the decision process to the Divine Will opens the door to true spirituality (that which is born of the Spirit is spiritual – John 3:6) and provides a victory over the strength of sin (1 Corinthians 15:56). In 1 Peter 1:14-16, *As obedient children, do not be conformed to the former lusts which were yours in your ignorance, but like the Holy One who called you, be holy yourselves also in all your behavior; because it is written, "YOU SHALL BE HOLY, FOR I AM HOLY."* Holiness is a willful decision to be set apart from worldly influences for a life in the kingdom under divine authority.

The Church Age believer finds fulfillment in his relationship with God as he is taught by the Holy Spirit the deeper meaning and personal application of the Scriptures. Instead of adding to the Word of God by utilizing the rational mind, he learns to trust the leading of the Holy Spirit. *It is the Spirit who gives life* [zoopoieo – makes alive]; *the flesh profits nothing; the words* [rhema – speech, discourse] *that I have spoken to you are spirit and are life* (John 6:63). According to Ellicott's Commentary:

These words are immediately connected with the thought of the Ascension, which was to precede the gift of the Spirit. (Comp. John 7:39; 16:7 et seq.). We are to find in them, therefore, a deeper *meaning than the ordinary one that His teaching is to be, not carnally, but spiritually understood. They think of a physical eating of His flesh, and this offends them, but what if they, who have thought of bread descending from heaven, see His body ascending into heaven? They will know then that He cannot have meant this. And the Descent of the Spirit will follow the Ascension of the Son, and men full of the Holy Spirit will have brought to their remembrance all these words (John 14:26), and they will then know what the true feeding on Him is, and these very words which He has spoken will carry their lessons to the inmost being, and be realized, not simply in a spiritual sense, but as spirit and as life.*

Chapter 29
Filling Man's Poverty with God's Riches

E. M. Bounds, a 19th-century pastor in the Methodist Episcopal Church, wrote several definitive books on prayer that are considered classics. Upon his retirement as pastor in 1894, he spent his final 17 years engaged in intercessory prayer, writing, and itinerant revival ministry. He would typically arise at 4:00 am to be alone with God in prayer until 7:00 am and was indefatigable in his study of the Bible. Because Bounds diligently practiced what he preached, he was able to capture the essence of prayer, and his works live on as a testament to the importance of prayer in a Christian's life. According to Bounds, *"The story of every great Christian achievement is the history of answered prayer."*

God's Abundance

"Prayer is the contact of a living soul with God. In prayer, God stoops to kiss man, to bless man, and to aid man in everything that God can devise or man can need. Prayer fills man's emptiness with God's fullness. It fills man's poverty with God's riches. It puts away man's weakness with God's strength. It banishes man's littleness in the face of God's greatness. Prayer is God's plan to supply man's great and continuous need with God's great and continuous abundance." **EM Bounds**

To receive the full abundance of God's supply, the believer must begin at the place where he believes that God is not only capable of meeting every need but He also desires to do it. Jesus said that *"with God all things are possible"* (Matthew 19:26) and *"apart from Me you can do nothing"* (John 15:5). These statements lead us to understand that God is capable and we are not, so we need Him. And how often do we pray, not knowing what we really need? Paul tells us that the Holy Spirit helps us by interpreting our groanings on behalf of the Father and the Son (Romans 8:26-27). These realities elevate the act of praying from a mundane obligation to appease conscience and bring prayer into a higher experience, a genuine communion with the God of all grace (1 Peter 5:10).

Ask

In James 1:5, *"But if any of you lacks wisdom, let him ask of God, who gives to all generously and without reproach, and it will be given to him."* So much of the Christian's shortages come not from his bankruptcy but rather from his unwillingness to ask. A generous God is anxiously waiting to demonstrate His generosity. James 4:2 says, "You do not have, because you do not ask. "The New Testament is filled with verses addressing the importance of asking God for the things that God desires to give. It starts with our willingness to believe that God wants to give. When a believer asks in prayer and believes, the answer will follow (Matthew 21:22). Additionally, there is John 14:13, which states, "Whatever you ask in My name, that will I do." It is in the character and the ability of God that prayer places its faith. The impossible answer can only come from the God of the impossible.

James 5:16 tells us that the effective prayer of a righteous man, the one who lives by faith (Romans 1:17), can accomplish much. The Greek word translated as 'effective' is *energeo*, from which we derive the English word 'energy'; it means that this prayer is working and operative. Jesus warns the religious man of the meaningless repetition of prayer, that his repetition of words or phrases will carry no weight with God. They will not work (Matthew 6:7). In the same passage, Jesus teaches that the righteous one who prays is not seeking recognition from others, but the prayer comes from an inner room where no one is watching. Those prayers have rewards attached to them.

Your Father Knows

Jesus also said in Matthew 6:8 that, *"Your Father knows what you need before you ask Him."* Prayer, then, is the process of the believer communing with God around something He already knows. But for what purpose? In Isaiah 65:24, *"It will also come to pass that before they call, I will answer; and while they are still speaking, I will hear ."* It means that God knows what we need before we do, and we can trust Him for the solution to our situation no matter what. Although the context of Isaiah 65 is the Millennial Kingdom, it speaks to new covenant believers in the church age as well. It means that His throne is a throne of grace, so we can have confidence that God's provision is never earned or deserved, but it is given in the exact time of need based on His grace and mercy (Hebrews 4:16).

> *"Prayer is a solemn service due to God, an adoration, a worship, an approach to God for some request, the presenting of some desire, the expression of some need to Him who supplies all need and who satisfies all desires, who, as a Father, finds his greatest pleasure in relieving the wants and granting the desires of his children. Prayer is the child's request, not to the winds nor to the world, but to the Father. Prayer is the outstretched arms of the child for the Father's help. Prayer is the child's cry calling to the Father's ear, the Father's heart, and to the Father's ability, which the Father is to hear, the Father is to feel, and which the Father is to relieve."* **EM Bounds**

Divine Solutions

It took a real commitment to prayer to bring E. M. Bounds to a deeper appreciation not only of its importance but also the intimacy it brings the believer and the expectation of divine solutions it creates. Depending on the situation, prayer can be a time of meditation and solitude and, other times, a wrestling match. In any case, prayer opens access to the riches of heaven like no other activity can afford. It is hard work with an eternal return.

Coming to live under and trust in the providence of God is the process of understanding that the Father is waiting to be gracious to His people, wanting to bless them according to His plans and purposes. The believer has come to trust in the Father's love as something above and beyond what the world understands love to include. It is unconditional! It means he learns not to place conditions on God's love. James Garfield, a Bible college president and war hero, became America's 20th president, never pursued any political office, and believed in divine providence. In this way, he gave the critical decisions of his life to God; he couldn't make a mistake.

It takes prayer to minister. It takes life, the highest form of life, to minister. Prayer is the highest intelligence, the profoundest wisdom, the most vital, the most joyous, the most efficacious, the most powerful of all vocations. It is life, radiant, transporting, eternal life. Away with dry forms, with dead, cold habits of prayer! Away with sterile routine, with senseless performances and petty playthings in prayer! Let us get at the serious work, the chief business of men, that of prayer. Let us work at it skillfully. Let us seek to be adepts in this great work of praying. Let us be master-workmen in this high art of praying. Let us be so in the habit of prayer, so devoted to prayer, so filled with its rich spices, so ardent by its holy flame, that all Heaven and earth will be perfumed by its aroma, and nations yet in the womb will be blest by our prayers. Heaven will be fuller and brighter in glorious inhabitants, earth will be better prepared for its bridal day, and hell robbed of many of its victims because we have lived to pray. **EM Bounds**

Begone Unbelief

John Newton, the author of "Amazing Grace," wrote many other poems that became well-known hymns. One of them is below, speaking to God's commitment to answer man's prayers:

Begone unbelief, my Savior is near
And for my relief shall surely appear.
By prayer, let me wrestle, and He will perform
With Christ in the vessel, I smile at the storm.
Though dark be my way, since He is my guide,
'Tis mine to obey, 'tis His to provide.
Though cisterns be broken and creatures all fail,
The Word He has spoken shall surely prevail.

Chapter 30
Three that Remain: Faith, Hope & Love

For we know in part [imperfect, obscure] *and we prophesy in part* [limited]; *but when the perfect* [finished] *comes* [the complete dispensation, the eternal state], *the partial will be done away. When I was a child, I used to speak like a child, think like a child, reason like a child; when I became a man, I did away with childish things. For now, we see in a mirror dimly* [ainigma – obscurely, an enigma], *but then face to face; now I know in part, but then I will know fully just as I also have been fully known. But now faith* [pistis – trust, firm persuasion], *hope* [elpis – desire of some good with an expectation of obtaining it], *love* [agape – God's unconditional, self-sacrificing benevolence to man], *abide* [meno – remain] *these three; but the greatest of these is love.* **1 Corinthians 13:9-13**

The Church at Corinth was a tremendously gifted church, with many exercising spiritual gifts, many times in an unrestrained fashion. It was Paul's priority in his first letter to address the definitions and limits of spiritual gifts, and he did so in 1 Corinthians 12, 13, and 14. Chapter 12 emphasizes the framework of those gifts, the right mode of exercising their spiritual gifts, and the degree of honor that was given to those who had been distinguished by God by the special influences of the Holy Spirit. He ended the chapter with the declaration: *And I show you a still more excellent way.* He would then spend the first eight verses of chapter 13 extolling the virtues of *agape* love.

In the above passage, Paul wishes to explain that the spiritual gifts that many times define the center of a believer's spiritual life have many limitations since *we see in a mirror dimly (obscurely)*. He was telling the church that those gifts have an appearance of spirituality, but they do not represent the fullness of Christ available to all believers who receive the love of Christ freely, without condition, and respond accordingly. As a result, **now**, faith, hope, and love are the perfection of God that remain during the Church age as an avenue into the deepest experience the believer has on this side of heaven. Spirituality should not be seen according to one's spiritual gifts.

Faith

Now faith is the assurance [hupostasis – guarantee, proof] *of things hoped for, the conviction* [elegchos – certain persuasion] *of things not seen. For by it, the men of old gained approval. By faith, we understand that the worlds were prepared by the word of God so that what is seen was not made out of things which are visible.* **Hebrews 11:1-3**

And without faith, it is impossible to please Him, for he who comes to God must believe that He is and that He is a rewarder of those who seek [ekzeteo – search diligently, seek to obtain] *Him.* **Hebrews 11:6**

Faith, in the theological sense, contains two elements recognized in the Scriptures: an intellectual element and another of even more profound importance, moral. Faith is not simply the assent of the intellect to revealed truth; it is **the practical submission of the entire man to the guidance and control of such truth**. *The demons also believe, and shudder* (James 2:19). The writer of Hebrews defines faith as the guarantee of things hoped for, the certain persuasion of things not seen. So much of one's faith is lived out in opposition to the seen world. Trusting in the invisible, as declared by God and His Word, is the foundation of a daily walk with the Lord. Pleasing God is based on believing that He is Lord moment by moment and that He wishes to reward each one who lives by that faith.

Trust in the Lord

Thus says the L*ord*, *"Cursed is the man who trusts in mankind and makes flesh his strength, and whose heart turns away from the* L*ord*. *"For he will be like a bush in the desert and will not see when prosperity comes, but will live in stony wastes in the wilderness, a land of salt without inhabitant. "Blessed is the man who trusts in the* L*ord and whose trust is the* L*ord*. *"For he will be like a tree planted by the water, that extends its roots by a stream and will not fear when the heat comes; but its leaves will be green, and it will not be anxious in a year of drought nor cease to yield fruit."* **Jeremiah 17:5-8**

Judah had been turning to false gods and foreign alliances for protection, but Yahweh indicates that a person who trusts in man for protection is cursed because his heart has turned away from God. Instead of prospering, he will wither away like a desert bush. God would make him as unfruitful as the barren saltland around the Dead Sea, unable to support life. A righteous person is blessed because his confidence is in God, *For he will be like a tree planted by the water*. When difficulties, represented by heat and drought, arise, he will not fear. Instead, he will continue to prosper like a tree that bears fruit and whose leaves remain green.

Hope

> *And not only this but also we ourselves, having the first fruits of the Spirit, even we ourselves groan within ourselves, waiting eagerly [apekdechomai – intensely anticipating] for our adoption as sons, [to be fully realized at] the redemption of our body [our glorified body]. For in hope we have been saved, but hope that is seen is not hope; for who hopes for what he already sees? But if we hope for what we do not see, with perseverance, we wait eagerly for it.*
> **Romans 8:23-25**

Elpis, the Greek word translated as "hope," is a favorable and confident expectation. It has to do with the unseen and the future. "Hope" describes three things: 1. the happy anticipation of good (the most frequent significance), as found in Titus 1:2; 1 Peter 1:21; 2. the ground upon which "hope" is based, (see Colossians 1:27 - *Christ in you the hope of glory*; and 3. the object upon which the "hope" is fixed. As the passage above illuminates, it represents waiting eagerly or intensely anticipating the promised future that all Christians have been given. Hope is the foundation for perseverance.

First Fruits of the Spirit

We groan because we have experienced *the first fruits of the Spirit*, a foretaste of the glory to come, just as the nation of Israel tasted the first fruits of Canaan when the spies returned (Numbers 13:23-27). Christians have tasted the blessings of heaven through the ministry of the Holy Spirit. We are eagerly waiting for our new redeemed body when Christ returns. At salvation, we experience the adoption as sons, as adults standing in God's family. When Christ returns, we enter into our full inheritance. In Titus 2:13, we are *looking for the blessed hope and the appearing of the glory of our great God and Savior, Christ Jesus.* When He returns, we will see Him as He is. *And everyone who has this hope fixed on Him purifies himself, just as He is pure* (1 John 3:2-3).

> *For when God made the promise to Abraham, since He could swear by no one greater, He swore* **by Himself**, *saying, "I WILL SURELY BLESS YOU AND I WILL SURELY MULTIPLY YOU"* [Genesis 22:17]. *And so, having patiently waited* [makrothumio – suffered long, restraint without retaliation], *he obtained the promise. For men swear by one greater than themselves, and with them, an oath given as confirmation is an end to every dispute. In the same way, God, desiring even more to show to the heirs of the promise the unchangeableness of His purpose, interposed with an oath, so that by two unchangeable things* [the promise and the oath] *in which it is impossible for God to lie, we who have taken refuge would have strong encouragement to take hold of the hope set before us. This hope we have as an anchor of the soul, a hope both sure* [asphales – that which cannot be thrown down] *and steadfast* [bebaios – fixed, sure, certain] *and one which enters within the veil, where Jesus has entered as a forerunner for us, having become a high priest forever according to the order of Melchizedek.* **Hebrews 6:13-20**

When Abraham was told to offer his son, Isaac, on Mount Moriah as a test of his faith, he passed the test. Since he was willing to offer his promised son (a type of the Father and the Son), the quality of the promises of God is confirmed by His oath; He was vouching for Himself, *He swore* **by Himself**. A willingness to wait patiently supposes that God cannot lie, that He is faithful even when we are faithless, *for He cannot deny Himself* (2 Timothy 2:13). If God were not to be faithful, He would cease to be God. This makes our hope *both sure* [*asphales* – that which cannot be thrown down] *and steadfast* [*bebaios* – fixed, sure, certain].

Faith and hope are made of the same substance, looking at things from a different perspective. According to one scholar, faith looks back 2,000 years to Jesus's first coming, while hope looks forward to his second coming. Still, everything God does is a byproduct of His love (1 John 4:8, 16).

The Work of God

Constantly bearing in mind your work [*ergon* – performance, the result or object of employment] *of* [produced by] *faith and labor* [*kopos* – wearisome effort] *of* [prompted by] *love and steadfastness* [*hupomone* – perseverance, the quality of character which does not allow one to surrender to circumstances or succumb under trial] *of* [inspired by] *hope in our Lord Jesus Christ in the presence of our God and Father.* **1 Thessalonians 1:3**

Each of these virtues found its object in the person of Christ, and each produced exemplary behavior. The Thessalonians had exercised saving faith in Christ in the past when they had believed the gospel, loving Christ in the present, hoping for His return in the future. These three are the clearest evidence of the believer's election. Their lives were certainly focused on Jesus Christ. No wonder Paul and his companions gave thanks for them.

Faith & Love in Action

But since we are of the day, let us be sober, having put on the breastplate of faith and love, and as a helmet, the hope of salvation. For God has not destined us for wrath, but for obtaining salvation through our Lord Jesus Christ, who died

for us, so that whether we are awake or asleep, we will live together with Him. Therefore, encourage one another and build up one another, just as you also are doing.
1 Thessalonians 5:8-11

A Roman breastplate covered a soldier from his neck to his waist and protected most of his vital organs. Isaiah saw the coming Messiah equipped with these pieces of armor: *And He saw that there was no man, and was astonished that there was no one to intercede; then His own arm brought salvation to Him, and His righteousness upheld Him. He put on righteousness like a breastplate and a helmet of salvation on His head, and He put on garments of vengeance for clothing and wrapped Himself with zeal as a mantle* (Isaiah 59:16-17). Jesus brings His righteousness in the form of faith and love and a helmet of salvation personified by hope.

That is what Christians' faith and love do. Faith in God protects inwardly, and love for people protects outwardly. These two graces cannot be separated; if one believes in God, he will also love other people. These attitudes equip Christians to live in anticipation of the Rapture. *For in Christ Jesus, neither circumcision nor uncircumcision means anything, but faith working through love* (Galatians 5:6). In addition, the hope of salvation guards their heads from attacks on their thinking. The salvation they look forward to is deliverance from the wrath to come when the Lord returns, as is clear from the context. It is not a wishful longing that someday they might be saved eternally. Followers of Christ have a sure hope; they are not like others who have no hope.

Bearing Fruit

*We give thanks to God, the Father of our Lord Jesus Christ, praying always for you, since we heard of **your faith** in Christ*

> *Jesus and **the love** which you have for all the saints; because of **the hope** laid up for you in heaven, of which you previously heard in the word of truth, the gospel which has come to you, just as in all the world also it is constantly bearing fruit and increasing, even as it has been doing in you also since the day you heard of it and understood the grace of God in truth; just as you learned it from Epaphras, our beloved fellow bond-servant, who is a faithful servant of Christ on our behalf, and he also informed us of your love in the Spirit.* **Colossians 1:3-8**

Faith is the soul looking upward to God; love looks outward to others; hope looks forward to the future. Faith rests on the past work of Christ; love works in the present, and hope anticipates the future. The Colossians' love extended to all saints (believers), probably not only at Colosse, but everywhere.

Faith and love spring from hope, confident in what God will do in the future. This confidence leads to a greater trust in God and a deeper love for others. This confident expectation of Christ's return influences believers' conduct. Hope is stored up in heaven because Christ, the essence of this hope, is there. Without Christ's ascension to heaven and His present ministry of intercession on behalf of believers (Hebrews 7:25; 1 John 2:1), they would have no hope. Epaphras and other fellow bond-servants found that this is the message of a fruitful life, centered on the life of Christ and His Word, and empowered by His Spirit.

> Faith will vanish into sight,
> Hope be emptied in delight,
> Love in heaven will shine more bright,
> Therefore, give us love.

Chapter 31
When Willingness Meets Divine Purpose

*This is good and acceptable in the sight of God our Savior, who **desires all men to be saved** and to come to the knowledge of the truth.* **1 Timothy 2:3-4**

A healthy relationship with God begins with the divine truth that He wishes salvation, an eternal relationship with Him, for all men. Acts 2:23 tells us that this was *the predetermined plan and foreknowledge of God* and that God Himself, through His Son, would be the solution. This solution would not be easy, but the result of an extended struggle, culminating in the seed of the woman, Jesus the Messiah, bruising the head of the serpent [Satan] (Genesis 3:15). This solution is intended for everyone, but there is a condition. It depends on man's heart attitude toward God.

Godly Fear

*Surely His salvation is near **to those who fear** [reverence] **Him**, that glory may dwell in our land. Lovingkindness and truth have met together; righteousness and peace have kissed each other. Truth springs from the earth, and righteousness looks down from heaven. Indeed, the Lord will give what is good, and our land will yield its produce. Righteousness will go before Him and will make His footsteps into a way.* **Psalm 85:9-13**

Romans 9:8 tells us that a relationship with God has always been based on faith in God's promises, a willingness to trust God for something one could not accomplish on one's own. Psalm 85:9 refers to it as a reverence for God, recognizing Him as savior and deliverer. Just as Paul wrote about the numerous supernatural blessings associated with salvation in Ephesians 1, this psalm provides an intimate glimpse into what salvation entails. Regarding this passage, Keil and Delitzsch Commentary on the Old Testament says:

> *The glory that has been far removed again takes up its abode in the land. Mercy or lovingkindness walks along the streets of Jerusalem, and there meets fidelity, like one guardian angel meeting the other. Righteousness and peace or prosperity, these two inseparable brothers kiss each other there and fall lovingly into each other's arms. The poet pursues this charming picture of the future further. After God's emet, i.e., faithfulness to the promises, has descended like dew, His faithfulness to the covenant springs up out of the land, the fruit of that fertilizing influence. And sedeq, gracious justice, looks down from heaven, smiling favor and dispensing blessing.*

Integrity & Uprightness

What connects the Old Testament believer to these divine realities? According to Isaiah 45:22, "*Turn to Me [panah – turn the face toward God] and be saved, all the ends of the earth; for I am God, and there is no other*. The uniqueness of God makes Him the only source. The fulcrum of the decision centers on man's willingness, a decision of the will, to place his total confidence in the God of Abraham, Isaac, and Jacob. King David understood this principle as a perfect heart, a heart of integrity and uprightness. In 1 Chronicles 29:14-19:

> *"But who am I, and who are my people that we should be able to offer as generously as this? For all things come from You, and from Your hand, we have given You. "For we are sojourners before You, and tenants, as all our fathers were,*

our days on the earth are like a shadow, and there is no hope. "O Lord our God, all this abundance that we have provided to build You a house for Your holy name, it is from Your hand, and all is Yours. "Since I know, O my God, that You try the heart and delight in uprightness [meyshar – rightness, equity, smoothness], *I, in the integrity* [yoeser – straightness, uprightness] *of my heart, have willingly offered all these things; so now with joy I have seen Your people, who are present here, make their offerings willingly to You. "O Lord, the God of Abraham, Isaac, and Israel, our fathers, preserve this forever in the intentions of the heart of Your people, and direct their heart to You; and give to my son Solomon* **a perfect heart to keep Your commandments**, *Your testimonies, and Your statutes, and to do them all, and to build the temple, for which I have made provision."*

Godly Examples

2 Corinthians 1:12 says it this way: *For our proud confidence* [glorying] *is this: the testimony of our conscience, that in holiness* [haplotes – singleness of mind] *and godly sincerity* [eilikroneia – sincerity, purity], *not in fleshly wisdom but in* [according to] *the grace of God, we have conducted ourselves in the world, and especially* [more abundantly] *toward you.* Paul makes it clear that it must be according to the grace of God, where the divine attributes of holiness and purity become the believer's motivation and an eagerness to represent these attributes as an example to the flock of God (1 Peter 5:2-3). Without this divine exchange of attributes, man will operate in his own limited ability and character, where there is no clear discernment of good and evil. Isaiah 5:19-21 says:

Who say, "Let Him make speed, let Him hasten His work, that we may see it; and **let the purpose of the Holy One of Israel** *draw near and come to pass, that we may know it!"* Woe to those who call evil good and good evil; who substitute darkness for light and light for darkness; who substitute bitter for sweet and sweet for bitter! Woe to those who are wise in their own eyes and clever in their sight!

Fulfillment of the Divine Will

The completion and fulfillment of the Divine Will are experienced **in Christ** within the new covenant relationship purchased by Jesus at His first coming and as defined by the Gospel. It is a mystery to the Old Testament believer but is realized in the fullness of the times, where redemption is complete, and forgiveness is *according to the riches of His grace*, as Paul documents in Ephesians 1. Paul used the term "in Christ" or "in Him" more than 170 times in his letters to identify the spiritual reality of knowing Christ. Jamieson, Fausset, and Brown Commentary says the following about "in Christ:" *The repetition of "in Christ" implies the paramount importance of the truth that it is in Him, by virtue of union to Him, the Second Adam, the Restorer ordained for us from everlasting, the Head of redeemed humanity, believers have all their blessings.*

This statement "in Christ" represents the fullness of the relationship each believer can have with God since it places its total confidence in who Jesus is and what He accomplished on behalf of the world. The believer's connection to this fullness is experienced in receiving the immeasurable love of Christ as Paul defines it in Ephesians 3:17-19: *so that Christ may dwell in your hearts through faith; and that you, being rooted and grounded in love, may be able to comprehend with all the saints what is the breadth and length and height and depth, and to know the love of Christ which surpasses knowledge, that you may be filled up to all the fullness of God.* Paul reveals that "in Christ" is the perfect position that is foundational for the many blessings associated with the new covenant in Ephesians 1:

> Blessed be the God and Father of our Lord Jesus Christ, who has blessed us with every spiritual blessing in the heavenly places **in Christ**, just as He chose us **in Him** before the foundation of the world, that we would be holy and blameless before Him. In love, He predestined us to adoption as sons through Jesus Christ to Himself, according to the kind intention of His will, to the praise of the glory of His grace, which He freely bestowed on us **in the Beloved**. **In Him,** we have redemption through His blood, the forgiveness of our trespasses, according to the riches of His grace which He lavished on us. In all wisdom and insight, He made known to us the mystery of His will, according to His kind intention, which He purposed **in Him** with a view to an administration suitable to the fullness of the times, that is, the summing up of all things **in Christ**, things in the heavens and things on the earth.   **Ephesians 1:3-10**

Under Compulsion

When Paul accepted the commissioning of God to be the Apostle to the Gentiles, he was sacrificing his will to the divine purpose for not only his life but for the very future of the New Testament church. It is not much different than the compulsion Jonah felt after spending time in the big fish. Paul speaks of this dynamic in Philippians 3:12 when he says, *but I press on so that I may lay hold of that for which also I was laid hold of by Christ Jesus*. Paul's labor to fulfill his call would be accomplished as he recognized and surrendered to the grace of God. He acknowledged that it would be the grace of God that was laboring with him (1 Corinthians 15:10).

> *But I have used none of these things. And I am not writing these things so that it will be done so in my case; for it would be better for me to die than have any man make my boast an empty one. For if I preach the gospel, I have nothing to boast of,* **for I am under compulsion**; *for woe is me if I do not preach the gospel. For if I do this voluntarily, I have a reward; but if against my will, I have a stewardship entrusted to me. What, then, is my reward? That, when I preach the gospel, I may offer the gospel without charge so as not to make full use of my right in the gospel.* **1 Corinthians 9:15-18**

Finding the divine purpose is for everyone who makes a conscious decision of the will to follow Christ no matter what the cost. Paul understood this when he spoke these words in Acts 20:27: *For I did not shrink from declaring to you the whole purpose of God.*

Man's willingness meets divine purpose at the cross. The religious man looks up and sees Jesus on the cross, but the spiritual man, in Christ, sees himself on the cross with Christ and, therefore, sees the world from a totally different vantage point, as the resurrected Lord sees it. Believers have *been buried with Him through baptism into death so that as Christ was raised from the dead through the glory of the Father, we too might walk in newness of life. For if we have become united with Him in His death's likeness, we shall certainly be in the likeness of His resurrection* (Romans 6:4-5).

Chapter 32

Where Deep Calls to Deep

As the deer pants for [arag – strongly, audibly longs for] the water brooks, so, my soul pants for You, O God. My soul thirsts for God, for the living God; when shall I come and appear before God? My tears [singular - weeping] have been my food day and night while they say to me all day long, "Where is your God?" These things I remember, and I pour out my soul within me. For I used to go along with the throng [sak – multitude] and lead them in procession to the house of God, with the voice of joy and thanksgiving, a multitude keeping festival. Why are you in despair [hamah – distress], O my soul? And why have you become disturbed within me? Hope [yahal – wait, hope] in God, for I shall again praise Him for the help [yeshua – deliverance, salvation] of His presence. O my God, my soul is in despair [sachah – brought low] within me; therefore, I remember You from the land of the Jordan and the peaks of Hermon, from Mount Mizar. Deep [tehom – depth, a wave or surge] calls to deep at the sound [qol – voice] of Your waterfalls [sinnor – water that drops suddenly]; all Your breakers and Your waves have rolled over me. The Lord will command [sawah – direct, command] His lovingkindness in the daytime, and His song will be with me in the night, a prayer [pillah – plea] to the God [el – mighty one] of my life.
Psalm 42:1-8

Although the above psalm is attributed to the Sons of Korah, several such psalms could actually have been written by David and given to them to put to music. One of the most eminent of the descendants of Korah, who was employed especially in the musical service of the sanctuary, was Heman (the singer, 1 Chronicles 6:33). The sons of Heman were appointed by David in connection with the sons of Asaph, and of Jeduthun, to preside over the music. If it was written by David, as seems most probable, it was with some reference to the Sons of Korah, that is, to those who presided over the music of the sanctuary. It was prepared especially to be used by them in the sanctuary, in contradistinction from psalms, which had a more general reference or which were composed for no such specific purpose.

David characterizes this psalm as *a prayer to the God [mighty one] of my life.* It begins with his confession that his soul audibly longs for and thirsts for God. He wrote in similar fashion in Psalm 63:1, *O God, You are my God; I shall seek You earnestly; my soul thirsts for You, my flesh yearns [kamah – longs] for You, in a dry and weary land where there is no water.* Jonah spoke a complementary sentiment in Jonah 2:7, *"While I was fainting away, I remembered the Lord, and my prayer came to You, into Your holy temple.* The holy temple, the sanctuary, is the place of God's presence, where intimacy is experienced. It is the place where deep calls to deep. This place is not visible, but the believer is brought there as a result of his longing. According to Isaiah 45:3, *"I will give you the treasures of darkness and hidden wealth of secret places, so that you may know that it is I, the Lord, the God of Israel, who calls you by your name."* The treasures of darkness are found in secret places.

Deep Things of God

Paul recognized that all the things God has prepared for those who love Him are available to man only by the Holy Spirit, according to 1 Corinthians 2:9-10, *but just as it is written, "THINGS WHICH EYE HAS NOT SEEN, AND EAR HAS NOT HEARD, AND which HAVE NOT ENTERED THE HEART OF MAN, ALL THAT GOD HAS PREPARED FOR THOSE WHO LOVE HIM." For to us God revealed them through the Spirit; for the Spirit searches all things, even the depths* [deep things] *of God.* The deep things of God speak of the deepest truths of the mind of God the Father on behalf of the ones who have demonstrated a love for God. Paul further declares in Romans 11:33, *Oh, the depth of the riches both of the wisdom and knowledge of God! How unsearchable are His judgments and unfathomable His ways*! The Holy Spirit has full access to God's deepest thoughts and will reveal them to those who long for and thirst after God.

Sudden Storms

And there arose a fierce gale of wind, and the waves were breaking over the boat so much that the boat was already filling up. Jesus Himself was in the stern, asleep on the cushion, and they woke Him and said to Him, "Teacher, do You not care that we are perishing?" And He got up and rebuked the wind and said to the sea, "Hush, be still." And the wind died down, and it became perfectly calm. And He said to them, "Why are you afraid? Do you still have no faith?" They became very much afraid and said to one another, "Who then is this, that even the wind and the sea obey Him?" **Mark 4:37-41**

In the above account, the disciples in the boat are facing what they believe is a life-threatening event, as *the boat is already filling up*. Notably, many of these disciples were fishermen, having spent much time in the Sea of Galilee catching fish. As the psalmist used the metaphor of the waterfalls and breakers to address the deep, it is the sudden storm with *a fierce gale of wind and waves breaking* that created the depth of the challenge to make the greatest impact on the disciples. They believed this was to be their demise, but Jesus had other plans. Not only did He solve the problem, but He demonstrated His deity by miraculously calming the wind and sea. The deep things of God were on display as Jesus confronted their fears. *"Why are you afraid?"* The deep things of God go as deep as the believer is willing to believe. To believe God for one's life is the ultimate faith in God.

Called of God

"Listen to Me, O Jacob, even Israel whom I called; I am He, I am the first, I am also the last. "Surely My hand founded the earth, and My right hand spread out the heavens; when I call to them, they stand together. "Assemble, all of you, and listen! Who among them has declared these things? The Lord loves him; he will carry out His good pleasure on Babylon, and His arm will be against the Chaldeans. "I, even I, have spoken; indeed, I have called him, I have brought him, and He will make his ways successful." **Isaiah 48:12-15**

Listen to Me, O islands, and pay attention, you peoples from afar. The Lord called Me from the womb; from the body of My mother He named Me. He has made My mouth like a sharp sword, in the shadow of His hand He has concealed Me; and He has also made Me a select arrow, He has hidden Me in His quiver. He said to Me, "You are My Servant, Israel [refers to Messiah], *in Whom I will show My glory."*
Isaiah 49:1-3

The two above passages address God's calling, first of Israel and then the Messiah. The Jews are God's chosen people, designated as belonging to Him just as the Father and the Son are one (John 10:30). At Pentecost, Peter declared, *"For the promise is for you and your children and for all who are far off, as many as the Lord our God will call to Himself"* (Acts 2:39). In both Isaiah passages, the call is that God provides everything necessary to protect and equip those whom He loves with everything needed to fulfill His will and make his ways successful.

The call to God is the place where He reveals His glory to the world. In Christ, the glory of the Father is manifested through His disciples: *"The glory which You have given Me I have given to them, that they may be one, just as We are one"* (John 17:22). That glory produces unity of mind and purpose.

Boasting in the Lord

For consider your calling [klesis – invitation to the kingdom of God and its privileges]*, brethren, that there were not many wise according to the flesh, not many mighty, not many noble* [eugenes – family of high rank]*; but God has chosen* [eklego – selected for Himself] *the foolish things* [moros – stupid, moronic] *of the world to shame the wise, and God has chosen the weak things of the world to shame the things which are strong, and the base things of the world and the despised God has chosen, the things that are not, so that He may nullify the things that are, so that no man may boast before God. But by His doing, you are in Christ Jesus, who became to us wisdom from God, and righteousness and sanctification, and redemption, so that, just as it is written, "LET HIM WHO BOASTS, BOAST IN THE LORD."* **1 Corinthians 1:26-31**

God's call on the believer has nothing to do with a person's wisdom, strength, background, or personal accomplishments but is entirely dependent on God's selection and choice. He purposely chooses those things for Himself that are not wise but weak and unlovely from the world's perspective. In so doing, He imposes a new value system that nullifies the things that are and opens the door for the new covenant relationship "in Christ" to integrate Christ's wisdom, righteousness, sanctification, and redemption as the believer's new identity. In this way, no one may boast, and God gets the glory.

Many Waters Cannot Quench Love

"Who is this coming up from the wilderness leaning on her beloved?" "Beneath the apple tree [tappuah – speaks of the love of Christ] *I awakened you; there your mother was in labor with you, there she was in labor and gave you birth* [the church]. *"Put me like a seal over your heart* [sealed with the Holy Spirit], *like a seal on your arm. For love* [ahbah – covenant love causing loyalty] *is as strong as death, jealousy* [qinah – intense zeal] *is as severe as Sheol* [place of the wicked]; *its flashes are flashes of fire* [passionate], *the very flame of the Lord. "Many waters cannot quench* [kabah – extinguish] *love, nor will rivers overflow it; if a man were to give all the riches of his house for love, it would be utterly despised." "We have a little sister* [Gentiles], *and she has no breasts; what shall we do for our sister on the day when she is spoken for? "If she is a wall* [separation from the world], *we will build on her a battlement of silver* [redemption – Finished Work]; *but if she is a door* [witness of the truth], *we will barricade her with planks of cedar." "I was a wall* [set apart], *and my breasts were like towers; then I became in his eyes as one who finds peace"* [justification – Romans 5:1]. **Song 8:5-10**

The Jews saw Solomon's writings allegorically, comparing Proverbs to the outer court of Solomon's temple, Ecclesiastes to the holy place, and Song of Solomon to the holy of holies. "Shulammite," Daughter of Peace being the feminine of Solomon, equivalent to the Prince of Peace. She is a vinedresser, shepherdess, midnight inquirer, and prince's consort and daughter; while He is a king in His palace, in harmony with the various relations of the Church and Christ. In the 8th chapter, she is beginning to experience the deeper chasms of His love. These verses sum up the nature and power of the love depicted in the Song.

According to Ellicott's Commentary:

This begins a new section, which contains the most magnificent description of true love ever written by poet. The dramatic theory encounters insuperable difficulties with this strophe. Again, we presume that the theatre and the spectators are imaginary. It is another sweet reminiscence, coming most naturally and beautifully after the last. The obstacles have been removed, the pair are united, and the poet recalls the delightful sensations with which he led his bride through the scenes where the youth of both had been spent, and then bursts out into the glorious panegyric of that pure and perfect passion which had united them.

The references to the new covenant relationship of the believer to Christ, the bridegroom, are profound. The sealing of the Holy Spirit as a seal over the heart and the reference to Gentiles as the *little sister* reveals the riches of His house for love. The reception of His love brings the believer to the Finished Work redemption of silver and a door to invite others into this fellowship of being accepted in the Beloved (Ephesians 1:6). The ultimate conclusion is peace (shalom), a tranquility that promotes rest and blessing. Nothing separates the believer from His love:

> *But in all these things, we overwhelmingly conquer through Him who loved us. For I am convinced that neither death, nor life, nor angels, nor principalities, nor things present, nor things to come, nor powers, nor height, nor depth, nor any other created thing, will be able to separate us from the love of God, which is in Christ Jesus our Lord.* **Romans 8:37-39**

Consider the words of A.B. Simpson from his hymn "The Mercy of God is an Ocean Divine:"

> *The mercy of God is an ocean divine,*
> *A boundless and fathomless flood.*
> *Launch out in the deep,*
> *Cut away the shore line,*
> *And be lost in the fullness of God.*
>
> *Refrain*
> *Launch out, into the deep.*
> *Oh let the shore line go.*
> *Launch out, launch out in the ocean divine,*
> *Out where the full tides flow.*
>
> *But many, alas! Only stand on the shore,*
> *And gaze on the ocean so wide.*
> *They never have ventured*
> *Its depths to explore,*
> *Or to launch on the fathomless tide.*

And others just venture away from the land,
And linger so near to the shore
That the surf and the slime
That beat over the strand
Dash o'er them in floods evermore.

Oh, let us launch out on this ocean so broad,
Where floods of salvation o'erflow.
Oh, let us be lost
In the mercy of God,
Till the depths of His fullness we know.

Chapter 33
In Your Presence

They heard the sound of the Lord God walking in the garden in the cool of the day, and the man and his wife hid themselves from the presence [paniym – face, figuratively of the person] of the Lord God among the trees of the garden. Then the Lord God called to the man and said to him, "Where are you?" He said, "I heard the sound of You in the garden, and I was afraid because I was naked [erom – without clothing]; so, I hid myself." And He said, "Who told you that you were naked? Have you eaten from the tree of which I commanded you not to eat?" **Genesis 3:8-11**

The first mention of God being present in a given situation or circumstance is found in the above passage, where Adam was looking to hide from the Lord after he found himself naked. The fact that he knew he was naked was just a symptom of the real issue; he had sinned by doing the thing, the only thing Elohim Yahweh told him not to do. Adam and Eve had to hide themselves from the presence of God, which they had always enjoyed. They would need to leave Eden, but God would give them a promise that the seed of the woman, Jesus Christ, would be man's provision and restore His presence to humanity. The Angel of the Lord, Christ in angelic form, would appear to some throughout Old Testament times to remind mankind that God had not abandoned him.

From Jacob to Israel

Then Jacob was left alone, and a man wrestled with him until daybreak. When he saw that he had not prevailed against him, he touched the socket of his thigh, so the socket of Jacob's thigh was dislocated while he wrestled with him. Then he said, "Let me go, for the dawn is breaking." But he said, "I will not let you go unless you bless me." So, he said to him, "What is your name?" And he said, "Jacob." He said, "Your name shall no longer be Jacob, but Israel, for you have striven with God and with men and have prevailed." Then Jacob asked him and said, "Please tell me your name." But he said, "Why is it that you ask my name?" And he blessed him there. So, Jacob named the place Peniel, for he said, "I have seen God face to face, yet my life has been preserved." Now, the sun rose upon him just as he crossed over Penuel, and he was limping on his thigh. Therefore, to this day, the sons of Israel do not eat the sinew of the hip, which is on the socket of the thigh, because he touched the socket of Jacob's thigh in the sinew of the hip. **Genesis 32:24-32**

Jacob had an amazing encounter with the Lord in the above passage, and he knew it. *"I have seen God face to face, yet my life has been preserved."* The wrestling match had to do with Jacob's strength and ability, and Jacob is left with a permanent limp. It was a constant reminder that man's strength may be his most significant obstacle to the presence of God in his life. Paul had a similar experience with a *thorn in the flesh*, as described in 2 Corinthians 12:7-9. Paul had prayed for its removal, but God told him, "*My grace is sufficient for you, for power is perfected in weakness.*" He was learning that his own strength was hindering his ability to experience God's presence.

Jacob had been a taker by the heel from his very birth, and his subsequent life had been a constant and successful struggle with adversaries. The thigh is the pillar of a man's strength, and its joint with the hip is the seat of physical force for the wrestler. When the thigh bone is thrown out of joint, the man becomes utterly disabled. Jacob now finds that this mysterious wrestler has wrested from him, by one touch, all his might, and he can no longer stand alone. In that condition, he learns by experience the practice of sole reliance on one mightier than himself. This is the turning point in the story. Jacob is given a new name, Israel, representing the new person he has become. Henceforth, Jacob feels strong, not in himself, but in the Lord and the power of His might.

Fullness of Joy

I have set [shavah – focus on] *the Lord continually before me; because He is at my right hand, I will not be shaken* [mot – unmovable]. *Therefore, my heart is glad and my glory rejoices; My flesh also will dwell securely* [betah – calm assurance]. *For You will not abandon my soul to Sheol* [sahat – pit, grave]; *nor will You allow Your Holy One to undergo decay. You will make known to me the path of life;* **in Your presence is fullness of joy**; *in Your right hand there are pleasures forever.* **Psalm 16:8-11**

In the above psalm, David expresses a confident expectation of eternal life and happiness founded on the evidence of true attachment to God. It represents the deep conviction that one who loves God will not be left in the grave and will not suffer permanent *decay,* corruption, or perish in the grave forever. David focuses his attention on his ongoing and continuous relationship with the Lord, as evidenced by his acknowledgment of the Lord with his right hand, the hand of honor and approval. David had a clear understanding of the Finished Work of Christ and the security and assurance it provides to each believer. He also understood that death and the grave would not separate him from the Lord. His attention to beholding the face of God in the details of life became a passion. In Psalm 17:15, *As for me, I shall behold Your face in righteousness; I will be satisfied with Your likeness when I awake.* The Apostle Paul echoed these sentiments in Ephesians 3:19, *and to know the love of Christ which surpasses knowledge, that you may be filled up to all the fullness of God.*

The above passage from David was quoted by Peter on Pentecost, marking the birth of the church (Acts 2:25-28). The application was not to David but to Jesus the Nazarene. He was *delivered over by the predetermined plan and foreknowledge of God* and put to death. *But God raised Him up again, putting an end to the agony of death since it was impossible for Him to be held in its power* (Acts 2:22-24). Peter tied David's testimony of God's faithfulness to Jesus as a fulfillment of the prophesy that He would live in His humanity in His Father's presence and survive His crucifixion without undergoing decay. Many Old Testament prophesies have multiple fulfillments.

The Burning Bush

Now Moses was pasturing the flock of Jethro, his father-in-law, the priest of Midian, and he led the flock to the west side of the wilderness and came to Horeb, the mountain of God. The Angel of the Lord appeared to him in a blazing fire from the midst of a bush, and he looked, and behold, the bush was burning with fire, yet the bush was not consumed. So, Moses said, "I must turn aside now and see this marvelous sight, why the bush is not burned up." When the Lord saw that he turned aside to look, God called to him from the midst of the bush and said, "Moses, Moses!" And he said, "Here I am." Then He said, "Do not come near here;

*remove your sandals from your feet, for the place on which you are standing is holy ground." He said also, "I am the God of your father, the God of Abraham, the God of Isaac, and the God of Jacob." Then Moses hid his face, for he was afraid to look at Go*d. **Exodus 3:1-6**

Moses spent forty years in the wilderness as a shepherd after his time in Pharaoh's household, and now the Lord commissions him from a burning bush. He finds himself in the presence of the Angel of the Lord, a reference to Jesus Christ. Moses was being instructed on how to experience His presence. The fact that the burning bush was not consumed is not by accident. F.B. Myers concludes that it is a picture of God's presence, not consumed because of His love for His people. In any case, the Angel of the Lord told Moses that to approach the Lord would require him to *"remove your sandals from your feet, for the place on which you are standing is holy ground."* Moses's response was similar to Adam's in Eden: *Moses hid his face, for he was afraid to look* God in the eye. Anyone entering the Lord's presence must approach Him as holy ground. The removal of shoes is a confession of personal defilement amid His unspotted holiness.

Moses was commissioned to be the one through whom Yahweh would deliver the people from slavery, receive the Pentateuch, and lead the people through the wilderness. His relationship with God was unlike that of any other Biblical character. In Numbers 12:8, *With him, I speak mouth to mouth, even openly, and not in dark sayings, and he beholds the form* [likeness] *of the Lord*. Exodus 33:11 tells us that *the Lord used to speak to Moses face-to-face, just as a man speaks to his friend*. He would meet the Lord in the tent of meeting when Moses would pitch his own tent outside the camp while the Tabernacle was still being constructed. In Exodus 33:8-10, *And it came about, whenever*

Moses went out to the tent, that all the people would arise and stand, each at the entrance of his tent, and gaze after Moses until he entered the tent. Whenever Moses entered the tent, the pillar of cloud would descend and stand at the entrance of the tent, and the Lord would speak with Moses. When all the people saw the pillar of cloud standing at the entrance of the tent, all the people would arise and worship, each at the entrance of his tent.

"My Presence Shall Go with You"

Then Moses said to the Lord, "See, You say to me, 'Bring up this people!' But You Yourself have not let me know whom You will send with me. Moreover, You have said, 'I have known you by name, and you have also found favor in My sight.' "Now therefore, I pray You, if I have found favor in Your sight, let me know Your ways that I may know [yada – to know relationally, experientially] *You, so that I may find favor in Your sight. Consider, too, that this nation is Your people." And He said, "My presence shall go with you, and I will give you rest." Then he said to Him, "If Your presence does not go with us, do not lead us up from here. "For how then can it be known that I have found favor in Your sight, I and Your people? Is it not by Your going with us, so that we, I and Your people, may be distinguished from all the other people who are upon the face of the earth?"*
Exodus 33:12-16

Moses found a friendship and an intimacy in his relationship with God, and he needed to know what the Lord's intentions were regarding His people. God had told Moses to lead the people, but without God's presence, and Moses was deeply concerned. God knew Moses by name, that is, that Moses was devoted to God. So, Moses wanted to continue learning God's ways and experiencing God's grace (favor). Moses interceded on behalf of the nation by reminding God that they were His people. In response, the Lord reversed His threat not to go with them and to give them rest.

Moses also needed confirmation that the Lord would indeed go with His people. The absence of God's presence with them in their journey to the Promised Land would pose serious problems. God agreed to Moses' request, assuring Moses that He was pleased with him. The Lord's presence was necessary for the nations of the world to recognize that these people were different and unique. When believers in Christ do not have regular fellowship with God's presence, the world cannot recognize the God of the Bible through their lives.

Job's Dilemma

> *"But He knows the way I take; when He has tried me, I shall come forth as gold. "My foot has held fast to His path; I have kept His way and not turned aside. "I have not departed from the command of His lips; I have treasured the words of His mouth more than my necessary food. "But He is unique [ehad – sovereign], and who can turn Him? And what His soul desires, that He does. "For He performs what is appointed for me, and many such decrees are with Him. "Therefore, I would be dismayed [bahal – troubled] at His presence; when I consider, I am terrified of Him. "It is God who has made my heart faint, and the Almighty who has dismayed me, But I am not silenced by the darkness, nor deep gloom which covers me."* **Job 23:10-17**

Job was in the midst of his trial, not understanding the meaning and purpose, but instead seeing God as terrifying. He is acknowledging God's sovereignty: *And what His soul desires that He does.* He is troubled at the presence of God, but he still holds to his devotion to follow God and His ways: *"I have not departed from* the command of His lips; I have treasured the words of His mouth more than my necessary food." It will not be until the end of his trial that he comes to see the nature of the living God. In Job 42:3-6, 'Who is this that hides counsel without knowledge?' "Therefore, I have declared that which I did not understand, things too wonderful for me, which I did not know." 'Hear, now, and I will speak; I will ask You, and You instruct me.' "I have heard of You by the hearing of the ear, but now my eye sees You; Therefore, I retract, and I repent in dust and ashes." The religious man follows the words of His mouth but is afraid of His presence. At Sinai, the people told Moses to go up on the mountain because they were afraid (Exodus 20:18-19).

Taking Refuge

How great is Your goodness [tub – that which is desirable for enjoyment], which You have stored up for those who fear [reverence] You, which You have wrought for those who take refuge in You, before the sons of men! You hide them in the secret place of Your presence from the conspiracies [contentions] of man; You keep them secretly in a shelter from the strife of tongues. Blessed be the Lord, for He has made marvelous His lovingkindness to me in a besieged [masor - fortified] city. **Psalm 31:19-21**

David recognizes the goodness of God; that which is desirable for enjoyment is stored up for those who reverence Him, who have taken refuge in Him. In Psalm 27:4-5, the secret place of His presence is further defined: *One thing I have asked from the Lord, that I shall seek: that I may dwell in the house of the Lord all the days of my life, to behold the beauty of the Lord and to meditate in His temple. For in the day of trouble, He will conceal me in His Tabernacle; in the secret place of His tent, He will hide me; He will lift me up on a rock*. It is a place of intimacy with God and protection from enemies. It is a besieged city, fortified by His lovingkindness.

A Spiritual Mindset

Therefore, if you have been raised up with Christ, keep seeking the things above, where Christ is, seated at the right hand of God. Set your mind on [phroneo – a mindset, devotion to, involving the will, affections, and conscience] the things above, not on the things that are on earth. For you have died [apothnesko – aorist active indicative – past action], and your life is hidden [krupto – concealed in a place of security] with Christ in God. When Christ, who is our life, is revealed, then you also will be revealed with Him in glory. Therefore, consider the members of your earthly body as dead [nekroo – aorist active imperative, keep putting to death] to immorality, impurity, passion, evil desire, and greed, which amounts to idolatry. **Colossians 3:1-5**

Paul saw clearly that the presence of God was experienced by a consistent entertainment of things above, spiritual thoughts that promote an intimacy with God. The spiritual mindset focuses its attention on things above, not on earthly matters. *In Him*, the believer recognizes that *you were also circumcised with a circumcision made without hands, in the removal of the body of the flesh by the circumcision of Christ; having been buried with Him in baptism, in which you were also raised up with Him through faith in the working of God, who raised Him from the dead* (Colossians 2:11-12). These are spiritual thoughts and convictions that affect the will, affections, and conscience of the believer. Once he accepts that he is dead to this world and his own interests, he is raised up with Him through faith in the working of God. In His presence in fullness of joy!

Twila Paris wrote a song on her *Kingdom Seekers* album entitled "Faithful Men" that highlights the importance of a life lived through the Holy Spirit and the fulfillment of a life lived by faith:

> Come and join the reapers
> All the Kingdom Seekers
> Laying down your life to find it in the end
> Come and share the harvest
> Help to light the darkness
> For the Lord is calling faithful men

Humble yourselves in the presence of the Lord, and He will exalt you. **James 4:10**